Advance Praise for
Enneagram in Real Life

'In *Enneagram in Real Life*, Stephanie Barron Hall provides a compassionate, accessible, and highly actionable, step-by-step pathway for growth using the Enneagram map—she takes the reader by the hand, as both a wise coach and fellow traveler, and shows how to take the journey of self-development that she is also clearly, courageously, taking herself."

—Beatrice Chestnut, PhD, author of
The Complete Enneagram and *The 9 Types of Leadership* and
coauthor of *The Enneagram Guide to Waking Up*

"Whether you're just beginning or are already familiar with the Enneagram, this book is all you need to discover your type and then—most importantly—learn how to do the work. Hall's style is conversational and 'real,' as the title suggests. She is vulnerable with her own struggles and acknowledges she is on the journey with you. There are so many Enneagram books in the marketplace now with most either veering off course of the original teachings of Naranjo and Ichazo, or simply repeating the same refrains. *Enneagram in Real Life*'s contribution is an ingenious approach of offering a comprehensive and accurate teaching of the current sum total of Enneagram understanding rooted in practical and specific applications. In other words, the teachings are precise and what you do with it is useful and clear. The OPEN framework is genius for its clarity and application."

—Dr. Chad Prevost, PhD,
author of *Shock Point: The Enneagram in Burnout and Stress*

"Tired of feeling stuck in unhealthy patterns? Stephanie Barron Hall's *Enneagram in Real Life* offers a fresh, actionable approach to self-discovery and personal growth. Hall, a certified Enneagram coach and the voice behind the popular Instagram account @ninetypesco, combines her expertise with relatable anecdotes and practical exercises to help you understand your core motivations, embrace your strengths, and navigate life's challenges with greater self-awareness and compassion.

"If you're ready to break free from old habits and create a more fulfilling life, this book is your roadmap to lasting change."

—Professor Jeff Karp, author of *LIT: Life Ignition Tools*

"Stephanie Barron Hall has written the new go-to book on the Enneagram. Filled with beautiful descriptions and relatable stories Stephanie has crafted a powerfully accessible resource that will educate and inspire both newcomers and Enneagram enthusiasts alike. With almost surgical precision, this book simplifies the complexity of the Enneagram system not by what it omits, but by what it emphasizes, as Stephanie expertly guides the reader toward immediate, practical application for personal growth. This is not another book on Enneagram theory . . . this is the Enneagram in real life."

—Scott Allender,
author of *The Enneagram of Emotional Intelligence*

"If you (like me) had your life changed after learning your Enneagram but aren't sure how to put it into practice, Stephanie has written the exact book for you! I love how practical, thoughtful, and actionable this book is. I can't wait to recommend it to my clients."

—Amanda E. White, LPC, therapist and
author of *Not Drinking Tonight*

"Stephanie Barron Hall's new book, *Enneagram in Real Life*, offers a fresh perspective on how the Enneagram can be applied to our daily experiences. It's always exciting to see new contributions to the field, and this book is a great resource for those looking to deepen their understanding of the Enneagram in practical, relatable ways. Whether you're new to the Enneagram or have been exploring it for years, there's something valuable to discover in her approach."

—Dr. Deborah Egerton, author of *Enneagram Made Easy*
and *The Enneagram Inner Work Journal Series*

"What's so enthralling about the sorting hat in *Harry Potter*? Many of us have been fascinated with the idea that a magical headpiece could somehow glean the students' characteristics and traits, thereby allocating each child to a house that suited them perfectly. In this sense, we've been interested in the science of personality types and categorization long before J.K. Rowling put pen to paper, with a slew of studies and theories supporting various typologies.

The Enneagram is a somewhat lesser-known system, which Stephanie Barron Hall beautifully explains with concrete case studies, clear descriptions, and importantly, actionable steps to improve the quality of life for everyone, regardless of type. The Enneagram is a complex framework, yet Stephanie guides readers through this self-discovery process with compassion—I can hear her kind, warm voice emanate from the page. Therefore, if you would like to learn more about yourself to make sustainable changes in important areas of your life, I would highly recommend *Enneagram in Real Life*. After all, 'Knowing yourself is the beginning of all wisdom' (Aristotle)."

—Dr. Meg Arroll, psychologist and author of *Tiny Traumas*

"Stephanie's approach to the Enneagram is the perfect balance of raw, emotionally honest, thorough, and adaptable. Picking up this book will actually take you on a deep journey of self-reflection and discovery. It requires your care, attention, and intentionality to absorb. Highly recommend to anyone who is interested in the Enneagram, but also for fellow experts in this space."

—Christina S. Wilcox, author of
Take Care of Your Type and *Take Care of Your Friends*

Enneagram in Real Life

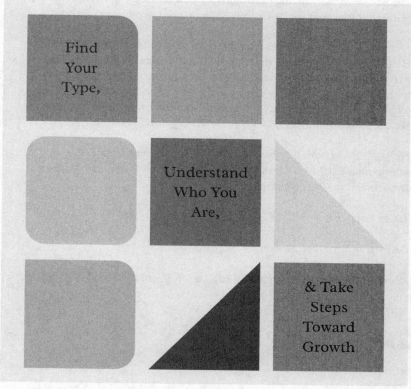

Find
Your
Type,

Understand
Who You
Are,

& Take
Steps
Toward
Growth

Stephanie Barron Hall

HarperONE
An Imprint of HarperCollins*Publishers*

ENNEAGRAM IN REAL LIFE. Copyright © 2025 by Stephanie Barron Hall. All rights reserved. Printed in the United States of America. No part of this book may be used or reproduced in any manner whatsoever without written permission except in the case of brief quotations embodied in critical articles and reviews. For information, address HarperCollins Publishers, 195 Broadway, New York, NY 10007.

HarperCollins books may be purchased for educational, business, or sales promotional use. For information, please email the Special Markets Department at SPsales@harpercollins.com.

FIRST EDITION

Designed by Bonni Leon-Berman

Library of Congress Cataloging-in-Publication Data has been applied for.

ISBN 978-0-06-331896-0

24 25 26 27 28 LBC 5 4 3 2 1

For Brandon, who believed when I didn't.

Contents

Introduction   xi

Part I: Start Here

CHAPTER 1–Laying the Groundwork   3

CHAPTER 2–How the System Works   13

CHAPTER 3–Finding Your Type   44

CHAPTER 4–OPEN: A Framework for Sustainable Change   58

Part II: The Body Types

CHAPTER 5–Type Eight   71

CHAPTER 6–Type Nine   95

CHAPTER 7–Type One   118

Part III: The Heart Types

CHAPTER 8–Type Two   143

CHAPTER 9–Type Three   167

CHAPTER 10–Type Four   192

Part IV: The Mind Types

CHAPTER 11–Type Five   221

CHAPTER 12–Type Six   245

CHAPTER 13–Type Seven   271

Author's Note   297

Acknowledgments   299

Notes   301

Introduction

The door to my second-floor apartment swings wide, and I drag myself over the threshold. Weariness creeps through my bones. With one glance, my husband jumps into action, his face stricken with concern.

"What do you need?" he asks. "Want me to draw you a bath?"

It's a struggle even to form words. "Sure, that sounds nice." I yawn.

By the time he returns, no more than five minutes later, I've collapsed in a heap on the entryway linoleum. Keys still in the door. I'm dead asleep.

FIFTEEN HOURS EARLIER

I park on San Julian Street. It's early, and most of Los Angeles is still asleep, so I don't even have to circle the block for a good spot. The morning is dark and still cool as I grab my notebook and head inside the Los Angeles Flower Mart. My wedding floral design business started as a hobby, but three years in, I'm dedicating every hour of PTO from my 9 to 5 job to it, producing increasingly ambitious weddings. This Thursday morning pickup is standard for a Saturday wedding, so my favorite vendor has already prepared the bulk of my order on a tall cart. After brief hellos, I wander the rest of the vast warehouse, crossing odds and ends off my list. Bits of texture and unique colorways will add something special to the bouquets I'll prepare over the next forty-eight hours.

Once I've found the perfect ranunculus and anemones for the bouquets, I pack the bundles of greenery and florals into prepared five-gallon buckets lining the trunk of my car. My favorite local coffee shop is still dark, so I hop back on the 5 freeway and take the 110 North. This wedding is special because I've known the bride for years, and we've designed a beautifully personalized backyard wedding reception. All day Thursday, my bride's family and friends gather to iron tablecloths, set up rented tables and chairs, and wrap greenery into long, lush garlands. It's also my first and only foray into event coordination, so I spend the afternoon coordinating vendor arrivals, delegating tasks, and assembling foundational elements of the centerpieces and bouquets.

By the end of the day, my Fitbit reading is over 25,000 steps. Only in my car on the ninety-minute drive back home does my body begin to relax from the buzzing energy of the day. The following days will sustain the same frenetic pace.

In retrospect, my husband was alarmed by my falling asleep on the floor, but he wasn't surprised. By that point, he'd seen this cycle many times. The thrill of this work kept me hooked. I embraced the hard deadlines and the ability to create something beautiful and tangible, but working a full-time job in addition to building a wedding business was unsustainable. I didn't know it then, but I had just begun my penultimate wedding season.

This event coincided with my early Enneagram learnings. I was just waking up to my tendency to place all my worth in my productivity and how impressive others found me. I'd always chased the magical warmth of success. There was something about it that made me feel proud and glowing. Accepted. Like I finally belonged. So when I found a creative outlet that people would admire in photos for years to come—something that would feature my work in my favorite publications, like *Style Me Pretty* and *Green Wedding Shoes*—I leaped, headlong. I knew enough about the Enneagram to know that as a type Three, I excelled when challenged. I loved to work hard and bask in the glory of a project well done. My mantra was, "If you're not falling over at the end of the day, you haven't worked hard yet." The first time I heard Brené Brown refer to exhaustion as a status symbol we wear as a badge of honor[1] I thought, "How's that a bad thing?" I was what I now call a #hustlemonster.

In the midst of all of this, I didn't truly know myself. I simply didn't have time to. When I started learning more about the Enneagram, I was shocked. I *thought* I was in tune with my emotions. I *thought* I was gentle and kind and compassionate. But the people around me mostly received a too-busy version of me who delegated tasks because, "You don't have much going on this weekend, do you, babe?" What's yours is mine, including your time! In short, I was a less people-oriented version of Leslie Knope. In other words, kind of a nightmare.

Soon, the tenuous balance I'd constructed came crashing down. It wasn't the first time I'd learned this lesson—I was even more intense before I came down with shingles after a series of all-nighters working on a ninth-grade English project. Nor would it be the last. Burnout hit me in a wave, and I simply couldn't care anymore. I was too sleep deprived and exhausted to care if I booked more weddings. The crushing weight of saying "yes" too often and "no" almost never left me depleted, wrung dry. I didn't want to carry any more buckets up three flights of stairs. A bride who asked for a daily proposal update was the final nail in the coffin. I announced I was not taking any more weddings, abandoned my inbox, and went on a non-work-related vacation for the first time in years.

During this time, I started reading about the Enneagram beyond the basics. I learned that flaming out is inevitable when you're burning the candle at both ends. I learned that my friends could see through the facade I'd subconsciously created and dutifully upheld. Early in life, I'd been labeled as "the sensitive one" (though I would now describe my young self as perceptive, image-conscious, or fearful), so I thought I had a natural connection to my emotional realm. But I've learned that being sensitive and expressing big emotions because your system can no longer bottle them is *not* the same as having a deep sense of emotional awareness.

While the "Achiever" moniker ascribed to Enneagram Threes immediately resonated, accepting this label allowed me to question my assumptions about myself and the world around me. Studying the Enneagram became a mirror for me. If a friend had said, "Steph, you tend to shift how you present yourself depending on who you're around. It sometimes makes me wonder what you really think and what's important to you," I probably would have rejected the notion outright. But reading about this type Three archetype allowed me to recognize traits that resonated and get curious about traits that didn't. Instead of rejecting a trait, I started to ask, "Hmmm . . . do I do that?" The depersonalization offered enough space that I could observe these ideas without defensiveness, thereby opening the path for inner work ahead.

In the intervening years, I've learned more about myself and more about the Enneagram. In 2017, I started Nine Types Co., an Instagram account dedicated to selling Enneagram-specific coffee mugs. They were great gifts, but soon I recognized that people followed and shared my posts more when I talked about the Enneagram tool itself. In 2018, I began teaching the Enneagram in team and small group settings, drawing on my past experience leading teams and using personality tools for professional development. By the end of the year, I had a semester of a master's degree in Strategic and Organizational Communication and Leadership under my belt, and I'd completed my first Enneagram certification program. Writing about the Enneagram became a fun pastime and not nearly as demanding as my years as a wedding florist. As my account on Instagram grew, so did my knowledge of the Enneagram. I crowdsourced responses to questions and then compared the answers to the well-established Enneagram texts on my shelf. Throughout my graduate studies, I focused on self-knowledge as a path for improved intra- and interpersonal communication. By 2022, I'd completed training with Integrative9 Enneagram Solutions, and later that year I graduated from the Chestnut Paes Enneagram Academy. To date, I've worked with thousands of individuals on six continents and dozens of companies who use the Enneagram to improve organizational effectiveness through stronger teams and productive communication.

Through this work, I've found that the challenge with the Enneagram is twofold. The first is that it's a complex system that looks deceptively simple. It's just nine numbers—how hard could that be? As we'll explore later in this book, there's a lot more to the Enneagram than that. When working with typing and coaching clients, I hear a lot of stereotyped assumptions about specific types, and sometimes, these are holding the client back from truly understanding themselves.

The second is that tools for real-life application have historically been sparse. In my years working with the Enneagram both personally and professionally, I've heard the same question time and again: "I know my type, but what do I do with it?" Advice can be abstract, in part because everyone is different, and tailored coaching requires a 1:1 relationship. But there is a middle way, and this book is designed to offer you practical, actionable tools that have worked for me and my clients.

That's why I wrote this book. Because I know that understanding yourself through the Enneagram will change your life, if you apply it. I've seen it happen time and again. It starts with a glimmer of insight: that moment of awareness, "Oh, *that's* why I do that!" Or the realization that your spouse is not using your very last nerve as a tightrope on purpose—they just see the world from a different lens. Or the alarming recognition that your way of leading is sending your employees running for the hills, resulting in cycles of burnout and constant turnover.

This is where our work begins.

That's not to say consciousness of these dynamics brings instantaneous change. My life story features many cycles of burnout, the latest of which occurred while writing this book. It was, as more sophisticated scholars might say, a doozy, which led to a deep depression and many months of feeling unrecognizable to myself. The sinkhole of hopelessness nearly swallowed me whole. What emerged was a new understanding of myself and what I value. The quest for admiration so central to the Enneagram Three's psyche comes at the cost of an essential concept of self. Until we have these seismic events in our lives, it can feel foreign for a Three to have a clear sense of identity or worth unrelated to the perceptions and expectations of others. I will never discount the unbearable darkness of depression, yet I can see how that season shifted my perspective and allowed more clarity in my own identity and unshakeable innate worth. My first draft of this introduction—submitted on the brink of burnout—was a succinct and polished story. I thought that made me credible. But here's what I know now, a year later: I am a full human, with flaws and gifts and strengths and humor and mistakes. I allow myself to be imperfect and still in progress, and I invite you to do the same.

Above all, I consider myself a student of the Enneagram on an inner work journey, just like you. Throughout the years, I've wrestled with my own process, too. While much of my growth work has centered Enneagram-specific coaching, inner work retreats, and other activities, working with licensed mental health professionals has been instrumental in my progress. The Enneagram is an incredible tool, but it's not the be-all and end-all for inner work; in my experience, all of these different angles can work in concert. This book is filled with exercises to challenge and support you on your path, but please consult with your personal mental health care provider if you are uncomfortable or uncertain about any of the practices offered, if you are able to access therapy. I've also included some resources for affordable therapy in the resource guide, which can be found at https://www .enneagramirl.com/resources.

As we embark on this journey together, you'll move beyond the basics of the Enneagram to embrace growth-oriented learning and actionable change. This book will equip you with the skills you need to apply the Enneagram in your real life. But here's the thing: to get the most from this book, you'll need to put it into action. Passively absorbing information won't move the needle. This book is all about the trial-and-error process of discovering the best way to apply the Enneagram in your life.

Thank you for entrusting me as a guide on your Enneagram journey. I can't wait to see where it takes you.

Always in your corner,

Steph

Part I

Start Here

CHAPTER 1

Laying the Groundwork

"Okay, fine! I'll do it," I acquiesced. My sister and husband had both urged me to take an Enneagram assessment, but I'd brushed them off for months. At the time, I was fascinated with a different motivation-based typology, but they persisted, knowing I would love the Enneagram, too. And that's how I found myself staring at the words "the Achiever" on my laptop screen.

My initial reaction was, *Yes! I won!* (fellow Threes will probably relate). But as I started reading, my joy dissipated, and searing dread crept up my spine. I was exposed. Scanning the page, I read about parts of myself I'd only recently started to recognize, and other parts that were completely outside my vision until I saw them plainly written. It laid bare traits that I disliked about myself, and while it was hard to read, I was intrigued.

I quickly found that the Enneagram wasn't like other personality tests I'd taken in the past. The Enneagram unearthed something deep, prompting self-reflection in a new way and directing my attention to some personal challenges and blind spots I habitually avoided.

Why the Enneagram?

The first time I became infatuated with interpreting personality was in elementary school. A friend had a book about self-concept, and it explained what different characteristics mean about us. Your favorite color (orange), favorite ice cream (mint chocolate chip), how you loop your cursive a's and dot your i's all had some qualitative meaning about your personality. I asked my parents and sisters for their selections and interpreted all of our results. Though the title of the book has since escaped my memory, I can still envision the chapter heading "Who am I?" scrawled across the page. This question is fitting. There's something innately human about the question "Who am I?" and the even more existential "Why am I here?"

Though personality assessments seem like a modern device, the act of sorting ourselves into identifiable typologies based on our personality traits is also a practice with a long history.[1] Innately, humans look for patterns. As children, we learn to identify a piece of furniture with four legs and a seat as a chair. These schemas allow our brains to save the processing power needed to relearn what a chair is every time we see one. This is essential to our functioning.[2]

As we move through life, our brains are wired to keep us alive.[3] We adopt all sorts of tricks to increase our odds of survival, many of which are excellent at keeping our bodies alive but miserable at instilling our lives with meaning, purpose, and happiness.[4] Ultimately, we all want to feel better. There's a reason why Bessel van der Kolk's *The Body Keeps the Score* has become a cultural touchstone, and books like *Atomic Habits* by James Clear have consistently topped bestseller lists. We want answers, and we're convinced that if we can puzzle through our trauma and change our behavior, we'll feel better. At least, I've always assumed so.

In part, I think this is why typologies like the Enneagram, Myers-Briggs, astrology, and others are so arresting. If we can discover some insight, we can be fascinated at the least, and transformed at the very best. Understanding our basic assumptions about the world—and where they came from—can help us identify how the patterns we've needed are no longer serving us and what we can do to change them.

This might be a surprise, given the title on the cover of the book you're reading, but I am an Enneagram skeptic. Sometimes I question how this one tool could be so broadly applicable, and I look for holes between accepted Enneagram theories and personality development concepts from psychology. So if you are a questioner, too, you've got company. However, I've also seen how powerful this material can be. When I hear friends struggle to understand their partner, or I consult with a team sans Enneagram teaching, I recognize how beautifully the Enneagram helps us understand ourselves and each other.

As you go through this book, think of the Enneagram as a map, a guide to help us find where we want to go and trace a path to get there. The process will still be imperfect, nonlinear, and several paths could lead to the same destination, but we have a full map furnished with a key, symbols, arrows, and descriptions to help us figure out where we are in the journey and how to move along to the next location. We just need to know how to read the map.

Cultural Overlay

The Enneagram is not about sorting all of humanity into neat little boxes. It's about understanding the perspectives we each hold within our complex systems. These systems are interconnected webs of culture, family of origin, class, gender, race, nationality, sexual orientation, and other social identifiers that make us who we are. These social identifiers are not personality based. They are socially constructed through relationships with others and the societies in which we live, and they affect how we show up in the world.[5] Personality psychologist Brian Little describes personality as cocreated with our innate selves and what we do in the world.[6] We cannot divorce the way we're socialized from who we are as individuals: humans are social animals, and even in ruthlessly individualistic societies, we remain interconnected. Who we are in relationship to others is indelibly linked to who we believe that we are.[7] Thus, the impact of the societal positioning, including positions of privilege, socioeconomic status, and the like, cannot be overstated when studying the armor of our types.[8]

While I've seen that the Enneagram is translatable across many different cultures, our understandings of the types themselves must be interpreted through the cultural context. Which is to say that my social identifiers (white, cisgender woman, millennial, middle class, American) do not make my perspective on the Enneagram "neutral." When working with clients, I research their cultures to understand how their origins might overlay with the Enneagram. In this book, I've tried to stay true to essentials of the type, and I conducted dozens of interviews with individuals of all twenty-seven subtypes across gender, sexual orientation, religion, occupation, generation, class, country of origin, race, and other differences that influence our perspectives. (Note that the stories and examples throughout the book came from these interviews and other firsthand experiences. In some cases, names have been changed.) Still, it's useful to identify how your culture, and even your family culture, might affect the way your type is expressed. For example, in some cultures, interrupting is perceived as rude, whereas other cultures perceive interrupting as a normal, expected part of communication. We cannot strip ourselves from these contexts, nor can we strip the Enneagram of them either. Your Enneagram type is not the only thing that is true of you. I prefer to see it as a part of your intricate human system.

While some of the ways we sort ourselves have to do with personality, as mentioned earlier in this chapter, some do not.[9] Humans have a long history of organizing power structures that inevitably oppress and marginalize some while centering others. The simple idea here is that the closer you are to the center, the more privilege and protection you have under these historical systems of oppression.[10] Because we all have various social identifiers, both marginalized and centered identities coexist in many of us. This matters because your specific expression of your type and your experience of the world depend on other factors, such as these social identifiers. This can make Enneagram typing trickier at times, but it underscores the necessity of Enneagram work as a collective activity. Author and therapist Chichi Agorom writes, "the work of healing and coming home to our truest selves is deeply personal, but it cannot be extricated from our collective healing."[11] In other words, let's move toward freedom and liberation together.

Guiding Principles

In our culture of constant self-improvement, we can get tripped up by this idea that we must be healthy or we're worthless. Then, we might assume that we must always move toward an up-and-to-the-right growth trajectory like we're a startup business pitching investors. But you and I are not businesses. And when we assume that we're only good when we're healthy or growing or constantly improving, we miss the whole point. Not only is this type of growth not the goal, it's also not possible. So I want to give you three guiding mindsets that will help you reframe the idea of growth to prepare for the work we're about to do.

Growth Mindset

Psychologist Carol Dweck has written extensively about this perspective, which she identifies as a "growth vs. fixed mindset."[12] Dweck illustrates the usefulness of replacing thoughts about our own deficiencies and shortcomings with curiosity and an assumption that we can grow. Instead of getting stuck in a fixed mindset, which assumes "everyone else is better and smarter," Dweck encourages the adoption of a growth mindset, marked by thoughts like "I wonder how they did that—I haven't learned that yet." When it comes to the Enneagram, instead of adopting a fixed mindset, which might respond to feedback by excusing bad behavior based on Enneagram type, we can pivot to a growth mindset that assumes that learning is not only possible but an essential part of the process.

Trust the Process

A few years ago, my husband and I replaced our weed-ridden front lawn with drought-tolerant native landscaping. Once the project was completed, I noticed a few of the plants weren't taking to their new homes. They weren't growing or flowering and seemed to be rather dormant, and the spring weather didn't seem to help either. In the fall, however, just as I was about to replace them, I noticed that they'd begun to thrive, while other plants had significantly slowed their previous growth trajectories.

Even though I knew that plants experience cycles of dormancy and growth, until I observed these cycles in my own garden with my very own eyes, it wasn't an obvious answer. What's more, it never occurred to me to think about myself and my personal growth in that way. Just like plants go through both dormancy and growth, we do as well. What if instead of expecting myself to grow at all times, I start to anticipate that I will experience seasons of expansion and seasons of settling in? What if the settling-in seasons, when our roots are growing deep and integrating into the soil, are just as important as those big, beautiful blooming seasons?

So when I talk about growth, I'm not just talking about always leaning into high-growth mode at all times. I'm also talking about getting comfortable with the equally good and necessary settling-in seasons when the roots are growing deeper even though you can't yet see it happening on the outside. Seeing yourself more like a garden and less like a self-improvement project can help your perspective when it comes to the Enneagram, especially if you're someone who can get critical when you haven't experienced a significant growth spurt in a while.

The Sleeper Effect

Similarly, expect growth over time, rather than expecting to see yourself change overnight. Real, sustainable growth takes work and time. Psychologist Richard Boyatzis has written extensively about the psychology of change. In particular, Boyatzis emphasizes the necessity for change to be intentional: true, sustainable growth is not only a longer process than most of us expect, but it also often requires a good bit of effort. In a paper about his aptly named "Intentional Change Theory," Boyatzis wrote about two phenomena related to personal change.[13]

The first is called the *honeymoon effect*, and it's a phenomenon many of us have experienced. When I think about the honeymoon effect, I think about that mountain-high feeling that we often experience when on a retreat or a weekend away. We can enjoy incredible spiritual experiences or life-altering insights. This is called a *change event*. Immediately after one of these events, there's an initial period when everything seems to be going well, the knowledge sticks, and the overall feeling is positive. At times, this can feel like the real change, but soon thereafter, we might revert to previous behavior or find changed behavior effortful. Discouraged, we succumb to the belief that we never changed at all, or that we're destined to be stuck in this place.

However, Boyatzis discovered a second phenomenon called the *sleeper effect*. The sleeper effect explains that six to twelve months after a change event, we will start to see and experience the real results of the event. Often, the change we worked toward has germinated and integrated in the background. Consistent effort toward change is what matters, even when it feels like transformation has not set in yet. Eventually, we can look back on how we've grown over six to twelve months, and this offers a more accurate barometer with which to measure growth.

Understanding that growth is not linear and takes hard work over time is helpful guidance for anyone seeking personal development to stay the course.

Guidelines for Use

Now that we've covered some key principles, I'd like to offer suggestions on how to use the Enneagram and this book. For many of us, looking inward can be a vulnerable and confronting process, so I want to make sure this journey of self-discovery feels safe and approachable for you and those around you.

START WITH SELF-COMPASSION. If you've studied the Enneagram for any length of time, you'll know that we often focus more closely on the not-so-lovely parts of each type. We can often see ourselves most clearly in our unhealthiest moments. And going further, we can't truly grow without seeing these challenging aspects of the self. But if you begin this process with a mindset of self-compassion and acceptance, this work can be positive in so many ways.[14] So be kind to your past, present, and future self.

CULTIVATE EMPATHY. This tool also offers you a path toward empathy because as you study it, you will discover that while some things are super easy for you (and your type), those same things are difficult for others, and vice versa. This is all helpful knowledge as you interact with the people around you. Expanding your awareness around the types can help you develop a deeper empathy overall because you start to see things from new vantage points; you're putting yourself into other people's shoes.

RESIST TYPING OTHERS. Saying something like "You're *such* a One!" can cause a loved one to feel misunderstood and unable to speak up about their own type. Putting an individual in a position where they have to argue for who they are is not helpful. Instead, I recommend sharing the Enneagram by explaining the insights you've learned about yourself and how much you appreciate it as a system. Seeing your growth process can be the inspiration a loved one needs to dive in on their own. Whatever you do, don't force it. I believe the Enneagram finds us all when we need it most.

DON'T WEAPONIZE THE ENNEAGRAM. This subject matter can be sensitive, so it's important to treat it with care. For example, saying, "That's such a Nine thing to say!" is often meant in jest, but it can be hurtful and cause others to shut down if you don't have a relationship that can support this type of joking.

With that said, seeing ourselves in our type descriptions can be fun and even funny. Against my own guidance—do as I say and not as I do and all that—my husband and I have taken to poking fun at ourselves and each other with our Enneagram types. Fortunately, we have a relationship that is safe enough to truly examine our ego activity, and this dynamic provides a bit of comic relief when we've overlooked the ways our habitual functioning is screaming our types.

The Path Ahead

The Enneagram is a deep and powerful tool, and I'm constantly looking to thread the needle between simplifying complexity and preserving the depth in this tool. Whether you are a seasoned self-development reader or a fresh-eyed learner, I hope this book can help you recognize not only your common patterns and characteristics but also something deeper. I hope you see glimmers of your truest and highest self along the way. If you choose to walk this path, you are embarking on a lifelong journey toward growth, healing, and self-compassion, and I'm honored to walk alongside you.

CHAPTER 2

How the System Works

What Is the Enneagram?

The Enneagram is a motivation-based personality framework oriented around nine core types. Because these are archetypes, you may not resonate with every little detail of your type description, but core aspects of the archetypal structure generally ring true for people of the same type.

While the term *personality framework* reflects an approximate definition of this tool, it is more accurate to think of the Enneagram as a map. The complexity of the system itself is part of what attracted me to it, and it's also what keeps a lot of us from fully accessing and understanding all that it offers. Using the Enneagram as a symbol to inspire curiosity and deeper self-discovery is the key to moving toward deeper self-awareness and awakening to our truest selves.

The word *Enneagram* is derived from Latin; *ennea* means "nine" and *gram* or *gramma* means "something that is written or drawn."[1] Thus, *Enneagram* refers to the system itself as well as the symbol shown in this section.

The Enneagram is a map for self-knowledge and transformation. As a map, there are inherent rules within the structure, and the image itself is full of symbolism. In this chapter, we'll walk through the concepts you need to understand to get the most from this book. With this tool, there's always more to know, and the paths of personal and collective development are lifelong quests toward meaningful change. There's no expectation we will arrive at the

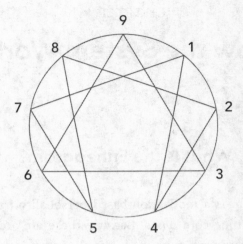

pinnacle of growth and graduate from inner work. To begin this journey, you'll need a thorough understanding of the tool itself.

This chapter will act as a guide to terms and concepts in the type chapters that follow. I know it's tempting to skip straight to your type, but I urge you, resist! You'll find important context to build on with type-specific information. Once you've read the opening chapters, feel free to skip around. In each type chapter, you'll find examples to illustrate how various aspects of the type manifest in real life, along with reflection sections to apply your new knowledge. You can also download a workbook featuring growth activities for your type at https://www.enneagramirl.com/resources.

Centers of Intelligence

If you've encountered other Enneagram material, you've likely heard the word *triad* floating around. *Triad* is the overarching term used to describe three groupings of three types. There are various triadic groupings, and each offers a unique perspective that allows us to gain a deeper understanding of the types. The centers of intelligence (or intelligence centers) are the most foundational of these triadic groupings. The three intelligence centers are the body, heart, and mind.

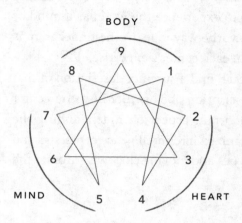

Each intelligence center has an underlying emotion that is a central theme of their lives and their inner work. Of course, we all experience all emotions, but the personality structure of each type in a given triad is organized to alleviate or obscure this core emotional theme. As I've studied the Enneagram, I've found it increasingly important to let go of some of the labels we place on emotions as we consider them "positive" or "negative." Anger (body), sadness (heart), and fear (mind) are often considered negative emotions, and this drives our desire to rid ourselves of intense expressions of them. But reimagining these emotions as neutral can free more space for us to recognize, work with, and process them.[2]

The Enneagram opens our eyes to observe ourselves in ways we typically haven't noticed before. Recognizing yourself in your center of intelligence may be easy, but it's more challenging to imagine how other centers see the world. During an Enneagram workshop a few years ago, a heart type shared he had an ability to take the emotional temperature of the room and immediately know what each person needed. A body type in the group started asking questions, trying to puzzle together exactly what mannerisms or observations about the individuals gave off certain signals. The heart type did his best to answer these questions, but describing this experience is like explaining the flavor of mango to someone who has never tried it before. It's so experiential that we often end up saying, "You just have to try it!" Unfortunately, in this case, that's not possible, hence the game of twenty questions. As a heart type, I'll never fully comprehend what it feels like to experience the world as a mind or body type, which is why my favorite way to learn the Enneagram is through group discussion from each center's expertise.

Before each new section, you'll find a succinct description of that center to supplement the descriptions below. Because the center of intelligence is such an important aspect of understanding the Enneagram, the types are organized into intelligence centers as you read, starting with the body types and moving clockwise around the Enneagram.

The Body Center

Types Eight, Nine, and One are in the body center. They are in touch with what is happening and what is going to happen on an instinctual level, as if their five senses are in overdrive. This center is sometimes called the "gut" center, which describes how they perceive the world through "gut feeling" and "felt sense." In moments of fear or anger, they might experience emotions physically as a stomach drop, or feeling their gut is on fire. All three of these types move through the world instinctually. In decision-making, they have a gut-level knowing of what to do next, but they will often validate that instinct with research, especially when they know others will expect further explanation. If you're a body type, you may have strayed from this instinctual knowing due to external influences, but remember you can make good decisions leveraging your natural inner resources.

Beneath the surface is an underlying anger or rage as well as a focus on structure or boundaries. Like many emotions, anger can be destructive or liberating. To use it well, it's helpful to recognize how anger can be a powerful, positive, and energizing force. For example, activists draw on anger to rise up and fight injustice; parents access anger to protect their children; you might use anger to set healthy boundaries. This is not encouragement to rage and constantly express destructive anger toward others around us, but a recognition of the truth that allowing more space for emotion can be helpful in accepting those emotions and moving forward in an integrated way.

Eights overdo anger, accessing it readily, even though another emotion might be hiding beneath the surface. Ones underdo anger, suppressing it because they believe it's inappropriate to express, and this often means it is turned inward as self-criticism. Nines fall asleep to their anger, believing they never feel angry. Nines and Ones miss that anger is a stronger driving force than they realize, both in a positive and negative way. It can be powerful for these types to lean into it a bit and truly accept it. The following images illustrate this concept. These are adapted from *The Wisdom of the Enneagram* by Don Riso and Russ Hudson.[3]

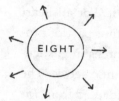

Energy (Anger) Directed Outward
Against External Control

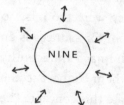

Energy (Anger) Directed Inward
& Outward to Maintain Calm

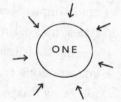

Energy (Anger) Directed Inward
to Contain Internal Impulses

The Heart Center

Types Two, Three, and Four are in the heart center. Heart types focus on relationships, building rapport, and creating mutual understanding and empathy. These types naturally sense the emotional context of interactions. Often, they sense what others are feeling simply by being in their presence.

Beneath the surface, heart types experience sadness. Some teachers label this as shame, but beneath shame is truly a sadness about the heart type's image or identity: all three of these types tend to believe they're not enough in some way. The loss of identity becomes a consuming focus of their attention. Each of these types wonders about who they truly are.

To establish a more stable sense of self, these types subconsciously present an image of who they are. All three of these types can have shapeshifting tendencies, but this is much more pronounced in Twos and Threes (Fours may counter-shapeshift, meaning they'll assess who they're supposed to be and will shift to become the opposite of that in some sense to stand out).

Threes often reject the idea of being a heart type, as in their daily lives, they find that emotions hinder their progress and productivity. Because Threes place such a high value on their efficiency, they set emotions aside and busy themselves with tasks. Once they slow down a bit, they might find emotional depth they haven't yet uncovered simply because they were too busy to notice it. For all heart types, making more room for sadness is an important part of processing their issues with image and identity. For Threes in particular, emotions can help them connect to their authentic selves. The following images illustrate this concept. These are adapted from *The Wisdom of the Enneagram* by Don Riso and Russ Hudson.[4]

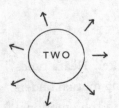

Image (Persona) Presented
Externally to Others

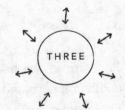

Image (Persona) Presented
Externally to Others & Internally
to Self

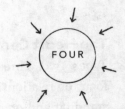

Image (Persona) Presented
Internally to Self

The Mind Center

Types Five, Six, and Seven are in the mind or head center. These types pay attention to strategy and security. While most people experience thinking several ideas at once, this is amplified for head types. They often experience thinking many, many thoughts at once, noticing connections between ideas, and building stronger connections as they process. The speed and intensity of these thoughts sets the head types apart.

Often, mind types experience that their thoughts move faster than they can speak, so some might seem to speak a bit slower as they are fully processing thoughts while speaking (this is more common with Fives and Sixes than with Sevens). For other head types, their thoughts move faster than others around them, and they find themselves interrupting because they're already on to the next idea. Because mental types experience so much excitement around ideas, they might unintentionally step on others' toes by interrupting.

The underlying emotion for head types is fear, and in this case, it is all about anticipation. Using their mental capacities, head types anticipate what might come and strategize for it. This is often portrayed mostly as a Six trait, but in fact, Fives and Sevens share this characteristic. In different ways, head types try to foster security and stability by attempting to predict the unknown. They use their mental strengths to analyze, strategize, and troubleshoot life as they move through it.

Head types also have a tendency to "think" their feelings rather than "feel" them. If you ask one of these types how they feel, they might say, "I think . . ." If you're a head type, it might be challenging to recognize that you're doing this! Some head types find it helpful for someone else to name their feelings for them at first. For example, if a Seven says, "it's like my shoulders are in my ears, I can't breathe deeply, and I am antsy," someone who knows that person well might be able to label that, "hmmm, that sounds like anxiety" or "that sounds like worry."

Mental types are also focused on patterns, systems, and models. It's common for head types to think about the rational, practical way to accomplish something. An Enneagram Seven I interviewed shared that when she starts meeting with a new therapist, it's important for her to understand the model they're using to approach therapy. She looks to a reliable, logical framework as a guide for her own processing, and that feels more secure than going in unprepared. The following images illustrate this concept. These are adapted from *The Wisdom of the Enneagram* by Don Riso and Russ Hudson.[5]

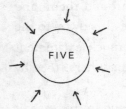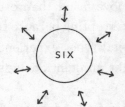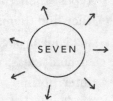

Flee Inward to Avoid External Threats & Intrusion

Flee Inward to Avoid External Threats & Outward to Avoid Internal Threats

Flee Outward to Avoid Threats of their Inner World

Motivation

The Enneagram is not about what we do but why we do it. These powerful, often subconscious "whys" are the driving forces underpinning our personality structure. In Enneagram theory, these are motivations. To some extent, our personalities are innate. While our environments influence how we turn out, "not all of personality comes from experience; some of it comes from genes."[6] Think of these heritable traits as a lens through which we see the world. Our perceptions of early childhood experiences are shaped by these lenses. This does not invalidate the pain you may have experienced, but it helps to explain why siblings can share experiences without becoming the same type. Each Enneagram type has unmet needs from childhood (internalized as messages called Unconscious Childhood Messages[7]), and these shape our motivation. Other aspects of the personality explored later in this chapter, like the passion, fixation, and focus of attention, weave together to form the fabric of motivation.

Though persistent and lifelong, these forces are tricky to recognize at first glance simply because we're not used to observing ourselves in this way. Understanding your own motivation may take longer than you expect initially, which is one of the reasons I see so many clients connect with one type's behavior only to later realize their driving motivation is that of a different type. Self-discovery is a lifelong process, so developing your skills to observe yourself even when you don't know your type will aid your development once your type is clear.

In my own inner work, I continually awaken to new ways my motivation is showing up in daily life. Like all of our automatic behaviors, our motivations are neither good nor bad but have been necessary coping mechanisms we've developed to ensure survival. With the wisdom of time, self-awareness, and self-observation, we can see that some of the habitual patterns we've developed are not working for our highest good. The aim, then, is to observe them and find space for choice, rather than continuing in worn-in patterns that are not producing the higher awareness we desire.

Even when we believe we are seeing all of life objectively, these subconscious motivating forces mean we are essentially looking through a pinhole.[8] Enneagram work enables us to notice this automatic narrowing of attention, so that we can learn to expand our view to be more clear and aligned with reality.

Motivations and Attentional Focus by Type

TYPE	MOTIVATIONS AND ATTENTIONAL FOCUS
BODY TYPES	
Eight	Strength, toughness, forward motion, autonomy, being a bold and powerful protector of oneself and others, pushing back against attempts at exploitation and power, self-trust
Nine	Peace, harmony, unity with humanity, feeling connected, togetherness, comfort, simplicity, keeping all perspectives and contributions in mind, creating and maintaining equality, fairness, taking a broad view on life
One	Clarity, integrity, balance, improvement, accuracy, excellence, bringing ideals to fruition, efficiency, creating a world that works well for the common flourishing of humanity, developing structure (internally, or by being a good role model, or by giving guidance) to make life better
HEART TYPES	
Two	Universal love, positive relationships, rapport, mutual enjoyment of one another, self-sacrifice for the common good, altruism, seeing the good in others, finding connections, claiming their place
Three	Achievement, self-motivation, adaptability, image awareness, admiration, self-belief and inspiring others, seeing potential, effective action, verve, success, dreaming big, finding validation and self-worth in accomplishment, getting things done
Four	Beautifying existence, appreciating the essential brokenness of life as precious and wonderful, generating creativity, a unique contribution through self-expression, seeing an ideal vision of the world, emotional acuity, being exceptional, extraordinary, and significant
MIND TYPES	
Five	Facts, data, rational, objective reasoning, steadiness, creating margin, developing competence, establishing certainty and clarity, self-sufficiency, managing demands, expectations, time, energy, mental and emotional expenditure
Six	Managing risks, analysis, predicting, safety, security, thinking through all possibilities, doing whatever they can to make sure everything turns out okay, questioning, establishing community, loyal relationships, reliability
Seven	Mental stimulation, freedom, possibilities, opportunities, experiences, planning, making time for fun and pleasure, activity, keeping a positive mood, sampling all that life has to offer, belief in the expansiveness of the ideal world

Avoidance

Each type is similarly motivated by specific scenarios they're habitually working to avoid. Avoidance can take the form of arranging life circumstances to ensure certain scenarios will not come to fruition or even erecting psychological barriers to avoid seeing reality. For example, a One might avoid feeling wrong or corrupt by having an incessant inner critic who constantly blames them for minor errors.

TYPE	AVOIDING
BODY TYPES	
Eight	Weakness, being betrayed, being vulnerable to external control, being controlled by others, exposing their inner softness
Nine	Being the cause of discord or disconnection, speaking up and causing conflict as a result, losing connection with loved ones, disunity or turmoil
One	Being wrong, corrupt, or deceitful, being morally inconsistent, being wrong and being the last to know
HEART TYPES	
Two	Experiencing rejection, feeling dismissed or discarded, being disliked, being selfish or lacking kindness, relational imbalance in which they have given less than others have
Three	Feeling worthless, falling short of their potential, failure (any whiff of failure is too much and to be avoided), being ineffective, others seeing them in a bad light, feeling embarrassed
Four	Not making a noteworthy impact on the world, blending in and losing distinct individuality, being too much, being out of alignment with their truest self, never reaching complete self-understanding
MIND TYPES	
Five	Being depleted, loss, abandonment, emptiness, feeling overwhelmed, carrying too much emotional weight, feeling unable to retreat and recharge
Six	Experiencing negative outcomes they did not foresee, betrayal of trust, being vulnerable to attack, submitting to an untrustworthy authority
Seven	Missing out, being left behind, limitations, restriction, feeling trapped, being forced to look at downsides

The inner critic can beat the One to the punch, so to speak. Or a Three might manage experiences of failure by only engaging in activities in areas of existing proficiency. Most of these scenarios are challenging for any of us, regardless of type, but we are particularly averse to specific scenarios that relate to our core type's personality structure.

Thresholds

Some of my favorite Enneagram learnings happen while in dialogue with others. When I'm teaching, I find that participants often experience glimmers of insight—those "lightbulb" moments where everything becomes perfectly clear, and we're not sure how we missed it before. A few years ago, I experienced one of these revelations as well. I developed this concept of thresholds during a workshop with a team. An Eight on the team asked why others experience Eights as argumentative or angry, even when Eights don't feel that way inside. A window of insight opened: Eights have a higher threshold for what feels like conflict.

I made a gesture around eye level and said, "For an Eight, this is their threshold for conflict. Anything below this feels like a conversation." Using my other hand, I signaled around shoulder height, and said, "For another person, maybe *this* is the threshold. Anything above this level feels like conflict. So you can imagine that if the conversation is happening here," gesturing halfway between the two levels, "the other person walks away thinking we just had a big fight, and the Eight walks away thinking we had a fun conversation."

In the intervening years, I've taught this concept countless times, and it is revelatory for interpersonal communication. The same general framework can apply to each type as a way to deepen our mutual understanding and gain empathy for our different perspectives.

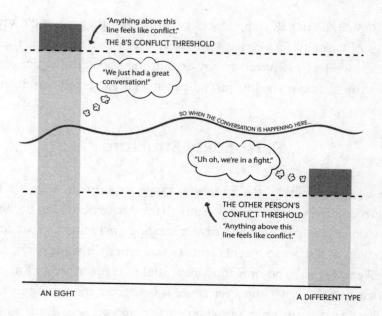

While workshopping this theory, I encountered the term *windows of tolerance*, developed by esteemed psychiatrist Dan Siegel.[9] When operating within our window of tolerance, we can engage, self-regulate, think clearly, and communicate with others. When outside the window of tolerance, those basic functions become fuzzy. The threshold concept is similar in acknowledging that each of us can tolerate different levels of different stimuli. Rather than looking at individual experiences of emotional regulation, my threshold theory identifies certain boundaries around the window of tolerance based on the psyche structures of each type. As we grow, the threshold becomes less absolute, and we gain flexibility and are able to stay in a regulated, centered state more often.

HIGH THRESHOLD: Experiences or situations that we have more capacity for, where we hold high expectations. It's the limit at which we become alarmed, start taking action, find a situation bothersome, or simply feel that we've done enough.

LOW THRESHOLD: Experiences or situations that we don't have a lot of capacity for. Perhaps we are more impatient about these topics, we feel motivated to say something about the topic, or if something crosses the line just a little, it feels extremely unsettling.

Personality Structure

It's useful to think of the Enneagram type structure as a shell. The shell comprises various components that we have needed to become functional and survive our early upbringing, including the passion, fixation, and defense mechanisms of our types. In some ways, the shell enables us to become functional adults, as described by Freud's concept of the ego.[10] But over time, we outgrow the coping mechanisms that were once developmentally appropriate. Enneagram work is about recognizing and reassessing these outdated operating behaviors to allow ourselves to flourish by getting in touch with our essence.

Inside the shell is our essence—the purest and most innocent self. This essence represents who we truly are, and it's innate. When I think about this essential self, I think of a concept from the therapy modality Internal Family Systems. In this modality, each of us has Self energy, which is marked by eight qualities: compassion, curiosity, clarity, creativity, connection, courage, calm, and confidence.[11] A key aim of IFS is engaging with the world from Self energy—this allows us to bring those eight qualities into our daily lives in a way that feels integrated, grounded, and mindful. The concept of essence I teach through the Enneagram lens represents a similar quality: it's marked by grounded, connected, compassionate presence. It is our truest self and is representative of our own inner knowing, which is often elusive when we are disconnected from it.

When we do Enneagram work, the aim is not to change who

we are but to return to our essence. This essence is precious, and early on in life, when we start to encounter the world around us, we quickly subconsciously recognize that it must be protected at all costs. This is where the personality shell comes in. This shell is a set of defenses that we need in order to survive. Most personality patterns were useful at some point, in that they ultimately serve to protect us and help us thrive.[12]

The shell itself is made up of defense mechanisms, the fixation and passion of the type, and other automatic habits that keep us safe. For each type, there are defense mechanisms that are commonly used, though all of us employ a variety of defenses. The fixation and passion are type-specific, and most Enneagram practitioners teach them in similar ways. Most of the personality patterns for each type either uphold or are supported by these components. These patterns keep us safe, they help us survive, and we have absolutely needed them to make it this far in life. However, most of us reach a point where our defense mechanisms become outdated, and we're no longer content to let them rule our lives. Each of the components below is powerful, and most of us never fully leave them behind. Instead, we become savvy to their tricks, and we learn to notice them, confront them, and choose differently over time.

Passion

We often think of passion as a good thing: it's something we use as fuel to pursue meaningful work, or we use it to describe what we care about in life. In Enneagram language, however, the term *passion* is better understood as in the context of "the passion of the Christ" in religious texts.[13] In this sense, passion is an overwhelming and uncontrollable emotional state; it's more powerful than we recognize, and it's often operating behind the scenes, buried deep in our subconscious experience. Even for those who would not describe themselves as emotional, the passion is a persistent emotional state that propels how we experience the world, what we think about, and how we act. The inner work of the Enneagram is, in many ways, learning to step out of the passion's grip. As we discuss the passion of each type, keep in mind that there's no expectation that you will be "cured" from your passion. You do not have to be free of it to be healthy or growing; in fact, I find that the more inner work my clients engage in, the more they notice their passion! This is not because they're somehow getting worse but because they are simply growing in awareness.

In each chapter, you'll find practical examples of how the passion plays out for each type so that you can gain awareness of the passion. You'll also find applicable tips to begin to move toward the opposite direction, which we call the virtue.

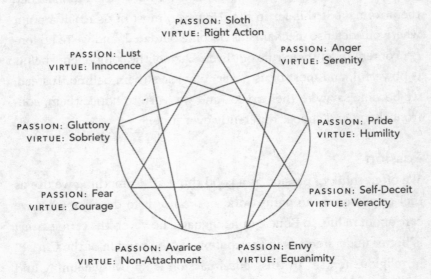

THE PASSIONS AND VIRTUES OF THE ENNEAGRAM

PASSION: Sloth
VIRTUE: Right Action

PASSION: Lust
VIRTUE: Innocence

PASSION: Anger
VIRTUE: Serenity

PASSION: Gluttony
VIRTUE: Sobriety

PASSION: Pride
VIRTUE: Humility

PASSION: Fear
VIRTUE: Courage

PASSION: Self-Deceit
VIRTUE: Veracity

PASSION: Avarice
VIRTUE: Non-Attachment

PASSION: Envy
VIRTUE: Equanimity

Virtue

The virtue is the opposite of the passion. It is who we are in higher self-awareness, and it represents our truest, most authentic expression of self. Where the passion represents our less aware egoic self, the virtue is who we truly are without the personality structure. Initially, the virtue can seem aspirational for a beginning Enneagram learner. I've even heard clients share that they cannot comprehend why they would want to return to their virtue as in their current life it seems less than ideal. However, over time, as we begin to see small glimmers of our true essence, we find more reason to lean in to the virtue inside wherever we can find it.

Defense Mechanisms

Defense mechanisms are unconscious strategies we use to avoid feelings of discomfort.[14] These work together with the fixation to keep us "safe," but this often inadvertently reinforces the passion once again. Each type has an assigned defense mechanism that they use frequently, but these are not the only defense mechanisms they employ. Any type can use any defense mechanism, and we often have a favorite cocktail of defense mechanisms to ensure comfort and to avoid damage to our psyche.

COMMONLY USED DEFENSE MECHANISMS

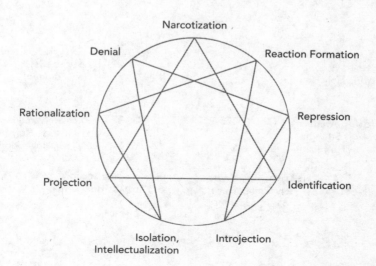

Fixation

The fixation is a mental strategy used to attempt to restore essence. Often called "ego-fixations,"[15] the fixations are the tools we use to try to get back to who we truly are, but they end up just defending the passions and keeping the entire personality structure intact. Each type has a specific favorite fixation, and because these are mental states (rather than emotional states like the passion), the work of undoing often requires a different type of attention than passion work. This book does not address them in detail, but you will find resources on this topic in the endnotes.

Holy Idea

The holy idea is the higher realm of the mental center—the opposite of the fixation. This is quite an advanced stage of inner work, so this book focuses on the passion, defense mechanism, and virtue as more approachable growth steps.[16]

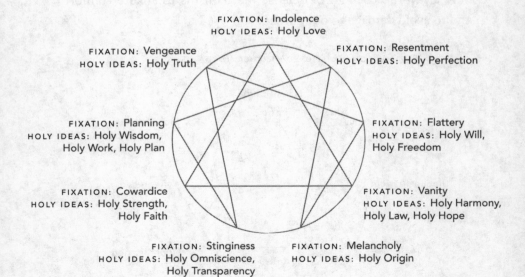

FIXATION: Indolence
HOLY IDEAS: Holy Love

FIXATION: Vengeance
HOLY IDEAS: Holy Truth

FIXATION: Resentment
HOLY IDEAS: Holy Perfection

FIXATION: Planning
HOLY IDEAS: Holy Wisdom,
Holy Work, Holy Plan

FIXATION: Flattery
HOLY IDEAS: Holy Will,
Holy Freedom

FIXATION: Cowardice
HOLY IDEAS: Holy Strength,
Holy Faith

FIXATION: Vanity
HOLY IDEAS: Holy Harmony,
Holy Law, Holy Hope

FIXATION: Stinginess
HOLY IDEAS: Holy Omniscience,
Holy Transparency

FIXATION: Melancholy
HOLY IDEAS: Holy Origin

Subtypes

Early in my Enneagram learning, I heard the advice that new learners should wait two years before they even begin to think about learning subtypes. I took that advice, and let me tell you: that is very bad advice. Subtypes are the most powerful and essential piece of the Enneagram because they lay out a specific, personally tailored growth plan for each type. They are especially useful for individuals who feel like they recognize themselves in the motivation or passion of their type but not in any of the behavioral depictions they read online.

Subtypes are distinct archetypes within each Enneagram type, which is the combination of the core type and the instinctual variant. The term *instinctual variants* refers to a specific set of three survival instincts we all have. These are not our only instincts, of course, but

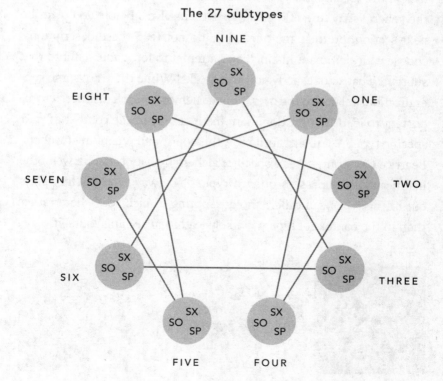

The 27 Subtypes

they are the important ones for this concept. Like our instinct to come up for air when underwater, the survival instincts we'll discuss here are animalistic in nature: they are engrained within the core of our being, and they dictate our behavior without conscious consideration.[17] Can you imagine needing to think about your heart beating or your lungs filling with air? Simply breathing is miraculous when we consider the mechanics, but it requires very little attention unless something has gone seriously wrong. In Enneagram theory, the three instincts are the self-preservation instinct, the social instinct, and the sexual instinct. Of course, we all have a drive toward each of these: the need to preserve one's own safety, the need for human connection, and the need for procreation and intensity are all essential to our survival.

When these three instincts are overlaid with the nine Enneagram types, we get twenty-seven distinct subtypes. In each chapter, we'll look at the specific subtypes therein, so this section will only focus on the general structure of the subtypes themselves. Before you read the next section, promise me one thing: do not read these descriptions, choose your dominant instinct, and attempt to force yourself into that subtype. That's not exactly how this works! While there are some generalizations related to the overarching themes for each instinct, it's important to identify your dominant instinct only in the context of your specific type. A primary author on this topic, and one of my teachers, Beatrice Chestnut, notes a specific "alchemy" that occurs between the instinct and the passion of each type.[18] The way each instinct plays out in the types can differ, and attempting to pick yours here rather than in the context of type will likely lead to mistyping yourself.

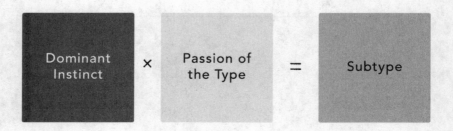

Dominant Instinct × Passion of the Type = Subtype

Self-Preservation (SP)

This instinct is about security, stability, and resources. Those **dominant** in this instinct have an underlying script that insists, "I am responsible for my own survival." Thus, they focus on financial security, health, well-being, home, and other material fixtures of life. While their attention is naturally drawn to these things, that doesn't mean they are necessarily skilled at attaining all the resources they need, simply that they are aware of the presence or lack of these creature comforts. They want to feel grounded in their daily lives, but they sometimes miss that avenues to accomplish this exist outside their natural inclinations. For example, a Self-Preservation Three might miss that they can feel more grounded and stable if they have better social connections or if they reassess their view of success. Externally, self-preservation subtypes tend to be more reserved and less expressive, but internally they are anxious and attuned to scarcity. Self-preservation subtypes are often warm, modest, salt-of-the-earth people. They are more calculated, intentional, and risk-averse than the other subtypes of their type.

When this instinct is **repressed**, a person's attention is less focused on the aspects of life listed above. They may not think about what is for dinner until it's time to eat or may forget to eat altogether. They might not consider their individual needs and may place others' priorities ahead of their own. Self-preservation repressed individuals can be more prone to burnout because they are less focused on their physical maintenance needs.[19]

Social (SO)

This instinct is about belonging, power dynamics, and social good. Those **dominant** in this instinct are concerned for the overall good of society, since they have an underlying assumption that "If the herd survives, I survive." These subtypes want to be a part of something bigger, they are cognizant of the roles we all play in society, and they live by a set of high ideals. Many social subtypes find themselves in leadership roles where they teach, train, or model for others how to be. However, they are not necessarily more sociable than others, and social dominants of some types can even be somewhat aloof if they are not working in a defined, purposeful role (in particular, this applies to types One, Three, Five, Six, and Eight). They are passionate advocates and supporters of humanity, though they may find it challenging to connect with individual humans. Sometimes social dominants feel they are a central part of the group dynamic, but even then, they may feel uncertain if they will ever truly belong. They may not realize how much they are sacrificing themselves for the group, but if they do, they're likely to wear it as a sign of pride.

When this instinct is **repressed**, a person is likely to be suspicious of groups, organizations, and foundations.[20] Because a social repressed person is not inclined to be a "joiner," it's easy to assume that others join such collectives for some ulterior motive. These individuals might also resist blending in too much with others to avoid losing their individual identity. For example, they might avoid participating in a school spirit day, or perhaps they overlook the role of societal forces on individual behavior.

Sexual (SX)

This instinct is about chemistry, attraction, and vitality. Those **dominant** in this instinct are always looking for a spark of fascination in life. They tend to swing to extremes, and very little in life is truly neutral to them. Everything is a polarity: they are attracted or repulsed, all in or all out.[21] They can be difficult to describe because they are paradoxical. Sexual dominants are often more emotional than the other subtypes, readily expressing big anger or excitement, but they can also be gentler, sweeter, and more sensitive. They merge with others, so even though they can be strong personalities in some ways, it's not uncommon for sexual dominants to feel a bit lost because they've blended too much with someone else (partner, parent, sibling, or close friend).[22] They mine for deep, intimate connections with specific others, but they can be highly idealistic, which makes it difficult to feel satisfied in their relationship. The adrenaline rush of the chase or the experience of merging can trump being good at the relationship itself. In all areas of life, sexual dominants seek that delicious electric feeling of newness and fascination.

When this instinct is **repressed**, a person might lack some intensity or zeal.[23] They are less animated and prefer steadiness, calm, and constancy over the variety and spontaneity sexual dominants prefer. They also might be less driven and less likely to go after what they truly want as they are more focused on what is the appropriate way to be.

Twenty-Seven Distinct Types . . . and Then Some

We all contain all three instincts, and we often find ourselves a bit in each. However, when moving through daily life, one instinct is running the show. This is called the dominant instinct.

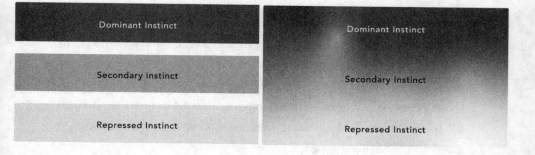

SUBTYPE SEQUENCE CONCEPT   SUBTYPE SEQUENCE IN PRACTICE

Dominant Instinct   Dominant Instinct

Secondary Instinct   Secondary Instinct

Repressed Instinct   Repressed Instinct

- The dominant instinct is the most prevalent in your life.
- The secondary instinct is often a very close second to the dominant instinct, so it may take time to decipher which is first and second.
- The repressed instinct is third and is often least prevalent in your life, even comically so.

Though one specific instinct is dominant, in practice, we subconsciously use the instincts as needed, typically vacillating between the top two. This can make identifying your subtype tricky, which is why I recommend looking at which one you use most often as evidenced by your behavior.

When the dominant instinct is combined with the passion of each type, the subtype is formed. The core motivation, or the essential why of each type, isn't changed with the subtype, but the subtypes differ in the way they perceive their needs and attempt to meet them. It's important to note that your subtype is not a different type (for example, you can't be a Four with a Social Seven subtype). It's also helpful to note that the core motivation is consistent across all three subtypes, but it shows up differently depending on the instinct.

Dynamic Movement Arrows

The arrows are another helpful way to see more dynamic movement within the Enneagram. Each type can access the two types it is connected to on the Enneagram diagram. When we access these lines in conscious ways, we tap into the higher levels of development of those types. But when we're not paying attention, moving through life in an automatic, less aware way, we tend to access the average to lower levels of those types.

Some Enneagram teachers consider one arrow the "growth" or

integration arrow, and the opposite arrow the "stress" or disintegration arrow. After a few years of working with clients 1:1, I found that this wasn't lining up in practice. Upon further research, I began to uncover new, more dynamic, ways of looking at the arrows, primarily through the book *The Complete Enneagram* by Beatrice Chestnut,[24] my in-person training with the Chestnut Paes Enneagram Academy, and Sandra Maitri's soul child theory.[25]

One of the main challenges to how I previously taught this is how my clients and I experienced them: the confines of "stress" and "growth" points seem simple, but the simplicity did not convey reality for many of us. Rather than strict guidelines around how we access these points, we can observe freer movement between them. The full access we each have to these other points is better represented when described as a flow between the types. Additionally, we can all access both the positive and negative aspects of both arrows. In my studies of the Enneagram, I've found there is often some aspect of another type that we need to borrow in an effort to be more integrated and balanced.

With this in mind, I've renamed the following points to convey these ideas.

In this image, Type Two is the Core Type. Type Four is the Recovery Point. Type Eight is the Transformation Point.

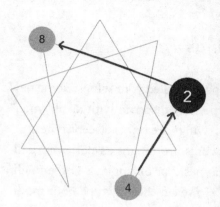

RECOVERY POINT: The recovery point features an aspect of the self that you need to recover and develop to pave the way for growth. This is sometimes called the security or growth number, but that doesn't quite capture the breadth of what can happen when accessing this type.

TRANSFORMATION POINT: The transformation point is the direction of sustainable growth. The term *transformation* conveys the metamorphosis that is available when we access this aspect of ourselves.

As already mentioned, when we're less conscious, we can easily pick up the lower or average aspects of either type. The growth path, then, is to use these types as assets. While the self-development you're looking for might be best described in the healthiest version of the transformation point, it's necessary to move to the recovery point first as a foundation.

Some authors, such as Sandra Maitri, have talked about the soul child theory, as an extension of the work produced by original Enneagram theorist Claudio Naranjo. I've found this work to be instructive in developing teachings around this topic. The concept states that a child we have disowned or neglected resides within each of us—not from malice but often because we've needed to do this to function. Something in that childlikeness is unresolved and needs to be recovered so that we can move forward into real growth.

When looking at these points, therefore, we can't hop straight into growth. We must first reach back into the recovery point to build the foundation for sustainable change.

In the chapters to come, you'll find descriptions of your arrows and how to access them as growth stretches.

Wings

Neighboring types to your core type are called your wings. Some new Enneagram learners name any type they resonate with as a "wing," but within the Enneagram system, wings are only adjacent types.

In some Enneagram schools, wings are taught as narrower definitions of the type, similar to subtypes. For example, a Three might claim a Four wing, signified 3w4. However, the way type Four modifies the Three is not always clear as descriptions of 3w4 (or any type/wing combination) vary widely. My teachers say, "Wings have been made to do the heavy lifting subtypes were meant to do."[27] Thus, I find it more useful to identify your subtype first, understand how it shows up in your life, and then clarify further

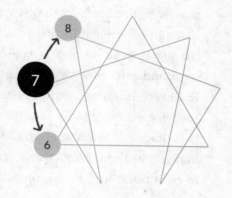

with the wing if it's an important part of your growth work.

Wings can be used for growth in that they offer smaller-scale stretches to balance. As you read the types, notice how neighboring types seem opposite. Claudio Naranjo says the types are the product of the tension between the wings, which pull each type in opposite directions.[28] If you identify strongly with one wing, work on integrating more of the other. For a Seven with a well-developed Eight wing, you might ask, what would a Six do here?

It's helpful to remember that you have access to your wing types and can use them when you need them. You may find yourself naturally shifting from one wing to another over the course of your life as you need different approaches. The whole idea of the Enneagram is not just to describe ourselves but to bring balance and integration into our lives.

Enneagram in Real Life: Foundational Practices for All Nine Types

In each of the following chapters, you'll find practical exercises for sustainable transformation. These are meant to be supportive for you, not to add another thing to your to-do list. Even if all you can muster right now is learning to observe yourself more consistently, that can be enough in this season. There's no rush to tackle all of the practices at once. You might find it useful to practice one per week and determine what is most helpful for you as you reflect on it. Each type has over a dozen suggestions to guide your development, so if something doesn't quite fit now or isn't a practical option for your stage of life, move on to the next one and come back to it later. Sometimes the simplest question, like, "What am I paying attention to right now?" can be eye-opening.

Context Matters

Most of us don't zoom out from our current moment to grasp a wide-angle perspective on our lives. If we did, we might be more understanding when we make mistakes or rely on old patterns that we know don't help us. Keep this in mind: *it all makes sense in context*. Your behaviors, patterns, emotional experiences, reactivity, struggles, and thoughts were at some point required to keep you alive, to protect your ego, or to escape harm in the context of your life story. Your story includes everything: your biology, family system, culture, religious system, racial background, socioeconomic class, minority status, disabilities, systematically oppressed social identifiers, microaggressions, trauma, and the like.

This is why I believe self-compassion is so important. When you imagine yourself as a child navigating so many difficult dynamics, you can appreciate the strategies you developed to make it through. Even if you're an adult now, it's difficult to unlearn these early experiences because they are deeply embedded in the way we *needed* to function in the world.[29] This is not to say that we excuse all of them now, especially the maladaptive ones, but to say: give yourself a break because unlearning takes time. When you get frustrated, remind yourself, *it all makes sense in context*.

The Power of Expressive Writing

In January 1991, one hundred senior engineers were terminated from their jobs at a software company in Dallas, Texas. Most had been with the company for thirty years and planned to retire there before the layoffs. Four months later, none had found new jobs, so a staffing company psychologist, Stephanie Spera, called psychologist James Pennebaker for help. Pennebaker, who was already pioneering a method called expressive writing, devised an experiment. The study included three groups. Two groups would write for thirty minutes per day, five days in a row, and the third group was the control and was not given any instruction. One experimental group wrote everything they felt about this experience: their deepest, darkest feelings, their mortification, fury, and rage. The other experimental group used a common time management strategy and wrote about how they used their time.

All of the men entered the study with hostility, frustration, and devastation toward their experience, but the men in the expressive writing group, who wrote about their sadness, fear, humiliation, and anger regarding the layoffs, reported feeling better immediately after writing each day. Within three months, 27 percent of this group had landed jobs, compared to just 5 percent in the other two groups. Several months later, that metric grew to 53 percent and 18 percent, respectively. Across all three groups, the men had gone on the same number of interviews. The feelers fared far better in their job search.[30]

James Pennebaker has written extensively about the healing power of expressive writing, noting the positive impact on short- and long-term health, anxiety, depression, coping with grief, and other challenging psychological issues.[31] Here's how you incorporate the practice:

- Choose a specific, emotionally charged topic to write about.
- Spend fifteen to twenty minutes a day, three to four days in a row. Set a timer! Using this time frame, expressive writers

experienced measurable improvements over the control group months after the experiment, even if they never journaled again.[32]

- As you're writing, don't worry about grammar or reading it over later. Write honestly about how you're feeling, what is challenging, what is stressful, and what feels frustrating.
- If it feels too vulnerable to leave all of this in a journal, consider writing on the same line or on the same page repeatedly, or have your shredder ready when the timer goes off.
- If writing by hand is difficult, you could write digitally or speak your thoughts out loud. Languaging your emotions is the important bit.

Any type can benefit from this practice! It's directly suggested for a few types, but your type will likely find it useful as well.

The Power of Emotional Regulation

Many of the practices in this book focus on your emotional world. Feelings wheels, journaling, reflection, oh my! It all can feel tiresome if you are disconnected from why this is so important. Maybe you're thinking, "Feelings are fine, but I need to stop procrastinating." Or, "I don't need to know about emotions, I need to stop being such a perfectionist." But that's precisely where feelings come in. Both perfectionism and procrastination are issues with emotional dysregulation.[33] Both inspire stress, anxiety, and self-criticism, and both result in poor health outcomes.[34] Therefore, we cannot skip the emotional processing part of this equation. Perfectionists and procrastinators share a sense of urgency to solve their problems, just as long as the solution is not to wade through the emotional mud on the way. The bad news: that's the only way through—trust me, as a certified procrastinating perfectionist, it helps! The good news: once you learn to process your emotions instead of shying away from them, your struggles with these troubled states will become much easier to manage.

Metacognition and Mindfulness

This book is full of invitations to pay attention to your thoughts, to observe how they make you feel, and to consider how you might change them to be more supportive. This way of thinking about our thoughts is called metacognition. It is a sophisticated brain behavior that we can access beginning in childhood, but sometimes we need to develop it to make it more effective. It's the mechanism that enables our self-awareness (and self-criticism), and it is one of the tools you already have to make sustainable change in your life.

Mindfulness helps you strengthen the muscles of metacognition. "Mindfulness practice [is] the driving lesson for managing the mind," according to psychologist Dr. Julie Smith.[35] Using this tool, you willfully direct your attention, which is helpful because "where attention goes, energy flows."[36] Mindfulness also helps you be present in the current moment because you're able to redirect your racing thoughts and bring your attention back to the task at hand. Throughout the book, you'll find suggestions for different types of contemplation, but if you are new to mindfulness, this can be a helpful first step. Various free apps and videos online feature basic guided meditations, which can offer a good foundation for building a mindfulness practice for you. You can find my favorite resources here: https://www.enneagramirl.com/resources.

Now, let's talk about your Enneagram type.

CHAPTER 3

Finding Your Type

In general, the most important part of Enneagram typing is the motivation. *Why* you do what you do is more important than what you do. However, this can be hard to identify at times. This guide details both motivational and behavioral aspects of each type to help you determine your type.

Before we begin, remember there are many valid ways to find your type. Online assessments can be useful tools to help you narrow it down, but even the best assessments get it wrong sometimes. Motivation is difficult to measure because it's deeply embedded, and unless we specifically discuss this facet of ourselves, we don't know how our internal workings compare to others'. Professional typing interviews from a well-trained practitioner can be useful as well, but they are cost-prohibitive for many. The steps outlined here will help you narrow your type using just this book. An online version of this assessment can be found in the resource guide here: https://www .enneagramirl.com/resources.

Steps to Determine Your Type

- As you read the statements that follow, keep track of each section's results on a sheet of paper. After each statement, write down 0 if you disagree, 1 if you somewhat agree, and 2 if you strongly agree with each statement. Try to answer quickly to avoid overthinking.

- Consider the entire statement: if you would describe yourself as curious but not as energetic or lively, you would mark 0 next to "I'm curious, energetic, and lively."
- After you've completed all nine charts, total your score for each type. This is a simple assessment, but it will offer enough insight to help you get started.
- Review the chapters for your top three results, paying particular attention to the motivation, avoidance, and passion of the type.

Section A

USE THE COLUMN TO THE RIGHT TO INDICATE YOUR RESPONSE. 0 = DISAGREE / 1 = SOMEWHAT AGREE / 2 = STRONGLY AGREE	
Anger is easy to access and is not a negative emotion for me: sometimes it offers me energy, protection, or guidance.	
Even though I have a tough exterior, I am very caring and compassionate toward my closest people.	
I enjoy a lively debate and find it fascinating to sharpen someone else's argument through conversation.	
While I don't necessarily enjoy conflict, I don't shy away from it either.	
I rarely let limitations hold me back; instead, I push through them and conquer them.	
I rely on my gut instinct to decide what to do next.	
I tell the truth, and I prioritize honesty and transparency above most other qualities.	
I tend to be direct and straightforward—what you see is what you get.	
It's easy for me to take charge of or control a situation.	
While it's nice if people like me, I don't need them to like me and won't sacrifice who I am to gain the approval of others.	
I never want to be weak or spineless.	
Total	

Section B

USE THE COLUMN TO THE RIGHT TO INDICATE YOUR RESPONSE. 0 = DISAGREE / 1 = SOMEWHAT AGREE / 2 = STRONGLY AGREE	
Even though I can easily sense what others need, I sometimes have a hard time knowing what I need and how to meet my needs.	
I am acutely aware of the relational environment around me. I can sense what others are feeling, and I intuitively know how to make them feel loved.	
I offer a lot of positivity, encouragement, kindness, and goodwill to others.	
I sometimes feel resentful that no one helps or cares for me in the way that I do for them.	
I spend more time focusing on others than on myself.	
I vacillate between feeling guilty for wanting more affection from others and feeling entitled to more attention.	
If I feel like a relationship is on the rocks, I'll go out of my way to help that person. Subconsciously, I believe that meeting their needs is what will make them like me.	
My attention naturally gravitates to what others need from me and how I can support them.	
People like me because I make them feel good.	
When I'm working on a project, I know I can rely on my network of connections to get things done.	
When someone doesn't like me, it's easy for me to sense their feelings, and I generally know how to get them to like me.	
Total	

Section C

USE THE COLUMN TO THE RIGHT TO INDICATE YOUR RESPONSE. 0 = DISAGREE / 1 = SOMEWHAT AGREE / 2 = STRONGLY AGREE	
I am highly attuned to my emotional experience of the world. I feel more deeply than others, and I can pinpoint emotions with great specificity.	
I approach life in my own unique way.	
I know I am distinct from others around me. I've always felt a little different—sometimes I love this about myself, and sometimes it makes me feel alone.	
I rarely run from big emotions. I may not always express them freely, but I find them important to understand and process in my own way.	
I sometimes feel like other people have an easier time in life, and I feel like I'm missing something that they intuitively understand.	
I spend a lot of time comparing myself to others. When I look at how deeply I think and feel, I know I'm deeper and more authentic than others. In other areas, however, I often feel inadequate or lacking.	
I tell the truth or surface unpopular ideas more than most: I think it's important to say what needs to be said, even when it's uncomfortable.	
I value authenticity above all else: I'm constantly searching for what feels most true, most aligned, and most resonant internally.	
I want to feel mirrored in relationships, and I'm easily frustrated when I feel misunderstood, but I also feel confined by others understanding me.	
In everything I do, I search for meaning and purpose.	
Self-expression is natural to me. I thoughtfully craft a sense of self that I can convey to others through words, creativity, clothing, art, my work, or other means.	
Total	

Section D

<table>
<tr>
<td colspan="2">USE THE COLUMN TO THE RIGHT TO INDICATE YOUR RESPONSE.
0 = DISAGREE / 1 = SOMEWHAT AGREE / 2 = STRONGLY AGREE</td>
</tr>
<tr>
<td>When I walk into a room, I naturally know who I need to be to fit in and be impressive.</td>
<td></td>
</tr>
<tr>
<td>Sometimes I expect robot-like efficiency from myself, and it's hard to see that this might not be attainable.</td>
<td></td>
</tr>
<tr>
<td>People typically describe me as confident.</td>
<td></td>
</tr>
<tr>
<td>It feels natural for me to set my emotions aside.</td>
<td></td>
</tr>
<tr>
<td>If I'm honest with myself, I worry what might happen if I slow down or take a rest.</td>
<td></td>
</tr>
<tr>
<td>I'm highly motivated by accomplishment: I like to get things done, mark things off my to-do list, and be productive and efficient.</td>
<td></td>
</tr>
<tr>
<td>I spend a lot of time thinking about what other people think of me.</td>
<td></td>
</tr>
<tr>
<td>I know that I'm technically going above and beyond, but I still don't feel like I'm doing enough.</td>
<td></td>
</tr>
<tr>
<td>I intuitively highlight parts of myself that will pull the most weight with a specific group of people.</td>
<td></td>
</tr>
<tr>
<td>I can get impatient when I feel like someone or something is standing in the way of my goal.</td>
<td></td>
</tr>
<tr>
<td>I can find a way to relate with almost anyone: I'm adaptable, and I connect with people through finding points of commonality.</td>
<td></td>
</tr>
<tr>
<td>**Total**</td>
<td></td>
</tr>
</table>

Section E

USE THE COLUMN TO THE RIGHT TO INDICATE YOUR RESPONSE. 0 = DISAGREE / 1 = SOMEWHAT AGREE / 2 = STRONGLY AGREE	
Because I ask so many questions, people assume that I'm pessimistic and planning for things to go wrong. I prefer to call myself realistic, prepared, and responsible.	
Others can always count on me. I'm a loyal friend.	
I am not always the most decisive person, but at least I think things through.	
I am often told that I am a bit of a contrarian. Taking the opposite perspective helps me see all different angles so I can feel certain I've covered all my bases.	
I am vigilant and aware of possibilities.	
I crave certainty in life, but I find that it is always just out of reach.	
I don't immediately follow leaders: I appreciate leaders who are strong and honest, but I tend to ask a lot of questions first.	
I intuitively know whether or not someone is trustworthy.	
I want to trust people, but I tend to be suspicious, especially at first. Honesty and consistency are important building blocks for trust.	
When I notice something that seems off, I often make a mental note and plan to avoid it, or I voice a concern.	
When I'm asking questions or conveying fear, I often use humor to let others know I know I'm doing the "asking too many questions" thing again.	
Total	

Section F

USE THE COLUMN TO THE RIGHT TO INDICATE YOUR RESPONSE. 0 = DISAGREE / 1 = SOMEWHAT AGREE / 2 = STRONGLY AGREE	
At times, I can be overly rigid or black and white about what I think is right.	
Focusing on doing my part will make the world a better place.	
I am conscientious and cognizant of my impact on the world.	
I believe I have a duty to improve myself.	
I feel compelled to correct errors, though I try to approach it the right way and be tactful about it.	
I have a strong inner critic. I know I can come off as critical or judgmental of others at times, but that is a fraction of the criticism I hear internally every day.	
I often feel tense and frustrated because I see the ideal world that could exist if everyone just did their part.	
I rarely let anger or frustration show, as this does not feel appropriate.	
I think everyone should follow the rules, though I often check the rules against my own understanding to make sure they make sense. If the rules are not sufficient, I'll often abide by my better rules.	
If everyone else could take things seriously, I wouldn't have to be so responsible all the time.	
There are definite right and wrong ways to do certain things.	
Total	

Section G

USE THE COLUMN TO THE RIGHT TO INDICATE YOUR RESPONSE. 0 = DISAGREE / 1 = SOMEWHAT AGREE / 2 = STRONGLY AGREE	
Delight, satisfaction, and pleasure are vital in my everyday life.	
I am a quick-minded seeker of fascination. Sometimes people assume I only care about fun or adventure, but I'm actually seeking engrossing, mentally stimulating activities.	
I am curious, energetic, and lively!	
I hate feeling trapped, and I'll do anything to keep moving mentally or physically.	
I have a wide variety of interests, and I love to dabble in everything.	
I instantly reframe negatives into positives, almost without thinking about it.	
If I don't like something about my life, I either accept it and move on or I change it. Life is too short to not enjoy it.	
Keeping my options open is important to me. I commit when necessary, but I don't like to limit myself prematurely.	
My mind is always spinning with new ideas and interesting thoughts.	
Problem-solving comes naturally to me because I am always thinking outside the box.	
Variety is the spice of life. I fill my days with new and invigorating opportunities.	
Total	

Section H

Even though I am often easygoing, I hate to be pushed around or told what to do.	
Even when I have strong opinions, I don't always share them readily. Some people have too many opinions about too many things. It's okay to be neutral.	
I am acutely aware of tension hanging in the air: when it arises, I often find a way to leave, whether through physically removing myself or turning my mind off.	
I am generally pretty even-keeled: I don't tend to have as many emotional highs and lows as other people seem to.	
Solving the world's problems isn't really up to me.	
I find myself looking for where I agree with others, and I can easily highlight the common thread among various perspectives.	
I have a really hard time saying "no" because wanting something different from someone else feels like conflict.	
I have simple wants and needs, and I tend to move toward comfort and simplicity.	
I need time to consider various angles before forming an opinion.	
I'm a good listener.	
It baffles me when conversations become needlessly contentious.	
Total	

Section I

USE THE COLUMN TO THE RIGHT TO INDICATE YOUR RESPONSE. 0 = DISAGREE / 1 = SOMEWHAT AGREE / 2 = STRONGLY AGREE	
I am highly introspective and observant. I love to get lost in learning about topics that interest me, and I quickly become an expert in my favorite subjects.	
I am very private, and I share information selectively to maintain a sense of control in my relationships.	
I can come off as aloof or unfeeling, even though this is not the case. I genuinely care, but I also prefer to keep my emotions to myself.	
I abhor inane chitchat. I enjoy deep, intellectual conversations, and I love to think through difficult puzzles.	
I highly value objectivity, data, and information.	
I often create organized systems or routines in my life to manage information, time, and energy more efficiently.	
I mentally compartmentalize different aspects of my life.	
I naturally distance my thoughts from my emotions. This allows me to maintain a steady, logical, and rational approach to difficult situations.	
I prefer dealing with challenges alone, feeling that others might not meet my needs.	
I create margins in my life to ensure I will not be depleted.	
If I become depleted, I need a significant amount of alone time to recharge.	
Total	

KEY		
SECTION	TOTAL	TYPE
A		8
B		2
C		4
D		3
E		6
F		1
G		7
H		9
I		5

When you read your top three results, focus on the type that fits best rather than looking for 100 percent alignment. You may identify strongly with the motivation, avoidance, and passion of the type, even if some of the behavioral descriptions are not a perfect fit.

MY TOP THREE TYPES	
TYPE	SCORE

When you find your type, you may experience a sense of discomfort. Recognizing ourselves in the weaknesses of our type descriptions can be challenging, but this is why it's important to embrace self-acceptance and practice observing ourselves without judgment. All nine types are equally good (and equally bad), but many of us readily see our weaknesses and overlook our strengths. Alternatively, some new Enneagram learners find great comfort in reading about their type for the first time. They suddenly feel less alone and recognize there's nothing wrong with them—they just see the world through different lenses.

If you can look at descriptions of your type as self-inquiry rather than self-description, you'll learn to observe yourself differently. Sometimes, what we might learn about our types doesn't instantly resonate with us. However, rather than dismissing the validity of your type, get curious.

You might notice that you find different results depending on various factors. While we change and grow over time, Enneagram theory says our types do not change. This is why I always recommend verifying your assessment results. It's possible to mistype, meaning you perceive yourself as a certain type, only to realize later that you are a different type. This is fairly common, especially if you are a Six, a Nine, or if the original Enneagram descriptions you read did not include subtypes. This is part of the self-discovery process for some people, and there's nothing to be ashamed of if it's part of your story.

Ask yourself:

- What resonates here? What doesn't?
- Is it actually untrue, or is it just something I've never noticed before? Or, is it that I don't want it to be true?
- If it's not true, what would be a more accurate self-observation?

If You Get Stuck

Here are a few guiding questions to help you observe yourself from a different angle.

- REFLECT ON YOURSELF AROUND AGE 20. Which statements would your young adult self resonate with? Our types are often clearest around 20–25. As we gain life experience, we learn to soften some of the dysfunctional edges of our types, and we become less like the stereotype of our core type over time. This does not mean the type changes but that we've adopted more functional habits.
- LOOK FOR INTERVIEWS OR PANELS OF DIFFERENT ENNEAGRAM TYPES ONLINE. As you listen, consider the following:
  - What resonates deeply with you? What feels uncomfortable to think about?
  - What doesn't resonate with you? Consider a word, phrase, or idea you heard that doesn't resonate: if you could make an edit to that phrase to make it resonate, what would that change be?
  - As an example, when I first learned the Enneagram, I heard that type Threes are "always successful" or "always chasing external measures of success." I struggled to resonate based on predetermined images of success (you know, what we typically see in movies). When I started to consider that measures of success can vary with every individual, it resonated a bit more. Now I think, "Threes are aiming at what success or worth means *to them*."
- KEEP IN MIND THAT THE "TEXTBOOK EXAMPLE" OF EACH TYPE IS EXCEEDINGLY RARE. It's expected that you won't resonate with every little thing about your type: we're looking for resonance with the core motivation, what the type is avoiding, and the passion.
- TRY PINPOINTING YOUR UNDERLYING MOTIVATIONS. Here are a few questions to guide your reflection.
  - When was the last time I felt a strong emotion? What caused

me to feel that way? What was it about this situation that touched a nerve?

- When you feel a strong emotion, especially an uncomfortable emotion like anger, sadness, or fear, what do you do with it? Do you express it? Do you bury it? Do you busy yourself with other tasks?

- What is your best quality? What is something you appreciate about yourself and the way you live your life?

CHAPTER 4

OPEN:
A Framework for
Sustainable Change

Early in my Enneagram journey, I knew I wanted to change. I knew that my lack of emotional awareness was rearing its ugly head in my daily life and that if I could learn to process my emotions more fully, I'd feel less like I was on a constant emotional roller coaster.

The framework in this chapter is based on my own personal inner work journey, along with formal Enneagram and personal development education, and my work with coaching, typing, and team clients. I always say that applying Enneagram is not rocket science (although at times it may feel that way). This framework isn't either. It's a simple, straightforward model that will equip you with a set of reflection questions and prompts you can reliably use to begin your own growth work, whatever form that may take. In each type chapter, you'll find type-specific examples of how you can apply this concept. This chapter is a broad overview of the framework with a specific story woven throughout.

O

Observe

Self-observation is always the first step in kick-starting self-development. Observing yourself is about noticing what's happening in your mind, heart, and body in the moment and being able to assess what's triggering different experiences or responses. This is a continual practice and the bedrock of much of our growth work. It might take time to get into the habit of observing yourself consistently, but once you get the hang of it, you'll be able to notice patterns popping up in real time.

A few important notes here:

- There's no expectation that you observe yourself 24/7. That would be exhausting. Instead, I think of self-observation as the ability to experience something and then choose to spotlight that internal experience or not. The key here is the choice: when we're stuck on autopilot, we don't have the ability to choose a different pattern or response, and we don't know why we're reacting the way we are. Self-observation is the first step to unlocking that choice.
- Self-observation and reflection are often used interchangeably, but they are different concepts. Self-observation is in the moment: What am I noticing? What am I experiencing right now? Reflection is retrospective: What happened earlier? What was going on inside me when I had that reaction? Both play a pivotal role in growth, and reflection can be a powerful tool to help build your skills of observation—over time, you'll start noticing things closer to real time.
- Self-observation doesn't necessarily require quiet isolation, but it does require a basic sense of psychological safety.[1] If you're in

a stressful season, do what you can. Maybe that means taking a deep breath and wiggling your toes at every stoplight on your morning commute. These are all building blocks for this work we'll continue together.

How to Build This Skill:
Exercise 1. Practice Self-Observation in Moments of Calm

The goal here is to notice what's happening internally during calm moments. In this step, we're not trying to change anything; we're simply cultivating awareness.

STEP 1. Start now by taking a deep inhale through your nose. Release your breath slowly through your mouth.

STEP 2. As you're reading this book right now, bring your attention to your body, notice if your feet are moving or if your ankles are crossed. Notice how your fingers are holding the book. Give yourself a few minutes to observe your body, see if anything feels tensed or relaxed. Just notice, no need to change anything.

STEP 3. Move your attention to your heart and your mind. Notice what emotions and thoughts are coming up. Use the same light awareness as above, and just notice what bubbles to the surface. There's no need to investigate your emotions or pull them apart to discover where they've come from. Simply observe what you're doing, feeling, and thinking in this moment. That's enough.

STEP 4. THROUGHOUT THE DAY: Whenever you have a calm moment during your day—maybe first thing in the morning, during your lunch break, or before going to bed—keep steps 1 through 3 in mind and bring your attention to your body. With a light awareness, scan down from the crown of your head to the tips of your toes. Notice where there might be tension, pain, comfort, relaxation—any sensation is okay. Just note what comes up and move along without trying to fix or change anything. Then move on to emotions. What are you feeling right now? How is it manifesting itself in your body? As time goes on, you'll be able to start building your awareness skill deeper and deeper until it becomes second nature.

For example, I started using mindful awareness while getting ready for work each morning. Instead of listening to a podcast or audiobook, I watched my hands make my lunch, I paid attention to the rug underneath my feet while I brushed my hair, I noticed the vise grip on my toothbrush. This can be a simple, effective way to integrate mindfulness in your day-to-day life.

Exercise 2. Journal and Reflect About Challenging Experiences

It's easier to observe ourselves when things are relaxed as we did above. Using reflection, the cousin of self-observation, can be an approachable method to learn how to mindfully examine more challenging moments while feeling calm and safe so that you have this skill when you need it in the thick of a difficult interaction.

Think about a recent challenge you experienced. Consider journaling through the following prompts:

a. What were you feeling in the moment?
b. What was happening in your body during the crisis? What happened afterward? Were you aware of any tension, sensations, or temperature changes?
c. What assumptions did you make about the world and about yourself in that moment?
d. What do you see now that you didn't at the moment?
e. How have you been feeling since this occurred?

Come back to this exercise every time you experience a difficult moment and need to work through it. Don't be shocked if you start seeing patterns!

Exercise 3. Observe Yourself in Difficult Moments

Ultimately, if you regularly practice exercises 1 and 2 in calm moments, you will be able to observe yourself in the midst of challenging experiences as well. This is the highest level of this observational skill. It might take a while to get to integrate this practice into moments of unrest, but eventually you'll be able to notice, "ah, I'm doing the thing," or "there I go again," and catch yourself repeating patterns amid turbulence.

Example: Janie

Janie grew up in a chaotic family environment with loving but busy parents and three younger siblings. She often played the role of the "family hero." Anytime anything went wrong, or her parent got mad, or something needed to be done, she leaped off the couch and fixed it. As an adult, Janie has been realizing this pattern doesn't serve her. Last summer, she arrived home after her family vacation depleted, resentful, and frustrated. She could see in hindsight how this pattern prevented any true enjoyment of her time at the beach. So, Janie has been practicing observing this impulse. This summer, she wants to do things differently. On the first day of their vacation, her brother couldn't find a mixing bowl in the kitchen, and Janie jumped up to help. As she walked over, she noted, "Oh, I'm doing this hero helper thing!" She still helped out, but it felt like a positive step to notice it.

P

Pause

Once you have built your skills of observation, work on adding a pause. Observation and Pause can begin to blend together, but I count them as separate steps because we must learn to observe ourselves before we can intentionally pause. Observing is about noticing. Pausing is about slowing our impulsive reactions. We all have these well-worn reactions that we've needed to make it through life thus far.

When we pause, we give ourselves freedom to choose: we can choose to lean in and understand what we're experiencing, we can choose a different reaction, we can gain insight into what we really need, and we can find clarity on how to move forward.

Most of us feel like one of our centers (head, heart, or body) rules our experiences. Pausing helps us tune into the internal feedback available to us when we stop acting on autopilot.

 How to Build This Skill:
Exercise 1.

As soon as you observe a trigger and feel an impulse or a reaction boiling to the surface, decide to pause instead by clasping your hands together and breathing through your nose a few times. This slows down your automatic response and allows you to make space to consider before reacting. In this stage, we are catching ourselves in the act, adding a moment of stillness, knowing that this will help us make supportive choices.

Exercise 2.

When you notice yourself jumping into automatic reactions, you could also build a pause by noting the antecedent. Put your hand on your heart, take a deep breath through your nose and a deep exhale through your mouth, and say, "Huh! That's interesting" or "Whoops, there I go again!"

Example: Janie on Vacation

Yesterday, Janie leaped off the couch when her brother needed a hand, but she was able to notice it in real time. So today, she's ready to do things differently. Before she even made it downstairs, she heard a crash. Her sister had elbowed a coffee mug, sending the mug to smithereens on the kitchen floor. By the time she reached the last step, her mom and brother were already there helping clean up the mess. Still, she noticed herself walking toward them, already thinking about holding the dustpan. And then she paused: "Ah, there I go again!" She took a deep breath and just waited for a moment, noticing what it felt like to dive into helping on autopilot. She had always assumed that stepping in was involuntary, but now she's recognizing she can make space for a different choice.

E

Engage Curiosity

Engaging curiosity will help you understand your reactions, and eventually, it can help you get more creative around the patterns you choose next. It can help you be more reflective around your self-observations as well. You don't have to be woo-woo to love the Enneagram, but this is the moment when we all need to tap into a little of that whimsy. Be creative. Get in touch with your intuition. If you have a gut instinct about what would actually meet a need, trust that there's something to it. This is all about being outside the box and using your imagination.

 How to Build This Skill:

Exercise: Engage Curiosity Through Reflection Questions

STEP 1. Take a moment to reflect on a pattern you observed recently.

STEP 2. Leave your judgments at the door. Imagine yourself collecting all your judgments and criticisms like you're picking up laundry or toys. Maybe some of these thoughts still have a place in your life, but for now, just pick them up and set them aside. If you can, literally envision boxing them up and setting them beside you (or far away! Wherever you need them to be). Now you can be curious.

STEP 3. Rather than assuming stimulus→ response is the only way to go, ask yourself:

- What root need is this typical response, feeling, sensation, or pattern meeting?
- Is this typical response still serving me or should I try finding other ways to deal with this stimulus?
- If this is not serving me anymore, what other options do I have?

STEP 4. Lean into awe, wonder, and creativity. Maybe you want to bring in a little humor here—chuckle at the way you keep doing that same darn thing. It must really be meeting a need! Wonder aloud, what ELSE is available? What ELSE might meet that need? Maybe it would feel good to take a longer pause or step back. Maybe it would feel good to ask someone for help. Maybe a silly little dance in your living room is the perfect solution. You don't have to do any of the things you think of—just brainstorm other ways to meet a core need that keeps popping up.

As you reflect on your options and keep practicing this skill, soon you'll be able to access all these other options in real time, when you need them the most.

> **Example: Janie on Vacation**
>
> So, Janie is frozen at the bottom of the stairs, uncharacteristically watching her mom, brother, and sister as they sweep up bits of ceramic. She's paused, which has given her a moment to think. What need does her normal behavior meet? As a kid, she stepped in to fill the gaps because she thought the house would run better that way; she thought being useful made her more valuable. She also thought that the best way to get love and connection would be to serve others, almost like she had to earn it. But now, she's noticing that true connection can be thwarted by resentment, which is a natural consequence of being a flurry of activity. And, she's seeing that other family members are happy to step in and fill the gaps. What else could she do right now to meet her needs for love, connection, and value? She could grab a book and head outside to connect with nature. She could prop herself up on the barstool and lovingly roast her sister for breaking a mug for the third year in a row. She could find her dad and ask him to go for a walk around the block. Really, there are no bad options here.

N

Next Right Thing

In the previous steps, you learned:

O: How to observe yourself

P: How to build in a pause

E: How to get intensely curious about what ELSE you might do

And now it's time to experiment! Choose what the next right thing is for you in the moment. I say "next right thing" because I want you to gain the skill of choosing and experimenting. I don't want you to feel stuck finding the perfect new pattern. You can always reevaluate later. In this moment, choose the next right thing based on what you've learned, and know that you can reflect later on what worked well and what didn't. Over time, you'll learn what works and build new patterns that serve you well.

 How to Build This Skill:
Exercise 1. Build this skill by doing it!

Try out one of the new responses you've brainstormed, or lean on the whole framework you've learned to Observe, Pause, Engage Curiosity, and then choose your Next Right Thing (for right now). You don't have to figure it all out mentally. You don't have to predict how it's going to feel. You've been putting in the work, and you have the skills you need to try it out, trust me. Trust yourself!

Exercise 2. Ask yourself these questions:

What is the next right thing you can do right now? What small change can you make right now? What can you experiment with? This is not about brainstorming like E; this is looking for opportunities for action now. Tune in to your experience and your reaction to it. This isn't a new set-in-stone pattern but another way to experiment. Don't forget to stay curious!

Exercise 3. Allow discomfort.

This paradigm shift may not feel comfortable at first, but that doesn't always mean it's wrong. Sometimes reflecting on it later can help you understand whether it's uncomfortable because it's stretching you or it's uncomfortable because it isn't right for you right now.

Example: Janie on Vacation

Now, imagine you're Janie. What will you choose? How do you imagine her morning will play out? Maybe she feels uncomfortable because she's still feeling a little guilty for escaping outdoors when tasks await inside. Or maybe she has the best conversation with her dad she's ever had. Or maybe she's teasing her sister and then Janie accidentally sends a mug off the end of the bar, and they end up at a thrift store together buying replacements. What is it like to try something new? How can Janie stay in a mindset of experimentation, no matter how the morning unfolds?

Applying the OPEN Framework for Each Type

In each type chapter, you'll find an example to apply the OPEN framework as you catch yourself in the passion of your type and move forward the virtue. As you recognize your passion and walk through the OPEN steps, you'll begin to shake off the ways your personality structure is keeping you bound. The virtue shows up after deep internal shifts, so it's not necessarily something you can journal your way into. However, part of the process can be observing yourself and building some of the inner practices you'll need to support your growth work. Coaching and therapy can also be useful tools to aid this process, if you're able to access them.

Part II

The Body Types: Overview

BODY TYPES	
Central Themes	Boundaries, control, autonomy, structure, containment, actionable information, experience, gut instinct, fairness, justice
Underlying Emotions	Anger, rage
Common Experiences	• Instinctual decision-making, i.e., having a gut sense for what they think they should do, even if they can't describe how they decided • Sensing emotions physically and needing alone time to stop "gut checking" everyone around them • Using anger as an energizing force for autonomy, boundaries • Wanting to feel held, for example, ending a coaching session on time and with a bit of wrap-up
Aversions	• Being told what to do • People who seem untrustworthy or shapeshifting • Disregard for structure

CHAPTER 5

Type Eight

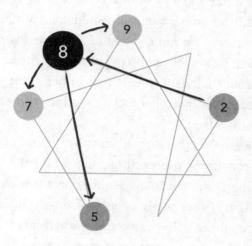

Jacqui possesses the trademark Eight's concrete approach to life: she's upfront, she says what she means, and she doesn't shy away from hard conversations. She also represents something I've observed in many of the Eights I meet in my line of work: *she goes all-in.* These days, going "all-in" means that she's committed herself to inner work and deep transformation. She's full of Big Eight Energy, and she's also kind and warm in her very Eight way. She has tapped into softness and surrender in ways that are remarkable to me, as an Enneagram educator, because I know how much effort it takes to stay open in a world you have every inclination to protect yourself against.

When Jacqui was in her twenties, she signed up for a wheel pottery class. The instructor, a German woman in her midfifties, skillfully illustrated how to center a lump of clay on the wheel in a way that looked artful and effortless. Like many skills that take years to hone, throwing pottery always looks *so easy* when experts show off their talents for centering and pulling and shaping. Jacqui watched her instructor and decided she'd be centering her own clay in no time.

After throwing the lump on the wheel and pressing the pedal, Jacqui applied water and a great deal of force to bring that clay into submission. But no amount of will would control the clay, and so Jacqui applied more and more pressure until the instructor yelled, "Halt!" Startled, Jacqui looked up to see the instructor rushing over and lifting Jacqui's hands to reveal that in her effort, she'd mostly only succeeded in bloodying her hands by grinding the sides of them into the spinning wheel.[1]

There's a lesson in this simple story for many of us who find ourselves in consistent overexertion, but I find that it highlights a common type Eight tendency. Eights operate with the subconscious belief that if they apply enough strength, mental fortitude, and physical toughness, they can conquer anything. By sheer power of will, Eights ensure that they are in the driver's seat of their own lives every single moment of every day.

How Eights Show Up

Eights are **motivated** by the need to be "against," but this doesn't necessarily mean they are intentionally contrarian. Pushing back against assumptions and expectations is a self-protective measure Eights subconsciously employ to let others know they will not be easily controlled or overtaken. Eights lead with strength, toughness, and intensity, as they are powerful, dynamic types who are fearless in the face of challenges.

Eights possess a keen understanding of their own instincts, and they tend to trust their gut to lead them through life. Eights often believe they are the only ones who are responsible for themselves, but this does not mean that Eights leave everyone else in the dust.

In fact, Eights tend to be highly justice-oriented. They stand up for those around them who are experiencing unfair treatment, and they protect innocence wherever they see it, which can also be a function of projecting their own innocence out into the world. Because Eights are unable to believe that innocence will be protected in themselves, they fiercely protect it in others.

Making an impact is an important driver for Eights. While Eights can work well on teams, they hate being hindered by arbitrary rules. Eights rarely accept "that's how it's always been" at face value, instead investigating different, more effective processes to accomplish their goals. They can be impulsive and impatient at times when they believe things are moving too slowly or when they perceive that emotions are getting in the way of moving forward.

Eights **avoid** being betrayed or controlled by another person, and as a result, vulnerability can feel dangerous because it implies letting someone else see a soft spot that could be exploited. Decisive action, an impenetrable exterior, and strong boundaries all work together to protect the Eight from being too vulnerable.

There's an important distinction to make here, however, because many Eights feel that they *are* vulnerable. Eights often say, "I'm an open book," or "I'm always honest, even when it makes me look bad." But it's important to note the difference between transparency, which includes that sense of honesty and straightforwardness, and vulnerability, which connotes a certain level of emotional self-disclosure. Often, Eights are quite open, and they're not interested in managing their image; however, showing the softer, emotional side of themselves is difficult since that could allow someone else to take a position of power or control over them. Note that they shield themselves from exploitation, but they are not self-conscious or easily embarrassed.

While many Eights don't intentionally intimidate others, the same external presentations that protect them can warn people away. They are grounded, secure, and unyielding in that you don't get the sense you can easily knock an Eight off course.

From a young age, Eights felt the need to stand up for themselves to ensure their own survival. Eights may have experienced the world as unjust, so they built mechanisms to protect their tender feelings from harm. A young Eight may have been thrust into maturity too soon, especially if a caregiver lacked some necessary skills to adequately protect them. Adult Eights often carry on the belief that they must be autonomous to survive since receiving help requires showing vulnerability to someone who could potentially harm them. If they are in charge of themselves, they know they'll be okay, and they know they'll be able to handle whatever life throws at them.

One common **misconception** around this type is their relationship with control. All body types have a desire for control and boundaries in their lives in different ways, and this is true of Eights as well. Many Eights (especially women who are Eights) are frequently labeled as bossy or overbearing simply because they speak with confidence that most other types do not. Candor and volume lend to an impression that they are too tough or angry, but their kindness and tenderness are evident to those closest to them. Eights are often black-and-white thinkers, and when unaware, an Eight might have a "my way or the highway" attitude, but more aware Eights recognize that controlling others is an exercise in futility. Thus, most Eights are not using their strength to take over others' lives, but to keep their own locus of control.

Thresholds

High Thresholds: Conflict and Discomfort

Eights have a **high threshold** for conflict. They can engage in heated debates without feeling like the conversation has transitioned into an argument. Eights often enjoy dissecting ideas, surfacing a counter-argument, and using energy and volume to get their point across. It can feel like sport more than dispute. They also disagree passionately without becoming embroiled in emotion; after all, most of these conversations are not personal in their minds. Because of this, Eights can leave conversations *thinking* they had a great discussion, only to be confused later when they learn that their conversation partner experienced distress due to the conflict. This means that Eights excel at having difficult conversations and fearlessly addressing sensitive topics, making them well suited for roles like counselors or therapists.

Similarly, Eights have tremendous resilience and a **high threshold** for situations that seem daunting or scary. Whether mentally, emotionally, or physically, they lead with strength and can delve into spaces others fear. Venturing into the unknown and putting themselves out there are not so scary for Eights because they know they can trust themselves and follow their gut whenever they need to restabilize. This makes Eights incredible forces for speaking out against injustice and doing what they need to do to support the causes they are passionate about.

Low Thresholds: Betrayal and Incompetence

Eights tend to have a **low threshold** for betrayal. Something that might not feel like a betrayal of trust to someone else can be cutting for an Eight. This extra sensitivity helps them to protect themselves as they're avoiding vulnerability, but it can also make building deeper connections challenging.

Eights also have a **low threshold** for incompetence or weakness in other people. Of course, at times, Eights move to protect others they perceive to be innocent or in need of advocacy (especially Social Eights), but often Eights experience visceral contempt for incompetence in leadership. It doesn't take long for an Eight to sense a power vacuum and step into it. When interviewing Eights, many shared that while they have had leaders they have admired, ultimately, they prefer working for themselves. Working for an incompetent leader leaves Eights feeling exhausted, frustrated, and wrestling between taking over and calling it quits. As Eights move toward health, they can be more intentional about stepping into the leadership vacuum.

Type Eight Personality

In this section, we'll dive straight into the type Eight personality structure, but you'll find a detailed overview of the terms in this section (Passion, Defense Mechanism, Virtue) in chapter 2.

Passion: Lust

The word *lust* is commonly associated with sexual lust, but here, it is meant more broadly, as a tendency toward excess. I've heard Eights say that "anything worth doing is worth overdoing," which aptly describes the Eight tendency to go all-in. Subconsciously, the passion of lust acts as a shield of forceful energy, which protects Eights from being too vulnerable.

For some Eights, lust manifests as a loud speaking voice, assertive movement, or impulsivity. Lust leads Eights to believe that excess, intensity, and reactivity will protect them from being conquered by outside forces. This is not a conscious choice but a way of moving that feels like breathing. While Eights can grow to become gentler, readily extending compassion, protection, and kindness to others, when living from lust, Eights are impatient and guarded.

The passion of lust could look like . . .

- Moving through life with force, intensity, and big energy.
- Powering through sickness, emotion, or anything else that could

be perceived as weakness without regard for your body or the experience of physical pain.

- Frequently being the first to act or take over a situation, especially when power or control are uncertain.
- An inability to moderate energy resulting in everything getting the full force of your anger, *especially* when autonomy or vulnerability become threatened, sometimes leading to exhaustion or burnout.

Reflecting on Your Passion Through Journal Prompts

How does the passion of lust (or if it helps, think of it as "excess") show up in your life? If you can think of an example, write about it. What was happening when you saw lust show up clearly? How did it feel? What were you paying attention to? In what ways did lust serve you? In what ways did lust *detract* from what you needed or wanted in that moment?

Defense Mechanism: Denial

A common type Eight defense mechanism is denial. Denial shields an Eight's vision by disregarding any hint of weakness. It often feels more like a gut reaction than anything, and it's a function of that tough exterior and tendency to be "against." Denying the existence of pain, limitations, and needs can be a natural expression of this defense mechanism. Many Eights subconsciously push pain to the periphery, as Jacqui did when throwing pottery at the start of this chapter. Unfortunately, that means Eights can miss valuable lessons pain offers, like letting a new pottery learner know to ease off, or helping an athlete recognize early signs of injury. Continuing to push may result in further destruction, but because the Eight isn't recognizing the signals, they keep pushing.

This insistence can leave an Eight (a) operating on autopilot and unaware of collateral damage left in their wake, or (b) hitting a wall of overwhelming exhaustion and burnout. Eights on a growth path must come to terms with how pushing themselves so hard is hurting them long-term. Begin by recognizing how denial shows up in your daily life and slowly shifting how you approach situations.

Reflecting on Your Defense Mechanism Through Journal Prompts

How does the defense mechanism of denial show up in your life? What red flags does your body offer as feedback? What happens when you try to recognize and honor your basic human needs or limitations? What might happen if you continue to use denial to conquer every obstacle in your path? Have you ever faced burnout or exhaustion? What did that look like? What support could have helped before you reached that point?

Virtue: Innocence

Moving toward innocence for Eights is about reconnecting with a childlike self who can experience the joy and delight of the world with undefended wonder. When Eights are connected to their virtue, they move through life with openness and a willingness to be affected by the world around them. Being undefended is a core aspect of innocence, but this is a state some Eights never got to experience. Even in childhood, they were always aware of the need to protect themselves.

While less aware Eights recoil at the idea of lowering their defenses, Eights connected with the virtue of innocence realize that they don't need that tough exterior to be okay, and they can integrate innocence with maturity. Instead, they are able to embrace their vulnerability and emotional state, understanding there is a sensitive and sweet inner child who is just as much a part of them as the fierce protector they've always been.

The virtue of innocence could look like . . .

- Responding to each day with an open, unguarded mindset, no longer holding to the assumption that others intend to control or overtake you.
- Recognizing vulnerability as strength, and accepting all parts of yourself, even the soft or sentimental parts.
- Practicing self-restraint and patience.
- Pausing before reacting.

OPENing Up to Innocence

As you recognize lust and apply the OPEN framework introduced in chapter 4, you'll begin to shake off the ways your personality structure is keeping you bound and slowly move toward the virtue of innocence.

OBSERVE: Notice when your impulse is from the passion of lust. For example, observe when you instinctively move to apply more force to make things work.

PAUSE: Through reflection, then self-observation, you'll be able to slow your automatic reaction. As you get better at catching yourself in the act, you'll be able to find a pause. As you pause, simply take a breath and ground yourself.

ENGAGE CURIOSITY: Get curious about a different reaction: What else could you choose? As you consider new options, keep in mind that this step is simply to think about how to step out of your normal reaction, which you'll try out in the next step. In our example, perhaps you can see that you have an underlying assumption that being slow to react is weak, or being anything less than fully decisive is too soft. What if you could trust your strength even when you move slowly? What if you let your knee-jerk reaction pass?

NEXT RIGHT THING: Experiment with different responses or reactions. You don't have to get it right! This is a way to try out different things, and again, you want to start small. So perhaps this time, you simply take a deep breath. Still your entire body and breath down to your toes. You might even place a hand on your stomach and one on your chest. After a long exhale, move forward. How was that experience? What possibilities opened up during the pause?

Subtypes

The three subtypes of type Eight represent different expressions of the passion of lust. If you're an Eight, you'll likely see a bit of yourself in each description. To understand which subtype is dominant for you, look at the evidence in your life: How does your behavior align with each description? Which subtype do you see in action? Which of the growth stretches feels most intolerable to you?

Self-Preservation Eight

Nickname: Satisfaction
At a Glance: Pragmatic, Concrete, Self-Reliant

Self-Preservation Eights focus on meeting their own needs. One Self-Preservation Eight I interviewed described himself as a "fight-for-my-life survivor type." These Eights have full confidence in their resilience, relying on their gut instinct and hard-driving nature to overcome setbacks. To be certain they will not be at the mercy of others, Self-Preservation Eights create insulation through resources like financial cushion, social capital, power, and influence. Financial resources are not always the key driver for these Eights, but this is an important aspect of their autonomy. They might choose to keep their investment accounts separate from their partner, or they may review their business revenue and expenditures multiple times per week to predict what's coming in. A Self-Preservation Eight might use their energy to find a specific entrepreneurial path that will be highly successful and will ensure that (1) they will never need to work for a boss again, and (2) they will have all their needs met through accumulating resources.

Even when facing difficulties, these Eights believe in their ability to figure things out. They are grounded, pragmatic, and no-nonsense. While Eights don't find themselves experiencing overwhelming fear in general, all Self-Preservation subtypes have a certain degree of anxiety related to ensuring that they will be able to survive and thrive in their environment. Self-Preservation Eights notice uncertainty and quickly move into concrete plans, systems, and preparation. In my experience with Eights, this approach is grounded, calm, and practical. Self-Preservation Eights in particular make fewer concessions when it comes to addressing and considering their emotional state, as they focus on staying logical as a means to ensure stability and autonomy. This detachment sometimes causes Self-Preservation Eights to mistype as Fives, but they retain the intense, gut-driven, action-oriented Eight nature.

Self-Preservation Eights value loyalty, dependability, and authenticity in their close relationships. They appreciate people with a solid sense of self and the ability to take care of themselves, but they don't hesitate to care for and protect their closest people.

Growth Stretch for Self-Preservation Eights

DEVELOP YOUR EMOTIONAL RANGE. Anger is the dominant emotion for Self-Preservation Eights, but it is useful to explore what pain might be lurking beneath the anger. What might your anger be protecting? Give yourself permission to feel these feelings. This work can be difficult, but it's important. Sometimes you can be too self-reliant, keeping others at a distance. Once you give room to other feelings, risk a bit of vulnerability and confide in someone, maybe even let them know you need support.

Social Eight

Nickname: Solidarity

At a Glance: Benevolent, Empowering, Courageous

Social Eights use their strength to support and mentor others. Because Social Eights are concerned for the common good, they will find ways to champion causes and people they care about to move society forward. They want to make a big impact in the world. While Eights in general can be intolerant of weakness, Social Eights are attuned to innocence in others, and they often move toward others to protect them or fight for them.

These Eights are often warmer, more congenial, and less "Eight-ish" than the typical Eight description. For this reason, Social Eights sometimes mistype as Twos. Outwardly, they are perceived as altruistic, loving, compassionate, and willing to do anything for their loved ones. While this is true, Social Eights don't feel the need to mold themselves to be who others want them to be. They have a strong internal compass and a sense of self-worth grounded in who they are (rather than who they are to others, which is a common Heart type struggle).

Though vulnerability is still a challenge, these Eights tend to be less focused on self-protection. Instead, Social Eights are willing to put themselves in situations that will challenge their resistance to vulnerability if it means fighting for justice and causes they care deeply about. Thus, "Social" refers more to the greater social good, advocacy, and solidarity work. Sometimes Social Eights are called "social anti-social"[2] because they care deeply about alleviating suffering and helping humanity, but they can be impatient with individual people. It's common for a Social Eight to go to bat for someone else without considering the personal cost to themselves. Of course, this can be valuable in some situations, but it is not a sustainable way of life.

Social Eights can be more controlling than other Eights, and at times, their desire for control and power can be a blind spot since they are simultaneously genuinely altruistic. This dynamic happens because Social Eights tend to think they know what's best for others, and they may even try to control or command that others do things in a way that is "best for them" from the Eight's perspective.

Growth Stretch for Social Eights

FOCUS ON YOUR NEEDS. Social Eights tend to relegate their needs to a later, less busy date. This is especially true if your self-preservation instinct is repressed. The problem is there will always be something that feels more important than listening to your inner dialogue. Bring attention back to your needs and desires. Notice your tendency to move toward advocating for and protecting others, especially when you have soft emotions bubbling up inside. Take a moment now to plan time for yourself, during which you will offer yourself space to process your feelings, do something you enjoy, and do something relaxing (like a massage).

Sexual Eight

Nickname: Possession
At a Glance: Animated, Magnetic, Irreverent

Sexual Eights are the quintessential seekers of spark and fervor. They can be openly rebellious, and they tend to revel in going against the grain and stirring the pot, especially as a means to upend existing structures and create change. Sexual Eights almost delight in being "bad," or at the very least nontraditional. They don't need others to like them, and they often prefer to be oppositional rather than falling in line. However, this penchant for nonconformity doesn't mean they are unlikable; in fact, these Eights have a natural charisma that helps them woo and influence others. They can be quite magnetic, but many Sexual Eights determine when to turn their charisma on and off.

Sexual Eights tend to be more emotional than the other Eight subtypes, though sometimes they externalize these emotions without deeply feeling them, meaning they might be expressive without processing the emotion. These Eights may even reveal vulnerabilities in a way that seems uncharacteristic of Eights, often as a way to connect with others to build a more satisfying relationship. While Eights overall are known for their strong boundaries, Sexual subtypes have a push-pull dynamic around boundaries: they feel drawn to dissolve themselves into another to feel complete closeness and gratification, yet they seek to push others away to keep enough distance that others will still find them intriguing. A Sexual Eight I interviewed, Anne, described this dynamic like a Venus flytrap: the cycle of attraction and magnetism, then engulfment, then nourishing and keeping others out.

When Sexual Eights are unaware, they can be quite domineering and will use their ability to woo others to keep others under their control. However, as Sexual Eights grow, they find themselves more aware of this tendency and are able to identify when drawing others in is an attempt at control and power versus when they are simply desiring closer connection.

Like all Eights, Sexual Eights go for impact: they make big gestures and they seem to be forces of nature. They tend to be passionate, dynamic, and confident in their ideas and abilities.

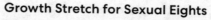

Growth Stretch for Sexual Eights

EXPERIMENT WITH SOFTNESS. You long for intimacy, but sometimes Sexual Eights fear being truly seen almost as much as they long to be seen. Strength, toughness, and intensity can be powerful defenses against vulnerability. Instead of trying harder to wring the spark out of life, what if you did the opposite? Being softer and gentler with yourself and with loved ones can help build the intimacy and depth you desire. Integrating the soft and innocent parts of you that you often work to protect will guide you on your path toward growth.

Dynamic Movement Arrows

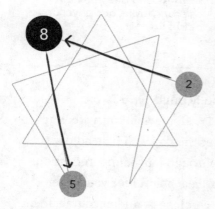

On the Enneagram, type Eight is connected to types Two and Five. These are the Eight's arrows, which means the other types the Eight can move to and freely access. I often use the term *move to*, but this does not mean the Eight *becomes* the other type—it simply means that the Eight borrows charac-teristics and motivations of the arrow types. If you've read other Enneagram books, you've likely heard this theory explained differently, so return to chapter 2 for further explanation if needed.

The most important thing to know here is that we can all borrow the higher (healthy) and lower (unhealthy) qualities of both arrow lines. When we're tired, stressed, overwhelmed, or otherwise not paying attention we tend to access these lower states.

When moving consciously, we can develop the higher side of our arrow lines.

RECOVERY POINT–TYPE TWO	
Unintentional Drift to the Lower Side Could Look Like . . .	**Intentional Movement to the Higher Side Could Look Like . . .**
• Being invasive and controlling, especially around fixing everyone else's life • Being dismissive of others' experiences if their advice is not wanted • Being emotionally expressive, but this can be used to manipulate others • Thinking, "You're either with me or against me" • Feeling that they don't want to be strong anymore (but still feeling that they must be, leading to resentment)	• Healthy attunement with others' feelings • Expressing empathy and love openly (even when it feels too vulnerable) • Acknowledging their need for love and reaching out • Offering themselves kindness and support • Embracing emotional softness and become more approachable, adaptive, and better listeners

Growth Stretch: Intentionally Build Type Two

• WELCOME VULNERABILITY. Note what strong feelings come up for you throughout the day, and instead of pushing through, let them out through journaling, reflection, a good cry in the car—whatever feels helpful for you. Offer yourself the support, kindness, gentleness, and encouragement your younger self needed.

• ACCEPT KINDNESS. Perhaps the most revolutionary act for an Eight is simply to believe in goodwill when it's easier to expect others to have ulterior motives for being kind. Instead, what if you accepted kindness from others as if it is genuine? How would it feel to see the best in others?

TRANSFORMATION POINT–TYPE FIVE	
Unintentional Drift to the Lower Side Could Look Like . . .	Intentional Movement to the Higher Side Could Look Like . . .
• Withdrawing so no one can use what they say or do against them • Self-protection through isolation and impenetrable boundaries • Gathering expertise to avoid making a mistake that would render them vulnerable to an attack, and then using it as ammunition • Use analysis and thought to form cutting arguments, push people away, and avoid deep, emotional connection • "I don't need anyone but myself"	• Pausing first to gather more information before reacting • Embracing curiosity and a willingness to see the world through fresh eyes • Practicing healthy restraint through a balanced use of their resources (not the trademark Eight 0 mph or 100 mph, no in-between) • Valuing their limitations as part of humanity • Thoughtful care of their inner child

Growth Stretch: Intentionally Build Type Five

• TAKE YOUR TIME MAKING DECISIONS. Rather than being quick and decisive, practice taking more time to gather information. You have a superior ability to recognize your gut instinct and go with it, but sometimes this leads to impulsivity. Use type Five to take more deliberate, considered action, rather than relying on brute force to push through.

• PRACTICE INTENTIONAL ISOLATION. Plan alone time to be with your thoughts and feelings. Use this time to get grounded, lean into contemplative practices like journaling and meditation, and allow yourself to be truly vulnerable with your emotions. This practice can be quite useful for Eights, especially as you're carving space for vulnerability.

Communication and Relationships

In this section, we'll explore both sides of communication: the Eight's side as well as those in communication with Eights.

How to Relate with an Eight

- BE AUTHENTIC AND ACCOUNTABLE. Eights can sense when others are not being forthright, especially if you're trying to endear yourself to an Eight by being overly effusive. Eights don't trust flattery, as they see right through it. Build a relationship on authenticity instead. Eights generally prefer spending time with people who have their own convictions than with those who tacitly agree with them. Own your beliefs, actions, and words.

- RESPECT THEIR VULNERABILITY. Even in very close relationships, it can be difficult for Eights to be vulnerable, so it's important to honor their choice to share with you. Sometimes people make a joke or attempt to lighten the mood because they're not used to their Eight sharing so vulnerably. Be careful not to poke fun at an Eight in this moment. It will backfire, leaving the Eight feeling hurt and regretful, and they're unlikely to share with you again. Instead, acknowledge their experience with kindness and compassion, and hold what they've shared in confidence.

- EIGHTS HATE TO FEEL PITIED. Sometimes sympathy feels like pity to an Eight, and before you know it, they'll be convincing you that whatever they've said is not a big deal (even if it was). Hearing "I'm so sorry," specifically in response to a challenging situation you had nothing to do with, can feel like pity. It might be more helpful to affirm, "Wow, that really sucks."

- CONTROL IS THE QUICKEST PATH TO CONFLICT. Eights are wary of any hint of someone else trying to control them. Of course, there are natural spaces for a hierarchical relationship, like at work, but even then, being told what to do is not an

Eight's favorite situation. In interpersonal relationships, feeling unnecessarily bossed around can cause a big reaction in which an Eight might become defensive, openly angry, or may retreat from the relationship for self-protection.

- BE DIRECT, BUT NOT BRASH. Some people, when talking with Eights, will try to be so direct that it's off-putting. Their thinking goes, "You're an Eight! You're fine, I can be a jerk to you!" But that's not the case: Eights are still humans, and while they may not show it, these interactions can sting. Eights value mutual respect.

Communication Skills for Eights to Develop

- SLOW YOUR IMMEDIATE REACTION. As an Eight your ability to know exactly what you're thinking and what you want is admirable. However, working on not saying everything you think will help you communicate more effectively. Sometimes Eights are resistant to this idea because it can feel dishonest or inauthentic, but moderating what you say a bit can actually be a marker of emotional intelligence and growth. Though, it's helpful to also have one or two people in your life who you can be unfiltered with.

- INTEGRATE EMOTIONAL VULNERABILITY. Eights are often very good at being transparent: they speak openly about things they've struggled with (even things that might make others uncomfortable!), but this type of self-disclosure is not the same as being vulnerable. Vulnerability involves disclosing deeper emotion, especially feelings they haven't fully processed yet. Developing trust can be a tenuous process because things that feel deeply vulnerable to Eights might not seem that way to others, or others just miss how personal it really is. It can help to share something like, "It's really difficult for me to say this . . ." or "This feels vulnerable . . ." to let a partner know that the vulnerability is coming and to be gentle (but not precious) and to listen well.

Practice Self-Friendship

In any relationship, interpersonal and intrapersonal (that is, within the self) communication co-occur.[3] As a result, I find it helpful to develop our relationships with ourselves as we're working to improve relationships with others.

The concept of self-friendship is simple: it's considering how we would respond to a friend who needed a little love and doing the same thing for ourselves. Here are a few ways you can practice self-friendship as a form of self-care.

- Remind yourself that it's okay not to be the strong one sometimes.
- Say no when you've got too much on your plate. Sure, you could push through, but this may be a moment to embrace gentleness rather than force in your relationship to yourself.
- Extend self-compassion for all your emotions instead of shaming yourself for feeling things.
- Listen to physical cues (exhaustion, hunger, illness) and move to meet your needs or ask a trusted loved one for help.
- Schedule regular alone time to refuel before you're feeling desperate for it.

Growth in Real Life

Growth for Eights involves integrating their emotional experience, learning to find softness rather than going for strength every time, and tapping into the power of slowing down. Even the invitation to slow down can inspire a hearty "Never!" from Eights who are not ready to begin on this path. Once they reach beyond this resistance, however, Eights experience more freedom in their daily lives, especially because they often use their "all-in" superpowers when beginning inner work. They cultivate fulfilling relationships, and they find healing along the way.

Thought Patterns That Might Be Keeping You Stuck

We all have thought patterns that keep us stuck. When they are subconscious, your initial response to the suggestion that these might not be helpful thoughts could be visceral discomfort. However, remember that we are focused on excavating and identifying these beliefs as a way to become free of them.

Notice how these thought patterns might come up for you:

- I don't need anyone—I'm better off on my own.
- If I show my feelings to my partner/roommate/best friend they will take advantage of that vulnerability. It's better to keep it to myself.
- Vulnerability will always be exploited.
- If I let myself need love, affection, or connection, I'm basically giving others control.
- I'm not safe with anyone else other than myself.
- I'm transparent, so I don't need to be vulnerable.
- If I let myself off the hook, I'll lose my edge.

Examine Your Assumptions

For each pattern above, journal about the following:

- Where does this belief come from?
- How long have I been attached to this belief?
- Is it true? Is it really true?
- What would be different if the opposite were true?

Everyday Practices: Finding Strength in Vulnerability

Sometimes, Eights find growth practices tiresome because they want to be able to apply forceful effort to get to the end result faster. Unfortunately, that's just not how personal development works. That said, if you're an Eight, your natural fortitude and your ability to be uncomfortable can support your process.

Feel your feelings all the way through.

This requires connecting to the most vulnerable parts of yourself and allowing those feelings to come to the surface. For many Eights, this practice elicits a visceral response. Building your ability to be vulnerable with yourself by creating more space for emotions is a great first step. Here are a few ways to do that. Read through the practices below and choose one to start this week:

- USE EXPRESSIVE WRITING TO OPEN UP. Try the journaling practice listed in chapter 2.
- EXPERIMENT WITH NAMING YOUR FEELINGS. Naming feelings aids emotional intelligence, which can benefit your life overall. Eights tend to express anger, even if they're feeling something else. When you're unaware of what's going on beneath the surface, you might find yourself constantly roiled in anger and frustration and unable to cool down. When you're upset or unsettled, use an emotion wheel (find one in the resource guide at https://www.enneagramirl.com/resources) and name the emotion beneath the surface. To practice this while calm, choose an emotion from the wheel and journal about what it feels like in your body, when you experience it, and how you express it.
- SHARE A BIT OF SOFTNESS WITH SOMEONE WHO IS SAFE. This simply looks like sharing how you're feeling with someone you

trust and allowing that person to sit in that feeling with you. It could also be sharing a challenge you're having without moving immediately into fixing it. This practice of letting safe people in can be valuable as you practice accepting your vulnerability.

Why so serious?
Eights can be a lot of fun, but sometimes they're too busy to let go of their serious drive. The most practical way to do this is to make more space for play and relaxation in your life. Think about times when you've felt at ease and relaxed, and plan a time (put it in your calendar!) to engage in those activities specifically. Afterward, observe how you feel. If it helped, make it a recurring thing you do regularly.

Honor your limitations instead of trying to conquer them.
Humans have innate limitations. In addition to practical needs like sleep and fuel, we are limited by time. Eights often try to overtake their human needs by conquering them, even in situations when they would encourage someone else to take it easy. Try the following journaling exercise:

* Bring to mind the last time you were sick and pushed through, regardless of how you felt.
* How did you feel in your body when you pushed yourself?
* Was there a moment when you decided to keep going rather than resting? Or did it feel second nature?
* What is your internal narrative about people who rest rather than persevering through similar moments?
* How might rest serve you?
* Next time you're in this situation, how can you remind yourself to slow down and take a break? What would it look like to honor your physical, mental, and emotional limitations?

Differentiate between empowerment and control.

Sometimes Eights tell others what's best for them. The intention behind this is normally good, but some Eights unwittingly take over, overstepping others' boundaries and controlling the situation. This isn't malicious: you desire to protect your loved ones, and you don't want to see them fail. As you become more in touch with your own feelings through growth—and increase your patience for letting others figure out their own lives—you'll also find the tenderness you need to sit with others as they process their pain.

- Bring to mind a situation you'd like to advise on. What are your intentions?
- How might you communicate your intentions in a way that is supportive but allows others to make their own decisions without losing your support?
- How can you be a gentle and loving presence when they face difficulty and disappointments?
- What is it like to feel the fear, sadness, anger, or whatever is coming up for you?
- How do you use your protective nature to avoid these soft emotions?

CHAPTER 6

Type Nine

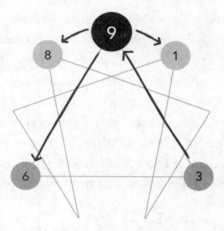

Dana exemplifies many of the characteristics we all love about Nines: she's easygoing, harmonious, and down-to-earth. She has little interest in presenting herself as more than she is; instead, she has a remarkable way of simply being in the world. Even though Nines are often treasured friends, it's easy for them to believe an underlying core belief that they don't matter, and that others are rarely thinking of them. They fear that they are forgettable.

A few years ago, Dana experienced this on her birthday. It was 2020, less than two months after the COVID-19 pandemic brought the world to a screeching halt. Naturally, Dana was uncertain what might happen as her birthday approached, so she planned a small get-together with a friend who shares her birthday and hoped for the best. When the day approached, only a few friends texted her to say Happy Birthday. Her type Nine response was measured and understanding: "Okay, that makes sense. People are busy. They've forgotten about me and my birthday. It's fine. No big deal."

Throughout the day, Dana tried to stave off her growing disappointment and worry that perhaps people didn't care about her after all. At the party that evening, Dana realized she hadn't checked Facebook, where her dad probably had sent her a birthday message. She found a quiet corner of the room where she opened the app and was surprised to see an outpouring of love, birthday wishes, and kindness fill her screen. No one had forgotten her, they had simply shared their wishes in a different format than she expected.

Because our types are so deeply ingrained in the core of who we are, it's easy to embrace the core messages of our types, unquestioned. This birthday experience helped Dana shift her perspective, and she can look back on the scenario with humor and compassion. Today it's much easier for her to remember that people care deeply for her, and she is not forgotten.

How Nines Show Up

Nines are **motivated** by a need to be at peace internally and externally. Beneath the surface, they are seeking comfort, harmony, and unity with others. Building a life that feels comfortable is essential for Nines. Because of this desire for peace and comfort, Nines are frequently described as operating at a lower energy level, but the reality is not quite that simple.

Navigating through life drains our energy in different ways. Nines expend energy by keeping the outside world, which is full of opinions, arguments, tragedies, and expectations, out, and the inside world, their thoughts, opinions, feelings, and curiosities, in. If these spheres collide, Nines dread the inevitable conflict, disappointment, and frustration. Nines subconsciously fear that they will not be able to navigate holding a different opinion from someone else, especially someone they admire. What if the difference turns into a big conflict or underlying tension? So rather than that unpleasant end, they spend their energy pressing the walls apart, creating a cozy space for themselves to exist unencumbered by all of this discomfort. No wonder Nines are exhausted! It's not for *lack* of energy but the constant *use* of energy to maintain their peace.

Along with guarding against mental and emotional discomfort, Nines **avoid** being the cause of discord or disconnection. Engaging in conflict is uncomfortable for most of us, but it's particularly challenging for Nines, who are focused on maintaining a sense of connection and harmony with those around them. Some Nines learned early on in life that relationships can be fragile, so they prioritize keeping them intact, even if it means not speaking up about what they truly think or feel. Rather than face the breakdown of a relationship, Nines fall into a pattern of turning down the volume on their own opinions and preferences (a pattern of self-forgetting) or internally adjusting their preferences or expectations to fit the desires of those around them (a pattern of merging).

This internal "turning down the volume" allows Nines to get through their days unscathed. Unfortunately, it can also cause challenging relational dynamics, often leaving others frustrated if a Nine comes across as absent-minded, not fully present, or even dishonest. In some cases, this pattern of behavior can degrade trust, which is opposite the intended effect. Also, because a Nine may allow others to assume they agree on something and then do the opposite (usually out of forgetfulness), others may perceive their behavior as passive-aggressive.

When Nines feel safe and secure in their relationships, and they sense that the other person is committed to continual growth together, they tend to share their honest thoughts more openly. This safety also leads them to feel an increased tolerance for tension that allows a Nine to build the deeper relationships they're seeking.

From an early age, Nines perceived that easygoing was the best way to be. They internalized the message "don't rock the boat," and made sure they wouldn't be too boisterous, too loud, or too attention-seeking. Caregivers may describe young Nines as relaxed, easy children who entertained themselves and rarely caused trouble. By being accommodating, they could maintain a safe distance from conflict, but this also required disconnection from their true self. As adults, Nines on a growth path actively work to find their inner voice and reconnect with their core desires, needs, opinions, and will.

A common **misconception** about Nines is that they are always okay with whatever others ask of them. In fact, Nines appreciate a bit of independence and can be stubborn when told what to do. It can be challenging for Nines to speak up, especially when more assertive parties have made decisions on their behalf without their consent. This causes internal dissonance by forcing the Nine to choose between speaking up and causing discord or acquiescing unwillingly. Both situations are uncomfortable, and the Nine resents being put in this position, which in turn inspires passive-aggressive behavior. Even though Nines enjoy togetherness and being with people they care about, they abhor being pushed around because it reinforces an early message that they don't matter. Nines are sensitive to being left out, and they work to include everyone, believing that if everyone belongs, they do too.

Thresholds

High Thresholds: Relentless Optimism and Acceptance

Nines have a **high threshold** for disorder, in the sense that Nines maintain their optimism that things will be okay, even when others might see disrepair. The "This is fine" dog illustration by KC Green depicts this well. In six panels, we see a cartoon dog sitting at a table as the room burns down around him. He lifts his coffee mug to his mouth and says, "This is fine."[1] This is not to say that Nines are devoid of any impulse toward action or that they are content with things falling apart around them. Rather, Nines hope for the best. Sometimes this is indicative of their head-in-the-sand approach to stress, but Nines also offer a sense of comfort and acceptance to those around them. They can be a grounding and steadying force since they are able to maintain composure when the world feels like a cosmic game of fifty-two-card pickup.

Nines also tend to have a **high threshold** for what feels important enough to require raising their voice. It's not that they don't care, but they perceive that even their strongly held convictions aren't worth getting too riled up about. Sometimes others fail to appreciate the gravity of a situation because Nines don't display obvious agitation. This doesn't mean they don't care, though. Nines often report communicating more enthusiastically about inconsequential ideas than deep convictions.

Low Thresholds: Conflict and Identifying Similarities

Consequently, Nines tend to have a **low threshold** for conflict. Nines sense even the residue of relational tension and become unnerved by it. As I said earlier, many Nines seek to preserve harmony in relationships above all else, and as a result, it can be difficult for a Nine to recognize which tension will undo a relationship versus which tension simply exists in most human-to-human interactions. Nines fear that sharing any kind of disagreement will destabilize the relationship, so they tend to err on the side of preserving steadiness by not outwardly disagreeing with a person.

Nines also have a **low threshold** for similarity, meaning that Nines easily spot points of agreement among people, even when they might seem subtle or unnoticeable to others. When wrapping an Enneagram workshop, one team member said, "It's interesting how different we all are!" A Nine in the room commented, "Wow, I was about to remark on how we're all so similar!" This Nine picked up threads of connection weaving through all the Enneagram types, and she was able to highlight commonalities across the different individuals. This ability opens the door for Nines to be fantastic mediators and conflict mitigators because they're able to see common ground where others only see difference.

Type Nine Personality

In this section, we'll dive straight into the type Nine personality structure, but you'll find a detailed overview of the terms in this section (Passion, Defense Mechanism, Virtue) in chapter 2.

Passion: Sloth

This passion of sloth is marked by a pattern of distracting oneself from experiencing too much emotional and mental discomfort. As Nines spend their energy keeping the outside world out and the inside world in, paying attention to themselves and their development falls by the wayside. Many Nines are interested in self-development work, but they also struggle to prioritize taking the time to know and understand themselves.

In general, Nines often describe themselves as slow processors, so even when they recognize that they need to get to know themselves better, it might take more time than they expect. Their emotional or mental experiences seem knowable but just out of reach—they are aware of them as background noise but the volume is turned down. Sloth feels like resignation, or, as many Nines have shared, "Que será, será." Whatever will be, will be. Sloth means taking a passive role in their lives with regard to their true wants, needs, and dreams.

The passion of sloth could look like . . .

- Subconscious barriers around difficult topics, such that when these topics arise in thought or in conversation, you are able to detach yourself from the experience of discomfort.
- Reluctance to feel deeply or confront ideas that are contradictory. Emotional upheaval can be overwhelming, so Nines subconsciously quiet their feelings.
- Comfort-seeking behavior, which can result in people-pleasing or ignoring your own beliefs and values.
- Taking a passive role in your life by going along to get along, and believing you don't really matter.

Reflecting on Your Passion Through Journal Prompts

How does the passion of sloth show up in your life? If you can think of an example, write about it. What was happening when you saw sloth show up clearly? How did it feel? Or, was it difficult to feel anything at all? How would you describe the physical sensation of sloth? What were you paying attention to? In what ways did sloth serve you? In what ways did sloth *detract* from what you needed or wanted in that moment?

Defense Mechanism: Narcotization

Type Nines often use the defense mechanism of narcotization, which is a way to numb the self as a protective strategy. Like sloth, narcotization allows Nines to create space between reality and their experience of the world as a way to increase comfort and decrease friction. Narcotization looks like creating a comfortable space in their minds to escape to, turning off their minds (intentionally or unintentionally), and drifting through life without awareness or attention. In many cases, it can mean using a substance or habit (such as drugs, alcohol, food, shopping, watching TV, reading, playing video games) to increase pleasant feelings and to avoid emotional pain. Narcotization helps the Nine feel safe and unbothered, but it does not help a Nine actually process the emotional experience that is causing the uproar to begin with. Narcotization contributes to sloth in that it is one of the mechanisms used to avoid experiencing deeper emotional or spiritual experiences.

Like a tortoise retreating into its shell when things get too loud or boisterous, narcotization offers a safe haven from external chaos. When unpleasant emotions rise, Nines can subconsciously flip a switch, either by falling asleep to themselves or the world around them.

 Reflecting on Your Defense Mechanism Through Journal Prompts

How does the defense mechanism of narcotization show up in your life? Narcotization allows space to set something aside for a while; however, just as a jigsaw puzzle does not piece itself together when left unattended overnight, abandoned emotions and challenges do not process themselves. Eventually we have to wake up and face the day. In what ways are you hoping things will solve themselves without your close attention and effort?

Virtue: Right Action

The virtue of the type Nine is right action. When in touch with right action, Nines are fully engaged in their lives, what they need, what they want, and what they will do next. They are committed to themselves and their values, which gives them a sense of strength, shielding them from the threat of conflict. When Nines are living from right action, they know what they need to do, and rather than turning away from it, they do it, even if it ruffles some feathers.

While a Nine acting from sloth may sidestep unpleasantness by tacitly agreeing with others through nonresponse, changing the subject, or giving a smile-and-nod rather than sharing a dissenting opinion, a Nine acting from right action is not worried about rocking the boat. This Nine is connected to their true purpose, and acting out of this purpose allows them to move forward with directed, well-considered, aligned action.

The virtue of right action could look like . . .

- Knowing what is right for you, acting on that information, and communicating needs and desires directly, even if this is unpopular.
- Trusting yourself to navigate discomfort or tension as it arises and being truly present in your life instead of shutting down when it feels like too much.
- Tackling the most important task first rather than getting caught up in procrastination or busyness with other, inconsequential but more comfortable activities.
- Being clear about your values and committed to your convictions, both internally and externally.

OPENing Up to Right Action

As you recognize sloth and apply the OPEN framework introduced in chapter four, you'll begin to shake off the ways your personality structure is keeping you bound and slowly move toward the virtue of right action.

OBSERVE: Notice when you start to slide into sloth, falling asleep to your needs and desires, or leaning into escapism.

PAUSE: Through reflection, then self-observation, you'll be able to pause. As you get better at catching yourself in the act, you'll be able to find a pause. As you pause, simply take a breath to ground yourself.

ENGAGE CURIOSITY: Get curious about a different reaction: What other reaction could you choose? As you consider new options, keep in mind that this step is simply to think about how to step out of your default reaction, which you'll try out in the next step. For example, even if you don't say anything, you could experiment with staying present in the moment and experiencing your physical reaction, or you could give an opinion or perspective to add to the conversation.

NEXT RIGHT THING: Experiment with different responses or reactions. You don't have to find the perfect action! This is a way to try out different things, and again. You want to start small. So perhaps in this moment, when you're feeling the desire to narcotize, you choose that your next action is to stay in the moment, breathe, and experience the sensation of discomfort the situation triggered. Spend a few minutes journaling about it to untangle more of your emotional experience. Slowly you'll build your tolerance for that sense of discomfort.

Subtypes

The three subtypes of type Nine represent different expressions of the passion of sloth. If you're a Nine, you'll likely see a bit of yourself in each description. To understand which subtype is dominant for you, look at the evidence in your life: How does your behavior align with each description? Which subtype do you see in action? Which of the growth stretches feels most intolerable to you?

Self-Preservation Nine

Nickname: Appetite
At a Glance: Companionable, Practical, Steady

Self-Preservation Nines focus on comfort above almost anything else. They create boundaries around themselves and their desires in pursuit of maintaining their peace. Even Self-Preservation Nines who may not consider themselves organized have unspoken routines and structures that help them create a predictable, pleasant day. These routines offer a sense of calm and predictability as a baseline for these Nines, who like to take care of practical needs for themselves and their families.

Creating their own personal life autopilot allows these Nines to focus on what matters to them, like their relationships, their work, and their alone time. They need time to sit in silence and sort through their day in their minds, solving any emergent issues. When stressed, Self-Preservation Nines might describe themselves "going through the motions" in a withdrawn, almost numb manner. Day-to-day tasks feel mechanical until they are able to settle the problem or conflict at hand. These Nines can also be more anxious than the other subtypes, though they are still easygoing externally.

Self-Preservation Nines gravitate toward concrete, practical applications rather than abstract ideas, and they are fairly accepting of life as it is. When they sense others are encroaching on them or placing many expectations on them, they can be stubborn. They may not always express their preferences to others, but they often have clear ideas of what they want in their daily lives, even if big dreams or concepts of purpose in life remain elusive.

Self-Preservation Nines are a stabilizing force for those around them, and they tend to be warm, loving, and generous toward others. In their close relationships, Self-Preservation Nines are more likely to share their opinions, especially if they feel psychological safety in that relationship.

Growth Stretch for Self-Preservation Nines

BREAK OUT OF AUTOPILOT. Making small changes to daily routines can be helpful to reengage in your life. For example, if you walk your dog the same loop every day, try going the opposite way. If you always watch TV before bed, try reading a book instead. If you spend your first fifteen minutes at your desk reading the news, try writing a to-do list or making a bullet journal. When you break your routine, how does it feel in your body? Where does your attention flow? Which actions allow you to be present and engaged in your life?

Social Nine

Nickname: Participation
At a Glance: Bubbly, Obliging, Neighborly

Social Nines focus on belonging, participating in the group, and investing in the common good. These Nines find themselves committed to various projects, and they place a higher value on the group's well-being than on their own. They tend to move through life with enthusiasm and energy, saying yes to anything that comes their way. Social Nines lack awareness around their capacity to take on more projects. In general, tuning in to their internal experience of their lives is challenging, but they also emphasize what the group needs to the extent that their own needs pale in comparison. Though Threes are often labeled the biggest workaholics of the Enneagram, I've met many Social Nines who are overcommitted, burned out, and still hustling to add more to their plate. This is both a strategy to retain group membership and a way of disconnecting from themselves. Even though Social Nines are important members of the group, they feel certain that they aren't, so part of their constant overextension is an effort to feel like they truly belong. Social Nines often believe that if they're not right in the thick of it, they'll be forgotten and empty.

Because Social Nines seek connection and belonging so intently, they can have a difficult time stating their real thoughts on a topic if they already know others disagree. Constant activity also leaves little time to consider how they feel, so Social Nines can also encounter challenges when asked for their perspective. They can be caught off guard by others asking for their opinion because to their mind, it's a foregone conclusion that no one really cares what they think, and they're trying to be okay with that.

In their interpersonal relationships, Social Nines are cheerful, talkative, and fun. They can seem more like Sevens in the way they convey, "I'm just happy to be here!" in contrast to more grounded, serious Self-Preservation Nines.

Growth Stretch for Social Nines

GET CURIOUS ABOUT WHY YOU SAY YES. Social Nines say yes to a LOT. Take some time to consider what need you're meeting by saying yes so often. Are you afraid you'll be left out or that you'll lose belonging? Are you convinced that your desires are second to everyone else's? What strengths do you already have that you can use to set an appropriate boundary around "yes" and "no"? Start small as you find ways to prioritize needs.

Sexual Nine

Nickname: Fusion

At a Glance: Impressionable, Compassionate, Amiable

Sexual Nines merge strongly with specific others. As they move through life, they typically have one person that they are very close to, such as a romantic partner, parent, sibling, or best friend. Nines naturally absorb their enthusiasm, dreams, and ideas like a sponge. While the Sexual Nine can sometimes be gentler and may be more insecure when they're unattached, they can be intense in the way they pursue relationships with specific others. A Sexual Nine friend once shared her frustration that her significant other was resistant to her merging with them. She only realized this level of irritation after doing intense inner work, which offered the space to reflect on this lifelong pattern.

In some ways, Sexual Nines can feel unfulfilled by their relationship with their life partner and might not be able to understand why. If their core relationship does not meet their need for emotional intimacy or provide the spark they're looking for, the Sexual Nine can struggle to understand what's not working. To feel more complete, they may dissolve themselves even further into the partner in search of the ultimate emotionally intimate connection.

Sexual Nines can feel a bit lost when they're on their own. They might recognize loneliness easily, but a deeper sense of emptiness may lurk beneath the surface. They might even ask, "How did I get here?" "Did I choose any of this?" They might even wonder if they are worthy of living a life that aligns with their own desires and dreams (or even having desires and dreams in the first place). Sexual Nines often can't see the warm, caring, fun, humorous, beloved person others experience.

While they are generally softhearted and generous, Sexual Nines can express big anger that might surprise or scare them (and the people around them!). It's important for Sexual Nines to learn to access this anger more steadily and use it to hold boundaries, express preferences, and speak for themselves.

Growth Stretch for Sexual Nines

GET TO KNOW YOURSELF. The growth work for Sexual Nines includes separating from significant others and becoming independent. This is incredibly challenging work at first. Plan alone time and get to know yourself. Consider what you would like to know about a new friend: What do they like to do in their free time? What is their favorite food or favorite morning beverage? That way, next time when someone asks how you'd like your eggs cooked, instead of saying: "Any way is fine!" you can say, "I'd love poached eggs, please!" This is simple, but when you start small, you can repeat the process with larger things.

Dynamic Movement Arrows

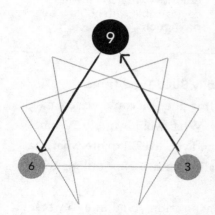

On the Enneagram, type Nine is connected to types Three and Six. These are the Nine's arrows, which means the other types the Nine can move to and freely access. I often use the term *move to*, but this does not mean the Nine becomes the other type—it simply means that the Nine borrows characteristics and tendencies of the arrow types. If you've read other Enneagram books, you've likely heard this theory explained differently, so return to chapter 2 for further explanation if needed.

The most important thing to know here is that we can all borrow the higher (healthy) and lower (unhealthy) qualities of both arrow lines. When we're tired, stressed, overwhelmed, or otherwise not paying attention, we tend to access these lower states. When moving intentionally, we can develop the higher side of our arrow lines.

RECOVERY POINT—TYPE THREE	
Unintentional Drift to the Lower Side Could Look Like . . .	**Intentional Movement to the Higher Side Could Look Like . . .**
• Taking on too much as they equate worth to productivity • Using busyness to disconnect from self • Becoming overly attached to how others perceive them • A tenuous sense of self that leaves them more deflated than before • Acting like they think they're important, but missteps send them reeling	• A well-differentiated sense of self • Confidence that they are important, needed, and strong • Applying themselves toward their goals and feeling inspired by their efforts • Communicating more assertively and getting to the bottom line effectively • Becoming self-interested in a positive way and feeling comfortable with healthy self-promotion

Growth Stretch: Intentionally Build Type Three

• WAVE A MAGIC WAND: Imagine you could wave a magic wand. Nothing is off limits. What would you do? What job would you have? Where would you live? Explore what that dream could look like by journaling, drawing, or talking to a friend.

• MAKE IT HAPPEN: Consider an aspiration you'd like to work toward. Advocate on your own behalf: What resources and support do you need? How can your strengths help you get there? Consider "no" a redirection: instead of getting discouraged, strategize how you can move forward differently.

TRANSFORMATION POINT—TYPE SIX	
Unintentional Drift to the Lower Side Could Look Like . . .	**Intentional Movement to the Higher Side Could Look Like . . .**
· Constantly overwhelmed and gripped by self-doubt and indecision · More suspicious of others and concerned others have ulterior motives · Being too in touch with fears, concerns, threats, and anxieties · Frustration that no one is looking out for them · Such intense connection to community that they're not sure if they could ever step out	· Becoming alert, aware of participants in their lives · Navigating threats becomes second nature · Trusting themselves to analyze possibilities, make decisions, and take action · Becoming more attentive to their inner experience (Sixes are often more aware of challenges and able to pinpoint the root of them) · Feeling connected to their purpose and willing to act on it

Growth Stretch: Intentionally Build Type Six

• BE A LITTLE CONTRARIAN: Because you often listen more than you speak, you probably know a lot more than you let on. Instead of resigning to others' will, try asking the question that's on your mind. Share your perspective, and remember that your contribution is valuable.

• TAKE STRATEGIC ACTION: Most Nines can do inconsequential tasks easily, but intentional action is another story. Develop your inner Six by prioritizing the most important actions for your specific goals. Consider building a rubric of questions a Six might ask. Am I saying yes because I don't want to cause any issues? What's most important to me? What do I need to say "no" to in order to say "yes" to what matters most?

Communication and Relationships

In this section, we'll explore both sides of communication: the Nine's side as well as those in communication with Nines.

How to Relate with a Nine

- RECOGNIZE THAT MINIMIZING DISHARMONY DOES NOT EQUAL AGREEMENT. Nines seek commonality in conversations—while they may not share ALL their opinions and beliefs unless they're comfortable, they will still highlight the areas of agreement. This can lead people to assume that Nines agree with them fully, but the truth is, they also see all the other perspectives as well. This ability to find mutual understanding can be a strength, but it can also be confusing or frustrating for people who don't understand their approach.

- PATIENCE IS KEY. It's important for a lot of Nines to be given the space to consider and process how they think and feel. It's common for other types to expect immediate answers, but rushing Nines will not help them think faster. As Nines avoid confrontation, relational issues can fester. In very unhealthy relationships, Nines can turn their brains off and disengage. When this shutdown occurs, the Nine might find it easier to remain unaware than to reengage, especially if they don't feel like their partner cares. Partners can sometimes read this as abandonment. Building openness in communication can help couples, friends, and family navigate these challenges with compassion and grace. Reassurance that the relationship will remain intact postconflict can also help.

- ENCOURAGE AND ACCEPT THEIR GROWTH. Nines often share that once they've begun to find their voice, other people in their life have gotten antsy or frustrated with them. They're not used to the Nine having boundaries or sharing their ideas, and it can cause frustration to those who are used to the

Nine's agreeableness. If a Nine is speaking up in this way, it's important to encourage it and see it as a sign of growth.

- DON'T INTERRUPT. Most of us interrupt because we're excited and want to show we're invested. However, Nines often wait until there's enough dead air to begin to speak, and they expect others to listen respectfully as they have. Jumping in or talking over them is the simplest way to get a Nine to clam up again. When this happens, the rest of us lose the contribution of a valuable, observant voice. Slowing the pace of communication can offer Nines adequate time to process.

Communication Skills for Nines to Develop

- USE YOUR VOICE. Work on speaking up and sharing on your own, without being asked. You have insight to share, but you often end up defaulting to silence when others don't ask or aren't ready to listen. Remember, your voice matters! Develop resilience when you don't immediately feel heard and understood by taking a deep breath and restating your point.
- STAY PRESENT WHEN TENSIONS RUN HIGH. Nines tend to withdraw when they feel uncomfortable. When do you notice yourself withdrawing? What are the specific circumstances that cause this? When does withdrawing protect you and when is it counterproductive? Work on expanding your ability to stay present in emotionally charged conversations so that withdrawing is an option but not the default.

Practice Self-Friendship

In any relationship, interpersonal and intrapersonal (that is, within the self) communication co-occur.[2] As a result, I find it helpful to develop our relationships with ourselves as we're working to improve relationships with others.

The concept of self-friendship is simple: it's considering how we would respond to a friend who needed a little love and doing the same thing for ourselves. Here are a few ways you can practice self-friendship as a form of self-care.

- Process your thoughts and feelings rather than avoiding them (journaling or verbal processing alone).
- Respect your need for alone time without judgment to tune in to what you want in life.
- Accept that some days you don't have energy for certain things.
- Observe when you have spoken up or moved toward an uncomfortable situation, and give yourself a high-five or a pat on the back. It sounds cheesy, but it works.

Growth in Real Life

For Nines, growth is all about learning to be with the uncomfortable aspects of life. Specifically, it can be powerful for Nines to tap into their anger. Often, Nines aren't aware of their anger, or they experience shame when they express it, as if they are a burden to others for having emotions.

Thought Patterns That Might Be Keeping You Stuck

We all have thought patterns that keep us stuck. When these are subconscious, your initial response to the suggestion that these might not be helpful could be visceral discomfort. However, remember that we are focused here on excavating and identifying these beliefs as a way to become free of them.

Notice how these thought patterns might come up for you.

- I don't actually impact the world or anyone around me.
- Really getting in touch with my desires sounds like a lot of work. It's more comfortable to drift through life.
- It doesn't really matter what I want or think: it won't change anything.
- It's better if I just keep things to myself.
- If I let myself feel what I truly feel, I will disrupt everything.
- Anger is unmanageable for me.
- My anger can be suppressed, and it won't impact me.

 Examine your assumptions.
For each pattern above, journal about the following:

- Where does this belief come from?
- How long have I been attached to this belief?
- Is it true? Is it really true?
- What would be different if the opposite were true?

Everyday Practices: Self-Differentiation and Self-Remembering

At the end of the day, I want you to know that you're valuable. You are worthy of love and attention. You don't have to make yourself small or unobtrusive to make space for others. Consider the ways you ensure that everyone else is heard and treated fairly and remember that you're one of the people who deserve to be heard, too. Growth for Nines is being able to experience the vibrancy of life, the uncomfortable, the joyful, the loving, and the sad.

Practice observing and expressing your anger.

Anger can be an energizing force. It allows you to set clear boundaries. It helps you move into the virtue of right action. But often, Nines spend energy keeping it hidden because it can be scary to allow yourself to express something that could be too big for you to handle, especially when you fear it might damage your relationships. Processing anger and making space for it might look different for everyone, but here are a few ideas:

- LET YOUR ANGER OUT PHYSICALLY. Use the physical experience of movement such as running or dancing to energize you and let some anger out. It can also help to act it out in a safe way by yelling, stomping your feet, or doing something that might *feel* a little overdramatic but is quite cathartic.
- SHARE IT WITH SOMEONE WHO IS SAFE. Let someone know how angry you feel. A third party, such as a coach or therapist, can be a good outlet. To begin, describe the physical manifestation of anger (for example, "my stomach feels like it's on fire," or "my face feels hot"), and an experience you connect it to (for example, "it makes me feel like I don't matter," or "I feel disregarded").

Give an unequivocal "no."
Nines often agree to more than they want to. Even if they don't agree, a firm "no" is rare. Instead, you might say, "We'll see," or "Sure, maybe," or "That sounds fun." All of these are noncommittal, placating words you might use when you want to say, "No way I'm doing that." Here are a few tips to find your "no":

- DEFINE WHETHER IT'S A YES OR A NO INTERNALLY. Sometimes you might not be certain what you think. Tune in to your gut using this quick practice: place your feet on the floor, take a deep breath, imagine the breath filling your body down to your toes. Take a second breath through your nose with your eyes closed. On the exhale, go with whatever answer comes up. Over time, you'll get better and better at tuning in to your instincts.

- USE A SCRIPT. "Thank you for the invite, but I will not be attending." It's polite, definitive, and clear. Or, my favorite, "I do not have capacity to do that, but I appreciate you asking." If the other person tries to argue or badger you, say, "I already gave my response. Let's talk about something else," and change the topic of conversation.[3]
- IMAGINE SOMEONE YOU LOVE NEEDS YOU TO STAND UP FOR THEM. Ah, yes. Nines can shine when standing up for others! Use that advocacy muscle for yourself. If you saw someone in the same situation, what would you say? What would you coach them to say? What would you say to fend off intrusive questions? Try that here. Don't forget, you are an important person, too!

Dream bigger.
Spend some time each week journaling about your dreams. You might not be aware of them at the moment, but the idea is to get curious about what is possible for you.

- EXCAVATE LOST DESIRES. What desires have you hidden, even from yourself? What is your gut instinct telling you? What is something you've always wanted to try?
- TAP IN TO YOUR CHILDHOOD WISDOM. If you're stumped, think about yourself as a child. What did you want to be when you grew up? What did you enjoy? What subjects fascinated you?
- MAKE A PLAN. Think about what small steps would help get you there. You are fully capable of choosing next steps and working toward your true desires. It might not feel like it at first, but as you get little wins under your belt, you'll get better and better at feeling confident in your dreams and actions.

CHAPTER 7

Type One

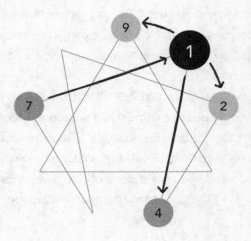

Attending staff meetings was never Peter's favorite activity, though he rarely let himself consider these preferences. Instead, he dutifully attended, took notes, and participated. One Monday morning, the entire team was on edge as they discussed their latest project. The scope was ambitious and one team member had just admitted that he had not completed his portion, which was a key function of his role. Peter wasn't proud of it, but he immediately thought, "How could you forget something like that?!" And, of course, Peter knew he'd never do something so reckless.

Then his boss turned his attention to the unprepared colleague. "What happened here?"

"You know what, I totally forgot. Slipped my mind. I'm so sorry, it won't happen again."

Dread coursed through Peter's veins. *I'm sorry?! I forgot?! That's it?!* Peter could only imagine the self-flagellation he'd be in for if he had forgotten something like that. Peter had organized his entire life around doing the right thing, being a good example, being the dictionary definition of a good employee, colleague, and person. Though he knew his colleague's apology was genuine, Peter couldn't fathom such a nonchalant response. Not even a hint of self-deprecation or groveling.

"Okay, thanks for letting me know, just please make sure you take care of it." The boss was relaxed, and even grateful. Peter was confused.

You're allowed to just apologize when you make a big mistake? He was certain he was going to witness his otherwise responsible co-worker's firing. Peter listened distantly throughout the rest of the meeting, sorting through this interaction in his head.

Upon reflection, he realized how often he arranged his actions to avoid blame. Peter had recently learned that he had a harsh inner critic berating him internally, and that not everyone has this voice. His inner critic wanted him to be good, but he was overdoing it all the time. Because it felt so awful for his inner voice to be proven right, Peter used perfection as a shield to avoid blame.

But this staff meeting interaction reframed Peter's perception of the world. From that moment on, he started saying, "I'm sorry, I got it wrong," and it was liberating. He suddenly realized that his reluctance to apologize or admit mistakes made him arrogant. His judgmental, hypercritical comments left others hurt and discouraged, even when he meant to offer support.

When he learned the Enneagram, he had a flashback of all the people he had hurt with his judgment, arrogance, and exacting standards. Deliberate, considered, and honest action, as well as scathing self-observation, offer Peter a sense of purpose in pursuit of balance and goodness. These days, intentionality is accompanied by a healthy dose of humor, conscientious relaxation, and fun, making all of the above more human and enjoyable.

How Ones Show Up

Ones are **motivated** by a need to be good, right, and morally correct. This is not about being the best or being good at specific tasks. Instead, Ones aim to find a deep sense that all is well in the world and in themselves. The good they are seeking is about virtue, integrity, righteousness, and fairness, and it includes warmth, balance, and the flourishing of all of humanity. For many Ones, pushing toward a standard of excellence and perfection feels like one way to get there, even though that's not the ultimate end. Ones are idealists who believe a perfect world could exist if everyone just did their part. Because they see all the ways the world around them does not meet their expectations, Ones work hard to fix and improve things to create the ideal world.

Of course, perfection is unattainable, and even when Ones recognize that, they still experience frustration around those shortcomings. Because Ones want to be existentially good, they carefully consider what is appropriate. When moving through life on autopilot, Ones can seem tightly wound and unable to relax. Unfortunately, when Ones operate from this space, they spend so much time forcing themselves and others into right, appropriate behavior that they end up inducing what they fear most. They become critical, judgmental, and intolerant of others who see the world differently.

Ones typically have an established set of principles and values that guides their lives. Sometimes, these are related to a religious tradition, but that's not always the case, as values differ vastly between individuals. While Ones are labeled as rule followers, they don't always describe themselves this way. In a sense, Ones don't see themselves as rule followers because they can perceive minute differences between how they show up and the rules: anything less than absolute adherence doesn't count. However, many Ones make their own rules that make more sense to them. These rules outline a stricter standard or a more efficient approach.

Ultimately, Ones **avoid** being bad or corrupt in some way, and they have a sneaking suspicion that they are somehow unknowingly corrupt. Because this experience is so disastrous for the One, they work hard to avoid it. Simple missteps or mistakes can feel destabilizing, so Ones avoid blame through strict adherence to their standards of excellence.

Ones also have another clever subconscious helper in their inner critic. Many of us experience negative self-talk, but Ones have a specific, berating voice that is constantly comparing their effort or their goodness to the ideal. This inner critic can be helpful in other ways, but it often serves to help the One ensure that when they are wrong, at least they're not the last to know. By beating an external critic to the punch, the inner critic helps the One psyche avoid being blindsided by their own inevitable corruption. "I might be terrible, but at least I know it" feels more tolerable than causing unintentional, irreparable harm.

The One's inner critic operates nearly all the time, and it focuses on improvement and admonishment. This knowledge can help us find compassion for Ones, especially when their critic becomes externalized in the form of judgment or nitpicking. Ones can see vast discrepancies between their daily lives and the ideal they'd like to create, but when Ones are more balanced, they can tap into small, thoughtful ways to show up as the earnest, conscientious, and discerning person they intend to be.

From a young age, Ones may have perceived that mistakes would lead to condemnation, blame, or ridicule. They worried about stepping outside the lines, so they drew even darker lines as protective barriers against straying from the narrow path expected of them. They may have felt like they needed to step up and be mature, whether because they needed to guide younger siblings or simply because they wanted to reduce chaos in the world around them. Ones crave order, clarity, and rationality. As children, they believed they must inhibit their impulses, and as adults, they might find freedom in reengaging with their gut instincts.

The most common **misconception** about Ones is that they are unkind or even cruel in their criticism. Ones want to support their loved ones and colleagues, so they help by giving advice and direct feedback. Their conscientiousness and sense of duty require them to speak up when they see issues. Likely because they are so accustomed to their haranguing inner voice, Ones can be unaware that their guidance lands as harsh critique, despite their good intentions.

Thresholds

High Thresholds: Effort and Accuracy

Ones tend to have a **high threshold** for what feels like "enough" effort. They put significant effort into activities that are important to them, doing whatever it takes to make things excellent. Ones can also feel like they've never witnessed "enough" effort by themselves or anyone else, leading them to be consistently self-deprecating, or—worse—searingly critical of others.

Ones also have a **high threshold** for accuracy. They continually work toward that definition of accuracy, looking for areas of ambiguity or falsehood that can be corrected and communicated to avoid confusion. Ones tend to think everything could be more accurate if we paid close enough attention, so they work to correct themselves and others. Though this can be perceived as criticism, Ones are motivated by a desire for excellence and don't understand why others might settle for less when excellence is attainable.

Low Thresholds: Criticism and Unethical Behavior

Ones have a **low threshold** for criticism. A small remark might make them feel like they're being blamed or accused, and they work hard to avoid ever being wrong or at fault. Even when they feel they're wrong, Ones who are less healthy may dig in their heels to justify their behavior, although they might also make sure never to repeat the offense. Some Ones also have a difficult time apologizing because they experience it as an admission of guilt.

Ones also have a **low threshold** for unethical behavior. If even something small seems out of alignment with their core ethics, Ones will speak up to address it however they can. If they are unable to take action, they may find themselves frustrated or anxious. Their ability to identify and correct bad behavior is admirable, though it's worth noting that Ones don't necessarily share the same ethical code across the board. Two individuals who are both Ones might disagree on the best course of action based on their distinct moral compasses.

Type One Personality

In this section, we'll dive straight into the type One personality structure, but you'll find a detailed overview of the terms in this section (Passion, Defense Mechanism, Virtue) in chapter 2.

Passion: Anger

The passion of type One is anger. Often, this type of anger is kept inside the body and causes Ones to feel tense or rigid because they are spending so much energy maintaining strict self-control. They produce tireless efforts to perfect and reform. Sometimes, this action is focused on the world around them, their partner, their work, or their children, and sometimes, it is about perfecting themselves.

Ones can experience that things are not quite right around them as a physical sensation, and this is challenging to ignore. Anger is not typically expressed directly. It's rare for a One to be openly hostile, but they can be subtly angry, frustrated, and resentful when living from the passion.

The passion of anger could look like . . .

- A constant low hum of irritation or agitation.
- Needing to fix and control everything to create excellence, accuracy, and balance.
- Holding yourself and others to extremely high standards and being harsh or critical toward yourself and others.
- Tension held within your body, such as through holding rigid posture, grinding your teeth, or holding muscles in a semiflexed position without realizing it.

Reflecting on Your Passion Through Journal Prompts

How does the passion of anger show up in your life? If you can think of an example, write about it. What was happening when you saw anger show up clearly? How did it feel? Notice especially how it felt in your physical body (for example, tense muscles). What were you paying attention to? In what ways did anger serve you? In what ways did anger *detract* from what you needed or wanted in that moment?

Defense Mechanism: Reaction Formation and Intellectualization

Ones frequently use a defense mechanism called reaction formation in which emotions and impulses are perceived as stressful or unacceptable and therefore counteracted by expressing the exact opposite of what one is truly feeling. This defense mechanism allows Ones to maintain appropriate behavior. This means that when they experience an unpleasant emotion, especially anger, Ones subconsciously transform the heat of anger into warmth. In this state, Ones can become endlessly accommodating as they dissolve their rage into a sweet, kind exterior.

While this modified reaction can be agreeable, sometimes Ones are unaware that others can still see them gritting their teeth or tensing their shoulders. It's not that Ones want to hide this, they just don't always recognize how powerful their anger is. They must learn how to process their anger to avoid inevitable ruptures.

Ones also use the defense mechanism of intellectualization. This method corrals their thoughts into rational, logical, proper approaches, disregarding their real feelings and attitudes about a given experience. Ones find solace in being reasonable and inadvertently block some of the wisdom they could gain from listening to their gut instinct intelligence.

 Reflecting on Your Defense Mechanism Through Journal Prompts

How does the defense mechanism of reaction formation show up in your life? Notice how challenging it is for you to share your anger directly. How does reaction formation prevent you from seeing situations as they are? How might feeling and processing your anger be more helpful? How might reaction formation make it more difficult to move on or let things go?

Virtue: Serenity

The virtue of type One is serenity. In this context, serenity is the ability to rest and to accept things as they are. Rather than using the strength of their will or the condemnation of anger to control, contain, or fix, Ones operating from a place of serenity let it all be as it is. The judgment of good versus bad and black versus white is replaced with a deep level of acceptance. Serenity represents a calm, quiet belief that much of life is as it is meant to be. This does not mean that Ones settle for injustice, however. This virtue allows Ones to apply themselves to bring serenity to the world around them with tolerance, discernment, and gratitude. Activism can be an outpouring of inner calm as it is no longer driven by the need to be a good person but simply by the desire to bring all of humanity to a sense of peaceful thriving. Serenity offers Ones freedom from the constant impulse toward self-improvement so that they can move fluidly with the ebb and flow of life from a mindful, centered place.

The virtue of serenity could look like . . .

- Self-forgiveness, self-acceptance, and self-compassion.
- Exuding balance, freedom, and acceptance—all of the ideals you appreciate but are unable to force.
- A sense of ease and softness in your body.
- The courage to take imperfect action on what you can control, the willingness to accept what you cannot, and the wisdom to know the difference, as in the Serenity Prayer.

OPENing Up to Serenity

As you recognize anger and apply the OPEN framework introduced in chapter 4, you'll begin to shake off the ways your personality structure is keeping you bound and slowly move toward the virtue of serenity.

OBSERVE: Notice when you start to experience the activation of anger. Pay specific attention to your bodily tension and rigidity.

PAUSE: Through reflection, then self-observation, you'll be able to pause. As you get better at catching yourself in the act, you'll be able to find a pause. As you pause, simply take a breath and ground yourself.

ENGAGE CURIOSITY: Get curious about a different reaction: What else could you choose? As you consider new options, keep in mind that this step is simply to think about how to step out of your normal reaction, which you'll try out in the next step. For example, even if you don't change anything, you could pay attention to where anger boils up for you physically, or you could get curious about what's making you angry beneath the surface.

NEXT RIGHT THING: Experiment with different responses or reactions. You don't have to get it right! This is a way to try out different things, and again, you want to start small. So perhaps in this moment, when you're feeling the desire to diffuse anger into sweetness, or even feeling the temptation to intellectualize what's happening, say out loud, "I'm feeling angry." Ones often have more excess physical energy than they recognize, so you could try expending energy through a workout and then using a guided meditation after. If you're new to meditation, this is a helpful way to begin!

Subtypes

The three subtypes of type One represent different expressions of the passion of anger. If you're a One, you'll likely see a bit of yourself in each description. To understand which subtype is dominant for you, look at the evidence in your life: How does your behavior align with each description? Which subtype do you see in action? Which of the growth stretches feels most intolerable to you?

Self-Preservation One

Nickname: Worry

At a Glance: Self-Refining, Mindful, Attentive

Self-Preservation Ones are the most overtly perfectionistic subtype, but they often don't feel "perfect" enough to call themselves a "perfectionist." Their idealism is primarily directed inward. They organize their lives around self-improvement, focusing on accomplishing optimal health, security, mental wellness, or another personal metric.

Self-Preservation Ones worry about violating their internal moral compass, constantly bringing awareness to how they are falling short and how they can be better. Even though they have a deep well of anger, these Ones repress it to ensure that they remain good and appropriate. They show up with genuine warmth, and they are inviting and kind. In their closest relationships, these Ones share some criticism, but they generally are not as focused on correcting or critiquing others as the other subtypes. Many around them might not be aware of how hard they are on themselves since many Self-Preservation Ones never speak it aloud. However difficult it might be to experience life this way, Self-Preservation Ones count it a worthy sacrifice to serve the ultimate good.

Self-Preservation Ones tend to accept critique readily and internalize it quickly. They often like to hear how they can improve, even if the words are difficult to accept. They can be quite anxious and may spend time anticipating criticism, perfecting and updating their actions to avoid errors.

When they're unaware, anger is a stronger force than they realize, and it's often keeping them stuck in this place of criticism, discontent, and discouragement. Understanding and expressing anger can be healing for Ones, even though it's uncomfortable.

Growth Stretch for Self-Preservation Ones

YOU ARE MORE THAN A SELF-IMPROVEMENT PROJECT. Self-Preservation Ones tend to see themselves as a project rather than a person with a full range of emotions, goodness, and imperfections. One way to loosen the reins on constant self-improvement is to take more time for things that are "unproductive" and just for fun. You may notice yourself wanting a break but thinking that you're doing the wrong thing if you take one. Consider indulging in a "guilty pleasure" once a week. You might feel guilty at first, but remember that this is your growth journey. Finding pleasure, fun, and relaxation is now your top priority.

Social One

Nickname: Nonadaptability

At a Glance: Resolute, Purist, Exemplary

Social Ones function as role models and teachers who show others the best way to live. They strive to set an example, and even if they don't specifically tell others how to be, they hope others will notice their conscientious, well-considered approach and follow suit. Social Ones place internal emphasis on knowing the right things to do, so they often dedicate themselves to research, learning, and attaining knowledge that will inform their decisions. Thus, they seem cerebral and more like head types than body types.

Social Ones typically come across as put-together and composed, but beneath the surface they have insecurities and questions like anyone else. Ultimately, they are working for the highest social good, desiring to make the world a better place for themselves and their progeny. Many Social Ones describe a sinking devastation on realizing that their sincere desire to help others lands more like judgment and arrogance. This revelation unravels their self-perception. On the other side of this unraveling, they can find a way of life that embraces their humanity.

Becoming less perfect allows these Ones to experience more freedom. While they want to exemplify integrity, morality, and all of these high ideals, these expectations can bar them from being honest with themselves and others when they are wrong. Their rigidity can leave them feeling trapped, as if any decision they make will be the wrong one. Though they lack the shapeshifting tendencies of

Threes, Social Ones often connect to the Three's brand of achievement, efficiency, and productivity.

Because these Ones place such emphasis on their morals, they find it easier to build close relationships based on shared values rather than common interests. Their black-and-white thinking can challenge their interpersonal interactions, and over time, they must learn the merits of introducing other perspectives in their life if they want to continue to grow in their relationships.

Growth Stretch for Social Ones

NOTICE YOUR RESENTMENT. Notice how often you model appropriate behavior and expect others to fall in line. Your intention is to be helpful, but there's also a strong desire for others to adhere to your proper way of doing things. When they don't, you can become resentful. Over time, as you learn to slow down this impulse, you might find more than one way to look at things (and that all of them can be right). Next time you want to correct someone else or model proper behavior, ask yourself the following questions before stepping in: Did this person ask for feedback? Is this a life-and-death situation? Am I overstepping a boundary by advising?

Sexual One

Nickname: Zeal
At a Glance: Passionate, Bold, Reformer

Sexual Ones focus on improving specific others, rather than considering themselves improvement projects. The trademark type One inner critic still exists, but these Ones are more openly directive toward others and less oriented toward the stereotypical tidiness or perfection often assigned to Ones. These Ones offer advice to help friends and loved ones improve themselves. Sexual Ones sometimes don't realize that they are attempting to exercise control over others, especially their partner, by "encouraging" them to do things in a specific way.

Sexual Ones find satisfaction in helping others get better, in part because it can feel like a distraction from their own inner critic. This externalization of the critic alleviates the frustration of facing down that critical voice or even engaging with deeper self-compassion. In their closest relationships, Sexual Ones subconsciously believe that after all their hard work, they deserve a partner who fits their ideal. This drives their reforming behavior and cements the One's place as the guide or director for their partner's life.

They are the most openly angry of the One subtypes as their focus is less about being appropriate and correcting themselves, and more focused on reforming others by whatever means necessary. Because of their quest to improve the world around them and their relative freedom of expression compared to the other One subtypes, Sexual Ones can be powerful, assertive forces in the world who can bring large-scale change in areas that need it most. They are often more energetic and less measured than other Ones, and this aids their endeavors.

Sexual Ones tend to be jealous of their partner's time and attention, and they may vacillate between feeling shame for acting "inappropriately" and feeling entitled to do what they believe they must do. Their growth work includes processing and naming their emotions, recognizing their desire for control, and increasing their compassion both internally and externally.

Growth Stretch for Sexual Ones
CULTIVATE MORE SELF-AWARENESS. Sometimes the root of criticizing others is in self-criticism. When you feel the need to correct a loved one, engage your curiosity. Let this be a signal

to look inward. Is it possible that you are running from or rejecting your own actions? Are you feeling jealous for their attention?
Sometimes insecurities and fears can be deeply buried for Sexual
Ones. Reflecting on what's going on under the surface of these emotions can diffuse some of the intensity, allowing you to see more of
your worth and lovability as you are.

Dynamic Movement Arrows

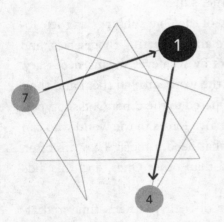

On the Enneagram, type One is
connected to types Seven and
Four. These are the One's arrows, which means the other
types the One can move to and
freely access. As already noted,
I often use the term *move to*, but
this does not mean the One becomes the other type; it simply
means that the One borrows
characteristics and tendencies of
the arrow types. If you've read other Enneagram books, you've likely
heard this theory explained differently, so return to chapter 2 for
further explanation if needed.

The most important thing to know here is that we can all borrow
the higher (healthy) and lower (unhealthy) qualities of both arrow
lines. When we're tired, stressed, overwhelmed, or otherwise not
paying attention we tend to access these lower states. When moving
intentionally, we can develop the higher side of our arrow lines.

RECOVERY POINT–TYPE SEVEN	
Unintentional Drift to the Lower Side Could Look Like . . .	**Intentional Movement to the Higher Side Could Look Like . . .**
· Being sarcastic or unintentionally biting at times · Expressing resentment that they feel like the "only adult in the room" because they actually want to have fun · Escaping into stimulation and behavior they'll later regret (such as overspending or excess) · Imagining too many options to think through, rendering them unable to commit · Pouting when they don't get their way	· Leaning in to playfulness and letting go of some inhibitions · Embracing the unlimited possibilities of life · Less perfectionism, more grace, lightness, and silliness · Attaching to joy as an essential aspect of life · Allowing for flexibility and freedom

Growth Stretch: Intentionally Build Type Seven

• MAKE SPACE FOR PLAY, FUN, AND LIGHTNESS. Go about your normal day with a playful attitude. Maybe do a little dance on your way to the kitchen for your morning coffee, put your coffee in a mug that makes you happy, watch a funny clip, and so on. Think outside the box! What is possible, even if impractical? Get creative when solving problems and trying new things.

• SPEND A DAY IN CHILDLIKE WONDER. If you go for a walk, breathe deeply and notice what is beautiful around you, examine the leaves on the trees and all their colors, find delight as if the world is beautiful and you've never experienced it before.

TRANSFORMATION POINT–TYPE FOUR	
Unintentional Drift to the Lower Side Could Look Like . . .	**Intentional Movement to the Higher Side Could Look Like . . .**
• Feeling more hopeless in their self-criticism • Moving beyond "I'm wrong, I need to do better," to "there's something deeply, irredeemably wrong with me" • Overidentifying with suffering and wallowing • Experiencing intense emotions, especially "negative" emotions • Taking feedback more personally	• Thinking outside the box by tapping into creativity, imperfection, and trusting the process • Relaxing some of their strict expectations and allowing life to unfold naturally • Seeing beauty in the mundane • Finding the gray area intriguing rather than something to be avoided • Leaning into introspection, thoughtful reflection, curiosity, and self-expression

Growth Stretch: Intentionally Build Type Four

• CULTIVATE A DEEPER RELATIONSHIP WITH YOUR FEELINGS. Sometimes Ones are challenged to articulate their emotions because they opt for sharing what they "should" feel rather than what they do feel. Accessing type Four can help you note and express more nuanced feelings. To begin, use a feelings wheel (find one at https://www.enneagramirl.com/resources) and choose an emotional word that best describes what you're experiencing. How would you define this word? Where do you feel it in your body?

• GET CREATIVE. Tap in to your creative side through some sort of creative expression. Choose something you can enjoy, but not necessarily something you're already good at. Remember, the goal is to get outside your normal box, not to create some sort of output. Painting, gardening, cooking, writing, or dancing are all great examples.

Communication and Relationships

In this section, we'll explore both sides of communication: the One's side as well as those in communication with Ones.

How to Relate with a One

- BE THOUGHTFUL, CONSIDERATE, AND CONSCIENTIOUS.
  Ones can get frustrated when others seem thoughtless or contradictory in communication. Staying on topic, rather than jumping around, can help this. Ones tend to be black-and-white thinkers who also communicate that way. They are more likely to talk about practical, logical ways to look at things, though they are idealistic about how things can be improved. While it may be tempting to point out the rigidity or the inner critic of a type One, this can cause Ones to feel more shame and frustration with themselves. A gentle "Wow, it sounds like you're being really hard on yourself" can be powerful in the right moment.

- LOOK FOR SOLUTIONS. Ones appreciate kindness, but they often prefer someone who will work through solutions with them. When others bring up issues, Ones try to help by giving advice, not realizing it's not what the other person wants. This is an opportunity for both parties to hone their communication skills by asking if their conversation partner is seeking a compassionate, listening ear or advice. When Ones offer advice, they're typically trying to be helpful, but unsolicited advice often comes across as criticism.

- BE GENTLE WITH CRITICISM. Because Ones have a strong inner critic, even the slightest criticism can be incredibly difficult for them to handle because it reinforces their preconceived notion that they are bad and irredeemable. They want feedback, but they don't need it endlessly reiterated: a gentle, honest approach is most helpful. By the same token, it's important for Ones to work on their own perspective with regard to criticism—to see that making a mistake or doing something wrong does NOT mean they're bad. Everyone makes mistakes! Sometimes, Ones can be intolerant of others' mistakes because they are so intolerant of their own.

 ## Communication Skills for Ones to Develop

- **WORK ON SEEING OTHER WAYS OF DOING THINGS AS VALID.** There is more than one "right" way to do most things, and gaining the flexibility to see that will help you in the long run. Practice asking more questions to gain insight rather than immediately sharing a judgment.
- **HIGHLIGHT THE POSITIVE.** When you are trying to help others improve, it can be disheartening when they respond negatively to your suggestions. Start by letting someone know that you see potential in them (or their project), and focus on the positives first. You often have these in mind, but it's less common for you to make them clear out loud.

Practice Self-Friendship

In any relationship, interpersonal and intrapersonal (that is, within the self) communication co-occur.[1] As a result, I find it helpful to develop our relationships with ourselves as we're working to improve relationships with others.

To me, the concept of self-friendship is simple: it's considering how we would respond to a friend who needed a little love and doing the same thing for ourselves. Here are a few ways you can practice self-friendship as a form of self-care:

- Remind yourself that things go wrong sometimes, and no one is at fault.
- Practice trusting what you instinctively know rather than listening to the "shoulds."
- Get curious about your desire to create structure and balance.
- Engage creativity or humor when you need to shift your perspective.
- Practice positive self-talk, especially around rest, productivity, and perfection.

Growth in Real Life

Growth Practices for type Ones must involve moving away from the pursuit of rigid ideals. Ones must learn to appreciate what is already good, even though it is imperfect. It means being able to see that they are good and that frequent self-condemnation isn't necessary for improvement. A lot of Ones feel that if they're gentler toward themselves they will suddenly become lazy, but again, this is leaning in to that black-and-white thinking. Finding the gray area will offer freedom.

Thought Patterns That Might Be Keeping You Stuck

We all have thought patterns that keep us stuck. When they are subconscious, your initial response to the suggestion that these might not be helpful thoughts could be visceral discomfort. However, remember that we are focused on excavating and identifying these beliefs as a way to become free of them.

Notice how these thought patterns might come up for you:

- If I let myself be less strict, I'll mess up.
- Mistakes should not be overlooked or forgotten.

- Expressing anger is dangerous and may make me unpredictable.
- I need structure, rigidity, and clarity to make sure I don't step outside the lines.
- I am in need of continual improvement.
- Being hard on myself is what keeps me going.
- If I miss something, and things fall apart, it will be my fault.

Examine your assumptions.

For each pattern above, journal about the following:

- Where does this belief come from?
- How long have I been attached to this belief?
- Is it true? Is it really true?
- What would be different if the opposite were true?

Everyday Practices: Self-Compassion and Letting Go

Growth Practices for type Ones must involve loosening self-control. Rather than getting better, Ones need to get worse. They need to embrace ambiguity, become more flexible, and appreciate that they are good even when they make mistakes.

Tend to your own garden.

When you see someone else doing something that you perceive to be not in their best interest or to be unethical or incorrect, it's tempting to want to step in and rescue them. Instead, try reminding yourself that they are in charge of their life, and you are in charge of yours. Instead of jumping in with advice or solutions, try offering an empathetic word and leaving it at that. How does this affect your relationships? What is it like to let go of needing to take responsibility for others?

Take time off.

Perhaps it's not always feasible to take time off of work, but learning to access a playful side is crucial for Ones. Plan a time to get away from responsibilities, whether it's an afternoon or a week. If you can, coordinate with others so that you will not be responsible for other activities during this time. For example, it might be tempting to procrastinate on your fun time by saying, "I'll go after I finish folding this laundry," or "I'll just multitask the fun thing with errands." Inevitably, it will get pushed aside. If this feels entirely foreign, here are some guidelines to help you invite more fun, play, and spontaneity into your life.

- Brainstorm: What makes you happy? What feels exciting? What makes you joyful?
- Make a plan: When will you take action on this? When will you make time for your play? I know I said spontaneity, but I also know Ones often need to schedule it in!
- And remember, investing energy in your happiness is worthwhile.

Work with your inner critic.

The inner critic is the most pervasive daily struggle for most Ones. While you may have heard the guidance to yell at your inner critic to get it to shut up, there are other methods of working with your inner critic that can offer more sustainable relief.

- TRY DISTANCED SELF-TALK. When your inner critic is berating you about something that has happened, restate it in the third person. Instead of "I made a mistake," think, "[Your Name] made a mistake." According to psychologist Ethan Kross, this method is less likely to lead to rumination and leads to fewer negative emotions, wiser reasoning, and better problem solving under stress.[2]

- TRY A PARTS-OF-SELF PERSPECTIVE. It might not always feel pleasant, but try getting to know this part of yourself. Recognize that your critic is playing an important role. Journal about the following questions: What does your inner critic want you to know? How old is your critic? What does their voice sound like? What are they afraid might happen if they don't correct you? What are they trying to protect you from? Acknowledge that your critic is trying to do something helpful (even if it feels misguided at times). When journaling, try to remain open and curious about this part of yourself.[3]

- RECOGNIZE THAT THE CRITIC'S PERSPECTIVE IS SKEWED. So much about you is already good, yet your vigilance around imperfections obscures seeing yourself clearly. Start to shift your mindset by offering yourself compassion when you feel the impulse to "should" yourself. Practice self-compassion by telling yourself, "I did my best," or "It's okay to be angry and disappointed," or "I'm okay," to validate your experiences.

Shake it off.

Have you ever seen an animal shake after a stressful encounter? That's their body's way of processing stress.[4] It's an intelligent design, but in our modern world, we rarely take a second for a head-to-tail shake. Fortunately, we can leverage other methods of movement to reconnect with our bodies, release stress, and reconnect with emotions.[5] Dancing combines various movements that help regulate our nervous systems, improve mood, accelerate heart rate, and invoke pleasure—yes, even if you have two left feet![6] Once a day, turn up your favorite feel-good music and have a ball.

Part III

The Heart Types: Overview

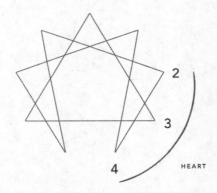

HEART TYPES

Central Themes	Relationships, identity, emotional attunement, attachment, expectations, adaptation, mirroring
Underlying Emotions	Sadness, Grief, Shame
Common Experiences	• Sensing what others are feeling • A sense of not truly knowing themselves except through relationship with another ("I'm lovable," "I'm admirable," "I'm different") • Wondering about their identity ("I am whoever you need me to be," "I am whoever you think I am," "I know who I am, but I think there's more, I just need to keep introspecting") • Seeing the world through the lens of relationships to others and self
Aversions	• Being dismissed as less serious or practical due to their focus on emotions • Others overlooking relationships

CHAPTER 8

Type Two

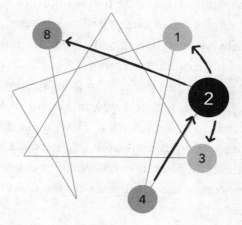

"Raise your hand if Bryan has ever given you a ride," Bryan's brother and best man polled the audience, his eyes scanning across a sea of wedding guests. All hands were raised. Bryan laughed and hung his head in mock shame at his brother's good-natured joking. They'd had this conversation before, so it was only fitting that it came up again here, in the best man's speech at his wedding.

"Please, whatever you do, don't let Bryan drive you home from his own wedding." A knowing laugh rippled through the crowd as they raised their glasses to toast the happy couple.

Bryan is well known among family and friends as the guy who will drive you wherever you need to go. Heading to the movies? Going out to dinner? Need to run an errand across town? No problem, Bryan will be there.

These car rides are an opportune time for deep conversations and building a sense of togetherness that feels special and meaningful for Bryan. He loves the experience of having quality time with others, and he never thinks about any inconvenience when it comes to chauffeuring his nearest and dearest (and the occasional acquaintance) all around the large metropolitan area he lives in. He's put so many miles on his car that his brother says he's costing rideshare companies thousands of dollars per year.

Bryan has always been like this; he loves the ability to be there for others, and his cultural background focuses on caretaking and the collective good of the family. Even from a young age, he wasn't certain what he liked, but he knew the warm feeling of making others feel loved. So he went with it. Now in his thirties, he's surrounded by deep, lovingly cultivated relationships and a wide net of friends and family. Sure, it costs him a bit extra in gas, but the relational connection and fulfillment he receives from his efforts feels priceless.

While he loves to engender mutual goodwill and foster positive relationships, part of him feels guilty when he's not pouring himself out for others. There's a certain fear of inadequacy underpinning his care and kindness—what will happen to this relationship if I'm not driving them here, there, and everywhere? What does it say about me if I'm not the one picking up a little extra cleaning or cooking at home? There's a deep sadness there, which relates to the type Two's concern about their truest self: many Twos wonder if others saw them for the full spectrum of their emotional world if they'd still be as loved and wanted. Twos subconsciously doubt anyone truly loves them beyond what they do for others.

So, they continue. But Twos who are starting an inner work journey, like Bryan, live with this constant tension of recognizing their own desires and taking kind, loving care of themselves, just like they do everyone else. Fortunately, Bryan has people around him who see the tension and encourage him to care for and value himself as equally deserving of his time and energy.

He still loves being everyone's personal driver. And yes, he did drive a guest home from his wedding.

How Twos Show Up

Twos are **motivated** by a desire to be loved, wanted, and needed, and they lead with warmth and affection. While Twos are often labeled "the Helper," many Twos are not primarily motivated to be helpful in the traditional sense, like helping a friend move or dropping off a casserole. Instead, they focus on securing warm, loving relationships, crafting heartfelt connections, and creating a positive environment where everyone is happy and taken care of. Deep down, Twos place much of their self-worth in how likable they are in the eyes of others.

They bank likability by sensing what others need and meeting those needs. If you seem down, they'll offer encouragement and advice to make life better. If they sense that you're stressed, they'll bring you coffee or alleviate your pain by taking something off your plate. Twos are action-oriented in that even when no one asks, they move toward the needs and expectations of others in an effort to build rapport and decrease tension.

Because their focus is on making others feel good, Twos can fall into a pattern of toxic positivity: the avoidance of difficult emotions or conversations.[1] Maintaining these positive "vibes" is so important that Twos will often repress their own experiences and show up as the upbeat, cheerful person everyone has grown to expect. Their internal world becomes disconnected as they meld themselves into this image of loving perfection.

Twos want to be there for others, but sometimes Twos feel like they have to play the role of the helper in others' lives or they will be forgotten or dismissed. Twos work hard to **avoid** rejection, as this would pose a threat to their sense of self. Subconsciously, they might wonder, "Who am I if I'm not beloved by others? Who am I if I'm not essentially likable?" Twos might continue in this role even when it's not serving them anymore. The challenge for Twos is that they are genuinely altruistic, and they are often praised for how well they care for others. This can be confusing because behavior that is not in their best interest is continually rewarded. It can be difficult for Twos to recognize that shifting their focus to themselves can be a healthy practice long-term.

Twos have a subconscious pattern of giving to get: part of them believes that if they show up for others, when they need someone, others will know how to respond without the Two having to ask. They are beautiful, thoughtful, relational, kind humans who find joy in loving others, and loving others is not *always* aimed at reciprocity, but they can be unaware of their expectations in this dynamic.

Sometimes, however, Twos can face challenges when respecting others' personal boundaries. They spend time and energy managing others' emotional experiences, and it can take years of intentional work to pull back from this behavior and let each person have their own experiences. For example, I consulted with a leader who struggled to delegate because she was afraid her employees would dislike her if they felt overwhelmed. She didn't realize that this behavior was causing her staff to miss out on valuable learning experiences and skill-sharpening opportunities. She prevented challenges by fixing issues before they arose so her team never felt stressed. Meanwhile, she felt undervalued and overwhelmed. This tendency often feels like deep care or genuine concern to a Two, so it can be challenging for a Two to recognize they are infringing, especially when they have pure intentions.

From an early age, Twos may have perceived that someone else in their family system needed more attention. They fit best—and got the love and nurturance they needed—when they served and supported others. Young Twos internalized the concept that the needs of others were more important, thus minimizing their own needs. As adults, Twos continue this pattern of repressing their needs because they fear becoming selfish, which was a major threat to their basic sense of self and belonging in childhood. Twos must invest in understanding their own experiences, feelings, and needs as they learn to break this pattern.

A common **misconception** in descriptions of Twos is the two-dimensional focus on their altruism. Like any type, Twos contain multitudes: they can be intellectual, humorous, creative, and strategic. They can be strong leaders, engineers, academics, and innovators. Their strength is that at their core, they think about all of this through the lens of relationships and connection. In organizations, Twos accomplish goals through collaboration, whether through tapping their network to connect all the right pieces or through leveraging each colleague's individual strengths.

Thresholds

High Thresholds: Expectation and Contribution

Twos have a **high threshold** for demands and expectations. In particular, Twos expect a lot of themselves and strive to be able to meet others' relational needs. They're okay with people they value having expectations, and they rise to meet or exceed them as a way of establishing rapport.

Twos also have a **high threshold** for what feels like a sufficient contribution, and they assume the only way to move forward is to continually go above and beyond for others. While some Twos do this by being overtly helpful, other Twos (especially the self-preservation subtype) may end up feeling like they continually must do more, even if they feel stressed out and anxious about it. They don't actually want to put themselves out there and help, but becoming unimportant to others would be worse.

Low Thresholds: Rejection and Appreciation

Twos have a **low threshold** for what feels like rejection. Dismissing their help, affection, attempts at building rapport, or encouragement all feel like rejection to Twos. They often find themselves believing that even the most subtle dismissal is an assault on their value as a person, despite rationally knowing that it's not true. They typically do everything they can to avoid that feeling of rejection, often by making themselves indispensable.

Twos also have a **low threshold** for what feels important enough to inspire deep care and appreciation. A Two will often notice a small gesture, a glance, or a feeling from someone else and give it room to flourish. A type Two friend of mine loves to go out for dinner, and she'll inevitably find something I've accomplished and entirely dismissed to highlight and celebrate. Nothing gets past her. This quality engenders deep connection, but Twos may become resentful, feeling unnoticed and unappreciated, as they often secretly hope others will offer the same perceptiveness and care to them, while having a difficult time making this expectation known. Others can help Twos feel important by extending care or excitement, even if a Two acts like something isn't a big deal. Part of the growth path for Twos is verbally clarifying their desire for this type of care.

Type Two Personality

In this section, we'll dive straight into the type Two personality structure, but you'll find a detailed overview of the terms in this section (Passion, Defense Mechanism, Virtue) in chapter 2.

Passion: Pride

For most of us, our passion is difficult to accept, but this is especially true of Twos, who experience themselves as intentional, conscientious, and even humble. Pride feels foreign. This is why this passion can be so pernicious. Pride manifests as an inaccurate self-perception: the inflation or deflation of the Two's importance. Inflated pride is the assumption that others need help, advice, and support, and they should take it without question. The Two knows best—why isn't anyone listening? They hold an unspoken expectation that everyone else needs help, except for the Two. When pride is deflated, they believe they are less deserving or worthy than others.

When giving from a place of pride, there are strings attached. Prideful giving is not about the one receiving the gift but the one giving. Prideful love says, "It's from the heart! All I require is your boundless gratitude and unending, uncritical friendship in return." This can be a major blind spot for sensitive Twos, who may have a hard time seeing how their generosity is not always genuine.

The passion of pride could look like . . .

- The belief that others need more help than you do, leading you to do more than required, even at your own expense, and regularly thinking, "What would they do without me?"
- Giving advice with the assumption that you have all the answers and know what's best for others.
- Hoping that when something falls apart in your life, those you've supported over the years will come running to your aid.
- Believing that you can determine how others experience you— and maybe even determine their thoughts—through your charm and strategic support.

Reflecting on Your Passion Through Journal Prompts

How does the passion of pride show up in your life? If you can think of an example, write about it. What was happening when you saw pride show up clearly? How did it feel? What were you paying attention to? In what ways did pride serve you? In what ways did pride *detract* from what you needed or wanted in that moment?

Defense Mechanism: Repression

Type Twos often use the defense mechanism of repression, which is a way to remain numb to their own needs, feelings, and desires in service of making space to serve others. Repression works together with the passion of pride to convince a Two that they don't need anything from anyone because they don't have any needs. However, a lack of awareness of their needs is not the same as not having needs at all. All humans have needs. Repression functions to help a Two hide information about themselves from themselves—feelings, desires, wishes, aversions, fears—that is too difficult to acknowledge consciously.

Repression also anesthetizes the impact of anger and resentment. As Twos double down on insisting they don't need anything, their unmet needs begin to scream for attention. Resentment festers when Twos expect others to meet their needs without any direct request, just as they do for everyone else. This resentment is also repressed until the fury of being so unsupported reaches a boiling point. In this state, the Two may scream and stomp that no one ever helps them. They may be uncharacteristically mean or sarcastic. For some Twos, the boiling point is the only time they're in touch with their needs, and they may become overtly demanding.

Reflecting on Your Defense Mechanism Through Journal Prompts

How does the defense mechanism of repression show up in your life? How is your aversion to being needy create intolerance to your own needs in the form of self-criticism when you have real, practical needs? How can you use your loving, caring energy generously toward yourself? The goal is not necessarily to meet all your needs yourself—humans need community, after all—but to get in the habit of being routinely attuned to your needs, your anger, and anything else you repress so that you can address issues from a calm, grounded place rather than from your boiling point.

Virtue: Humility

The virtue of type Two is humility, which is the ability to allow themselves to be as they are; they don't need to be more or less important than others to gain love or affection. Humility allows Twos the freedom to be exactly as they are, knowing that they are not so powerful that their word or deed will change the course of history. They can offer love and genuine care from a place of true altruism as their worth is not defined by how likable or lovable others find them. They do not need to ingratiate themselves with others or make themselves indispensable to earn love, connection, or kindness. They are simply loved, exactly as they are.

The virtue of humility could look like . . .

- Recognizing that you are a normal human with needs. Seeing yourself as worthy of experiencing tender, loving care, even if you don't do anything for anyone else.
- Feeling free to help others (or not) from a place of genuine altruism, no strings attached.
- Experiencing openness to feedback because your worth is not dictated by how likable or lovable others find you.
- Acting with intentionality in accordance with your values, and holding the awareness that you are not responsible for others' feelings or reactions.

OPENing Up to Humility

As you recognize pride and apply the OPEN framework introduced in chapter 4, you'll begin to shake off the ways your personality structure is keeping you bound and slowly move toward the virtue of humility.

OBSERVE: Notice when your automatic activities are a function of pride. For example, when you call a friend to check in or offer to bring them coffee, observe that impulse.

PAUSE: Through reflection, then self-observation, you'll be able to slow your automatic reaction. As you get better at catching yourself in the act, you'll be able to find a pause. As you pause, simply take a breath and ground yourself.

ENGAGE CURIOSITY: Get curious about a different reaction: What else could you choose? As you consider new options, keep in mind that this step is simply to think about how to step out of your normal reaction, which you'll try out in the next step. In our example, perhaps you start to notice that a tinge of loneliness creeps in just before you pick up your phone, or perhaps you identify that you're feeling very much in need of the kind of care you're extending to others.

NEXT RIGHT THING: Experiment with different responses or reactions. You don't have to get it right! This is a way to try out different things, and again, you want to start small. So perhaps in this moment, when you're feeling the desire to do something for someone else and repress your own needs, you can try a different approach to meeting your need for connection or care. Maybe you call your friend and say, "Hey, I really need to talk. Do you have a minute?" or you take yourself to a coffee shop and get the no-holds-barred order you'd usually only get for someone else.

Subtypes

The three subtypes of type Two represent different expressions of the passion of pride. If you're a Two, you'll likely see a bit of yourself in each description. To understand which subtype is dominant for you, look at the evidence in your life: How do you actually show up in life? Which subtype do you see in action? Which of the growth stretches feels most intolerable to you?

Self-Preservation Two

Nickname: Privilege
At a Glance: Endearing, Tentative, Receptive

Self-Preservation Twos convey warmth through their endearing and youthful demeanor.[2] These Twos can be playful and loving, but they may also be self-protective, avoiding situations in which they'll have to go out on a limb. They are more reserved than other Twos, and they don't move as quickly to help others, especially if they have not been asked. When they do help, they might feel resentful of the expectation that they play this "helper" role because it feels like the exchange they must make to receive the care, protection, and provision they crave from others.

Self-Preservation Twos sometimes operate in a way that invites others to take care of them, whether through a degree of self-neglect, or through hinting about what they need. This can be a subconscious tactic to meet their practical needs. When Self-Preservation Twos are unaware of their patterns, they might do this hoping someone else will step in and take care of them, but more often, they fear it's too selfish to ask for much, too self-important to take care of themselves, and too bold to believe they are worthy. In this subtype, the self-preservation instinct is not about securing external resources on their own but preserving their own energy and effort by helping others help them.

Self-Preservation Twos are kind and genuine friends who tend to be more mild-mannered than other Twos. They are often studious and quietly competent (even though they rarely announce that to the world). These Twos grow when they practice advocating for themselves and being more straightforward about their thoughts, feelings, and needs.

Growth Stretch for Self-Preservation Twos
NOTICE YOUR TENDENCY TO SELF-ABANDON. You tend to give your power away to others, believing they are the ones who can protect or hold you. Redirect your attention to how you can give yourself what you truly need. Because Self-Preservation Twos fear doing things themselves, playing big, or taking care of themselves, you might have a tendency to shrink yourself. You might be afraid to take bold action or draw attention to yourself because deep down, you wonder if you're worth it or if others might judge you. Try stepping into your power by pushing this envelope just a bit.

Social Two

Nickname: Ambition
At a Glance: Magnanimous, Poised, Industrious

Social Twos are engaging, positive people who are good at knowing the right people and getting things done. They build influence through giving of themselves and constantly find more they can do to support others (which also helps support them in subconscious ways). The name often given to these Twos is "ambition," as they often move toward positions of leadership, power, and influence.

Social Twos give advice, encouragement, gifts, assistance—whatever they think others need. They tend to think they know what's best, and they habitually forget to ask others if whatever they're giving is actually wanted or needed. These Twos have high expectations of themselves and others. One Social Two I interviewed said that "collecting so many blank checks that I can cash in at any time" set him up for failure. He drove himself into burnout fueled by the resentment toward others who didn't follow through on these unspoken exchanges. It can be difficult for Social Twos to slow down long enough to recognize their own needs because they tend to feel they are carrying the weight of the world on their shoulders.

Social Twos have a hard time acknowledging how little control they actually have over the earth's constant spinning on its axis. Much to a Social Two's chagrin, they can stop, and the world will go on. This feels extreme, but Social Twos often don't realize how much they've assumed they have power over so many different aspects of life leading them to giving excessively or beyond what is reasonable or necessary.

Growth Stretch for Social Twos

NOTICE YOUR STRATEGY. Your tendency to extend strategic generosity is a tactic that has helped you get through life. You might think that there is no other way to get your needs met. But this pattern is hindering the true love, connection, and belonging you desire. Who do you help most? Why? Bringing attention to this (and then shifting that effort back to yourself) can help you find the care you long for.

Sexual Two

Nickname: Persuasion
At a Glance: Captivating, Sensational, Winsome

Sexual Twos are inviting, kind, and exuberant. They are magnetic personalities who draw people in, which is why they are often described as "seductive." However, this could also be described by the more general "woo," or winning others over.[3] For these Twos, seduction is not always about a sexual conquest and can exist as a powerful force even in platonic relationships. Regardless of the relationship type, these Twos want to be "the one," or at the very least, a very special someone, to their chosen person.

When Sexual Twos form relationships, they seek to be very close, dissolving much of the boundary between themselves and the other person. Attachment offers the Two closeness, the assurance that the other person will meet their needs. The subconscious assumption is that most people look out for themselves; if the Two is one with another person, that person will begin to meet the Two's needs by default. In general, these Twos are more assertive in expressing their needs than the other subtypes.

Beyond this pattern, Sexual Twos find strong relationships fulfilling, and they are skilled at forging deep, connected relationships. A Sexual Two described his approach to friendship as, "I'll go wherever you go, as long as I can stay connected to you." Whether he's driving friends to the movies, running errands with a co-worker, or playing video games with his partner, the central focus is always the joy of simply being with his closest people.

It's easy to fall in love with a Sexual Two, but sometimes Sexual Twos believe no one would want to be connected to them if they weren't enchanted by the Two's schemes. Sexual Twos can find the genuine, vulnerable relationships they desire once they allow themselves to be seen and loved for who they truly are.

 Growth Stretch for Sexual Twos
CHALLENGE YOUR INTENTIONS. Cultivate some awareness around what you're hoping to gain through your generosity

and seduction. Are you in need of love? Connection? Affirmation? It's not bad to connect with others, but manipulation will never offer you the real, deep relationships you desire. Start to notice what it feels like when you're "seducing," and get curious about another way to meet that need.

Dynamic Movement Arrows

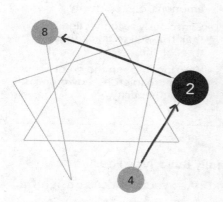

On the Enneagram, type Two is connected to types Four and Eight. These are the Two's arrows, which means the other types the Two can move to and freely access. I often use the term *move to*, but this does not mean the Two becomes the other type—it simply means that the Two borrows characteristics and tendencies of the arrow types. If you've read other Enneagram books, you've likely heard this theory explained differently, so return to chapter 2 for further explanation if needed.

The most important thing to know here is that we can all borrow the higher (healthy) and lower (unhealthy) qualities of both arrow lines. When we're tired, stressed, overwhelmed, or otherwise not paying attention we tend to access these lower states. When moving intentionally, we can develop the higher side of our arrow lines.

RECOVERY POINT–TYPE FOUR	
Unintentional Drift to the Lower Side Could Look Like . . .	**Intentional Movement to the Higher Side Could Look Like . . .**
• Lashing out against others, especially those who aren't paying attention to or catering to their specific needs • Mourning not getting what they need from life, and feeling unappreciated • Expressing intense anger and frustration when feeling abandoned, rejected, or misunderstood • Feeling or expressing that, "no one is taking care of me or my needs!" • Being more moody or pouty than they would typically be	• Making space for and acknowledging normal human needs, like the need for love, attention, belonging, self-care • Operating in tune with their internal emotional world • Becoming deeply introspective about their ideas, dreams, emotions, and creativity • Consciously reconnecting to their true self to guide them through life • Working through their real issues with more tolerance, awareness, and authenticity

Growth Stretch: Intentionally Build Type Four

• TURN CURIOSITY INWARD: Ask yourself deep, insightful questions, like, what made you feel something today? What do you daydream about? What do you long for in your life? Tap into the type Four tendency to find a sense of distinction from others. What is different about you? How is your true self special? As you learn to get more curious about your desires, you might find yourself more prone to prioritizing your needs.

• EXPRESS YOURSELF: Practice sharing more of the low side of your emotional range. You can start small, but allow yourself to share some of your difficult feelings that you assume might make others unhappy or disappointed in you. How do YOU feel about yourself when you're sharing? How do YOU feel about yourself when you're expressing your needs?

TRANSFORMATION POINT–TYPE EIGHT	
Unintentional Drift to the Lower Side Could Look Like . . .	Intentional Movement to the Higher Side Could Look Like . . .
• Becoming demanding, bossy, and controlling • Feeling inflated by the power they've gained by making themselves indispensable to others • An overtly angry or even a my-way-or-the-highway mentality • Becoming excessively self-indulgent to make themselves feel better since their needs have been denied for so long • Feeling entitled to command what others do	• Being more assertive about taking action on meeting their needs • Feeling powerful and capable, even if they don't feel supported or mirrored by others • Navigating conflict without people-pleasing or self-sacrificing • Courageously working in their own interest without guilt or shame • Knowing what is theirs to do and what isn't—they can say no, and they know the world will go on, they don't always have to be the one to step up

Growth Stretch: Intentionally Build Type Eight

• GET BACK ON YOUR SIDE OF THE NET: It can feel difficult to directly ask others for what you need when you spend more time in everyone else's thoughts and feelings than in your own. Channel your inner Eight and learn that getting the ball over the net is your job; it's not your job to return it, too. Instead of overworrying about how others will feel if you ask for help, simply trust that others will lend you a hand when they want to and can. If they do help, trust it's ok to simply say "thank you so much" and move on!

• GET COMFORTABLE WITH THE WORD "NO": Here's your challenge: say no once a day. I know it might seem like you don't agree to do much, but notice how often you tacitly agree to various activities, let alone how often you accept your position as the emotional laborer of your friend group, family, coffee shop, running club, and so on. Level up this challenge by hearing no once a day, too.

Communication and Relationships

In this section, we'll explore both sides of communication: the Two's side as well as those in communication with Twos.

How to Relate with a Two

- EXPRESS GENUINE CARE. Twos care deeply about their loved ones, but sometimes they feel like no one else cares quite as much. This could be due to a lack of emotional attunement from others or simply a gap in expressing care or concern. Remembering little details, showing a bit more emotional resonance, and verbally communicating your affection for a Two can go a long way. Asking good questions, checking in on how they're doing, and inquiring about their day or their interests can all be ways to build mutual rapport with Twos. Sometimes other types can neglect their relationships with Twos because the Two consistently puts in so much effort. But they won't stick around forever! Being the first to reach out is always appreciated.

- SHARE HOW YOU FEEL WITH KINDNESS. Twos work hard to meet everyone's expectations, therefore, feedback can be tough. Offer feedback gently, and be sure to also share positive thoughts and appreciation. It helps to start with reassurance that the relationship is secure. Keep in mind that even though feedback can be hard for Twos, they invest deeply in their relationships and want to maintain the connections they build. If there's something wrong, they would rather hear that (even when it's tough) than be blindsided by the dissolution of the relationship without the opportunity to fix it.

- DELVE BENEATH THE SURFACE. Twos often feel that others don't really want to know their truest self: they may hide less appealing aspects of themselves if they feel openness will lead to rejection. With repression at play, they may hide these less appealing qualities even from themselves. Twos can be quite sensitive and emotional, but it takes effort for them to be comfortable sharing how they're feeling aside from their typical cheerful, affectionate energy. When a Two shares this side, offer kindness, encouragement, and validation in response.

- BE KIND. Twos struggle to connect with people who they feel are needlessly unkind or inconsiderate. Sometimes this is because the Two is assigning their motivation to the other person's behavior ("If I were that rude, I would have to be very, very upset!"), but either way it can be a common cause for conflict.

Communication Skills for Twos to Develop

- WORK ON BEING MORE DIRECT about what you need from the people around you. Sometimes Twos fear that if they are too direct, they'll come across as mean or cruel, but we know that's not your tendency. Practice being more direct when lower-stakes issues come up so that you have the skill when you need it. We're all more likely to come across as demanding if we wait until we're on the brink to make our needs a priority.

- PRACTICE SETTING BOUNDARIES around your time. It's easy for Twos to overload themselves by saying "yes" to everyone who needs them, volunteering to help, and assuming that others know how much they already have on their plate. Communicating that you care and support others but don't have time to offer them more material help can be a good way to start.

Practice Self-Friendship

In any relationship, interpersonal and intrapersonal (that is, within the self) communication co-occur.[4] As a result, I find it helpful to develop our relationships with ourselves as we're working to improve relationships with others.

To me, the concept of self-friendship is simple: it's considering how we would respond to a friend who needed a little love and doing the same thing for ourselves. Here are a few ways you can practice self-friendship as a form of self-care.

- Set and stick to boundaries with self-compassion; it's okay that this feels difficult—you're still learning, and you can take your time to make this adjustment.
- Notice when you reach out to support others when YOU need support instead.
- Recognize when you're sending a gift because you want something (love, affection, gratitude, attention) in return. Then take yourself out for a "date" or buy yourself a gift when that feeling arises.
- Remind yourself that you don't need to do anything spectacular to be loved.
- Practice putting yourself first a little bit every day.

Growth in Real Life

Growth for Twos is about returning to themselves. It's about starting with the inside when considering who finds them lovable and likable, and learning that while it's lovely that they are so encouraging and helpful, that's not what makes them worthy as humans. These shifts seem small, but they can be terrifying and painstaking to untangle. As Twos begin to recenter their attention, they'll find greater freedom, love, and connection with others and with themselves.

Thought Patterns That Might Be Keeping You Stuck

We all have thought patterns that keep us stuck. When they are subconscious, your initial response to the suggestion that these might not be helpful thoughts could be visceral discomfort. However, remember that we are focused on excavating and identifying these beliefs as a way to become free of them.

Notice how these thought patterns might come up for you:

- If I let people see how I really feel, they won't find me lovable or even likable.
- I don't have as many needs as other people.
- I have to get it all right the first time or I'm letting everyone down.
- If I try expressing myself or my needs and someone reacts poorly, that's proof I shouldn't have tried in the first place.
- I need affirmation and approval from others to be happy.
- People love me because I'm so generous and loving. If I give less, they'll want me less.
- It will take too much time each day to pay attention to myself.

 Examine your assumptions.

For each pattern above, journal about the following:

- Where does this belief come from?
- How long have I been attached to this belief?
- Is it true? Is it really true?
- What would be different if the opposite were true?

 Everyday Practices: Reconnect with Your True Self

Twos can experience shame when they have needs, believing that they should be the ones helping others. Or they might feel like their needs don't need as much attention. Or they might believe that if others saw their real feelings, they wouldn't find them lovable. When they hide from these, they end up fulfilling that prophecy: no one has the chance to show up for them or love them exactly as they are. These practices will support you as you establish a new narrative.

Think about your future.

What do you dream of doing? What's on your bucket list? If you didn't have to care for anyone else's feelings, dreams, or goals, what would you love to do? What's standing in your way? Are there things you feel you MUST do? How might you support a friend in working toward these big dreams? What if you gave yourself that same support? For example, write an encouraging note to yourself (i.e., I see you and how hard you're working! I'm so proud of you!). As you continue to think about your future, how can you lean on yourself to be the person you've often been for others?

Reconnect with yourself.

Twos can benefit significantly from increased alone time, but life can get busy, and it seems there's never enough time in the day. While a solid thirty minutes of solitude per day might be ideal, here are a few ideas to try if that's outside the realm of possibility:

- "STICKY FEET." This is a practice from Dr. Aditi Nerurkar.[5] Imagine your feet are sticky, like spider webs. Branch your toes as far apart as you can, and sense all sides of your feet. Ground yourself by sensing the sturdy support you're getting from them.
- STEAL TIME. Perhaps you can't get extended alone time, but maybe you can steal quiet moments in your day to reconnect. If you can do so safely, close your eyes and place a hand on your

belly and one on your chest. Try a breathing exercise, such as box breathing. Breathe in for four counts, hold for four counts, exhale for four counts, and hold for four counts.[6] This simple breathing technique will help you recenter, and you can repeat it for a full two minutes, or just do one cycle.

- GIVE YOURSELF A HUG. Cross your arms over your chest as if you're giving yourself a hug. Rub your arms with light pressure. This practice, along with those listed above, helps you reconnect with your sense of self and define your physical body. Remembering you are your own person can help as you work to establish boundaries, advocate for yourself, and convey your true emotions.

Challenge the assumption that you don't need or deserve support.

Try this journaling method to reclaim your need for support:

- Depersonalize by writing in third person. You could use your first name, or you could even try using your best friend's name.
- Write about the challenges you're facing in detail.
- Reread your journal entry. How do you feel toward this person?
- What advice would you give? Should she reach out to ask for support? Should she give herself a break? Really try to depersonalize this. If you keep thinking of this through your first-person lens, you might be tempted to say, "I should suck it up, other people are suffering more," but you'd never say that to someone else, even if you might say that to yourself.

Be honest with yourself and others about how things are.

Twos often believe they must be cheerful, happy, and positive all the time. Sometimes, this is because you want to be lovable, and sometimes it's because you don't want to burden anyone else with your problems. But this requires you to abandon certain aspects of yourself that are less desirable, and it reinforces your belief that you're only lovable when you are in a good mood. Experiment with being totally honest with close people in your life and let your full self be seen.

CHAPTER 9

Type Three

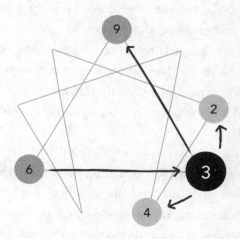

As an Enneagram Three, Charity is well acquainted with pushing herself. Working in community development tapped into her desire to make monumental change in the world, especially in her sphere of social justice and equity. Her work was stressful but meaningful, and she knew she could handle it. Being effective at her job involved pulling people together to work toward a common goal, putting in long hours, and streamlining her energy into work. Her intent focus relegated her physical and emotional needs to some ambiguous future—"I'll get to them after I accomplish this," she thought. It was that last piece that landed her in the emergency room.

One morning on her way to work, terror ripped through her system. She found herself doubled over in pain, convinced she was dying. Or having a stroke. Maybe a heart attack? Also, possibly, a brain tumor. Based on WebMD, she was certain she was going to die.

Half a dozen blood tests and an echocardiogram later, Charity was sent home with antacids for stress-induced heartburn and a suggestion to cool it on working so hard. She was "fine," medically. But she wasn't fine. She'd had a panic attack.

Over the preceding months, her anxiety had become a daily foe. She loved her work, but the urgency of building a more equitable world weighed on her. She'd always been so capable and sparkly and energetic, making change through strategic action and enthusiastic dedication to the cause. Her emergency room excursion revealed the personal cost of placing her entire self-worth in her accomplishments, especially when what she was working toward was so complex and daunting.

Her productivity-first mindset sputtered to a halt. She took a leave of absence from her job and filled her days with every sort of self-care task she could manage. She finally had space to tune in to herself and wonder about the life she wanted to build. She set out on meandering morning walks and midday nap breaks, she reached out to friends and enlisted help painting her newly purchased home (another task she'd previously insisted she could handle alone), and she found an excellent therapist. Nothing was safe from reevaluation. As she processed, her anxiety waned, her heartburn dissipated, and she found a deeper connection with her truest self. "It's been a long process of divorcing my value from what I do, and I'm still untangling all of it."

As a Three, Charity sees other Threes online or in her social groups, all polished and impressive, just like she seemed when she was falling apart. Deep down, she wonders if they're struggling, too, and if they know that there's a different way to be in the world.

Charity's story is poignant to me because it's so familiar. I've met many Threes who reach this crash-and-burn moment, a wake-up call sent by the body to bring awareness to their constant attempts to progress at any cost. Though Threes try to release some of the pressure, freedom for this type requires first evaluating where they find value.

How Threes Show Up

Threes are **motivated** by a desire to be seen as valuable, successful, and admirable. Threes overfocus on how others see them, subconsciously crafting an image that will be prized and rewarded. By showing up as the perfect version of themselves in any situation, they draw their feelings of worth from success and admiration. Even though Threes are typically unaware of this "shapeshifting" mechanism, they often feel exposed on learning about it through the Enneagram. It can be jarring to recognize that not only do others operate differently, but others can potentially see the Three's actions as a facade. Other types misunderstand this chameleon-esque behavior as intentionally deceitful, but most Threes state that they are not inventing a new self, they're just emphasizing different aspects of their current self. It doesn't feel disingenuous, even when it is; it feels like a necessary survival strategy. For Threes, being such a chameleon means they can relate to a variety of people, but the hidden cost is that they lose themselves in the outer image they project. Threes focus on the perceptions of others as they shift and adapt to any environment, but they often have a harder time understanding their own identity.

In all of this, Threes exhaust themselves to **avoid** failure, worthlessness, and falling short of their full potential. Threes overidentify with failure, believing that if they fail, they *are* a failure. As a result, Threes habitually work to achieve a sense of worth through being effective and successful, as defined by the meaning of success in their family, cultural context, or environment. While some Threes aim at big, bold, public success, many focus on smaller-scale versions of the successful person they aspire to be, such as an excellent spouse, employee, or parent. Deep down, they rely on external measures of worth to feel good enough, believing that if others value them, they are valuable. Beneath the chase for success is the belief that their image (how others perceive them) is the most important piece of the puzzle.

In much of Western society, and especially corporate America, this behavior is handsomely rewarded. Threes often find it hard to believe that their ability to be incredibly hardworking and successful is actually perpetuating their internal disconnection from self. As Charity said, "All my life, people have told me that everything I touch turns to gold." Threes tend to wonder why they'd ever abandon their natural Midas Touch, forgetting that in the tale of King Midas, food, drink, and even his loved ones turned to gold, too. Lacking practical and relational sustenance, King Midas faced starvation and loneliness.[1] Threes often miss that turning everything to gold seems appealing, but the pursuit can leave them feeling overworked, unrelatable, and empty.

From a young age, Threes started performing, and they heard the feedback that they have endless potential. This is almost always meant as a compliment, and it seems positive, but it can feel like stifling pressure. Even if they reach the highest heights, a Three can still feel like a failure because there was infinite unmet potential they could have achieved if they'd just optimized more, felt less, or stayed more focused.

When Threes are unaware of this hidden dynamic, they tend to be incredibly efficient, but they may also wreak havoc in their relationships. They soar in the corporate world, but then they wake up a decade in to realize they never even liked their job in the first place. Or they are the most incredible parent you've ever seen, but they are unable to truly connect with their partner or even friends because their lack of self-knowledge renders true intimacy elusive.

A common **misconception** held by Threes and their loved ones is that Threes are often a lot more emotional and sensitive than they let on, especially once they begin to do some inner work and let themselves feel. Appearing to be sterile and unemotional is often a function of trying to keep it all together. It is excruciating for many Threes to allow others to see them struggle. These intrinsically human experiences feel too vulnerable, so they apply gargantuan effort to make life seem easy, efficient, and polished. Slowing down jeopardizes their ability to outrun their emotional reality, sometimes leading them to spiral and question the point of all their efforts. Beneath the poise and industrious, can-do attitude is the question—am I enough? Am I doing enough? These questions are difficult to face. Threes find it even more challenging to recognize the truth that being worthy enough has nothing to do with their output.

Thresholds

High Thresholds: Productivity and Accomplishment

Threes have a **high threshold** for productivity, and they always believe they have capacity to do more. "Doing" is not just about working, but it's also about chores, to-do lists, goals, and commitments. Threes sometimes expect superhuman output because they can easily identify tiny inefficiencies in their day, like a moment when they sat down while cleaning the house or got distracted scrolling through their inbox. They expect the same on a larger scale, too, believing that if they just work hard enough, they'll be able to do more than is reasonable.

Threes also tend to have a **high threshold** for accomplishment. Nothing they do is ever quite enough to be worth celebrating. Many Threes "celebrate" by starting on their next project. Or they downplay their accomplishment because now that they've done it, it was "easy" rather than a unique achievement. Or they simply move the goalpost: if they were going to celebrate once they could lift 150 pounds, now they'll only feel accomplished if they can lift 200. When the bar is always moving, the approval they're chasing feels unattainable.

Low Thresholds: Failure and Slowness

Alternatively, Threes have a **low threshold** for what feels like failure. Experiences others may not consider failure, such as the end of a relationship, a project not going as planned, or even a dish being slightly less tasty than the last time they'd cooked it, can all feel like failure. To bar against the pain of this experience, Threes work extremely hard to show that they're worthy of admiration. Deep down, they believe that if they hit that goal or get that stamp of approval, they'll feel like enough. Some Threes subconsciously forget about failure, and it can easily become a blind spot. Sometimes Threes say they hate failure, so much that they can't recall the last time they failed.

Threes also tend to have a **low threshold** for anything that is slow moving, emotional, or interruptive. Patience is not typically a strong suit for Threes. Their intolerance for others slowing them down materializes in a sense of irritation or grumpiness, especially when the hindrance is an obstacle between themselves and what they're attempting to accomplish.

Type Three Personality

In this section, we'll dive straight into the type Three personality structure, but you'll find a detailed overview of the terms in this section (Passion, Defense Mechanism, Virtue) in chapter 2.

Passion: Self-Deceit

The passion of type Three is self-deceit. The delineation of *self*-deceit is crucial. Threes are not intentionally deceitful fibbers, rather, they tend to believe that who they are is the image they present to the world. The image they craft in a given context informs their self-perception, and they believe they are as worthy, valuable, or successful as others perceive them to be. They equate their sense of self to their performed identity. Deep down, Threes believe they're not enough as they are (or they don't even know who they are because they're so caught up in being this persona).

Unaware Threes operating on autopilot don't even notice the fallacy in this belief. When entrenched in the thought "I am as you believe I am," how they feel is peripheral. They're typically unaware of a dichotomy between these two selves. It's like looking in a mirror and believing you are looking at yourself, even though you're technically staring at a reflective piece of glass. You can see an image there, but your essence is not in your reflection but within yourself.

The passion of self-deceit could look like . . .

- Doing what you're good at without considering if you enjoy it. Or, sometimes, continuing to pursue accomplishments, even when you know you don't enjoy them.
- A sense of uncertainty about who you are. The adage "just be yourself" is panic inducing as it would feel simpler to be whoever others expect you to be.
- Crafting an image of having it all together even when you don't. If others believe you're a mess, you're a mess. But if they're impressed by your cool, calm, collected exterior while you excel at everything you touch, you're impressed, too.
- Becoming overly focused on external measures of worth such that you feel like output is the only thing that matters. You might be especially afraid that if you pause, you'll fall behind or cease to exist.

Reflecting on Your Passion Through Journal Prompts
How does the passion of self-deceit show up in your life? If you can think of an example, write about it. What was happening when you saw self-deceit show up clearly? How did it feel? What were you paying attention to? In what ways did self-deceit serve you? In what ways did self-deceit *detract* from what you needed or wanted in that moment?

Defense Mechanism: Identification

Threes often use the defense mechanism of identification. Identification asks the question, Who do I need to be to be successful? This leaves a Three subconsciously absorbing attributes and characteristics of someone else into their sense of self. In psychology literature, this defense mechanism often describes patterning oneself after an important other, such as a parent.[2] For example, a young Three admiring her mother's career as a surgeon may move through life fashioning herself after her mother, attending medical school and becoming a surgeon without ever pausing to discover what she truly wants from her life. Becoming just like her mother solidifies an identity of success, defending against internal challenges of her worth. To an extent, many children experience wanting to be just like a parent when they're young, but this becomes maladaptive when a Three is unable to differentiate that from their own desires, even into adulthood.

For other Threes, this defense mechanism extends to a specific role or identity, rather than an individual. Threes subconsciously bolster their self-esteem by forming an assimilation with the role they admire, to the extent that they overidentify with the role or image it presents. For example, a Three might hustle for a big promotion, not because they love their job but because they find validity in having a certain title. Or they may place their entire identity in attending a certain university, or associating with specific others.

**Reflecting on Your Defense Mechanism Through
Journal Prompts**

How does the defense mechanism of identification show up in your life? Sometimes this can be tricky to spot, but it often takes the form of identifying with being a *certain type of person* as a way to feel worthy and valuable. When will accumulating accolades make you feel like "enough"? How often do you move the goalposts? What external vestiges of worth are you leaning on to make you feel admirable?

Virtue: Veracity

The virtue of type Three is veracity. When aligned with veracity, Threes release all of the effort they've invested in becoming some-one important. Instead, they rest in the authenticity of their truest self. Because they are no longer hustling for worth or projecting an identity, they have space to slow down without the threat of losing their value. They can embrace themselves as they are, apart from the ideas and opinions of others, and this allows them to be in touch with their true feelings. Threes devote significant time and energy to distancing themselves from their emotional realm, but veracity allows them to be exactly as emotional as they are, with full ac-ceptance, compassion, and ease. While they often avoid this side of themselves, veracity allows Threes to settle into their full range of emotion as the heart of the Heart center.

The virtue of veracity could look like . . .

- A strong sense of self, unencumbered by the opinions of others. You can show up as you are, even if you're messy, unfinished, emotional, or falling apart.
- Being in touch with a wide array of emotions, especially a deeper sense of comfort with sadness and challenging feelings.
- Being centered and in tune with the ebb and flow of life with full recognition that your worth is unattached to output. A deep

inner peace and contentment with being a human being, rather than a human "doing."

- Seeing the value in others, regardless of their contributions or status.

OPENing Up to Veracity

As you recognize self-deceit and apply the OPEN framework introduced in chapter 4, you'll begin to shake off the ways your personality structure is keeping you bound and slowly move toward the virtue of veracity.

OBSERVE: Notice when your automatic activities are a function of self-deceit, and especially the part of you that avoids emotions. For example, observe the activities or busyness you use to avoid experiencing feelings.

PAUSE: Through reflection, then self-observation, you'll be able to slow your automatic reaction. As you get better at catching yourself in the act, you'll be able to find a pause. As you pause, simply take a breath and ground yourself.

ENGAGE CURIOSITY: Get curious about a different reaction: What else could you choose? As you consider new options, keep in mind that this step is simply to think about how to step out of your normal reaction, which you'll try out in the next step. In our example, perhaps you start to notice yourself drowning out a feeling by going for a run, listening to a podcast, or launching into a new project.

NEXT RIGHT THING: Experiment with different responses or reactions. You don't have to get it right! This is a way to try out different things, and again, you want to start small. So perhaps in this moment, when you're looking to escape your experience of sadness, anxiety, or something else you can't quite put your finger on, you can get curious: What am I really feeling? Grab a journal, and spend ten minutes writing about how you're feeling right now.

Subtypes

The three subtypes of type Three represent different expressions of the passion of self-deceit. If you're a Three, you'll likely see a bit of yourself in each description. To understand which subtype is dominant for you, look at the evidence in your life: How does your behavior align with each description? Which subtype do you see in action? Which of the growth stretches feels most intolerable to you?

Self-Preservation Three

Nickname: Security
At a Glance: Self-Composed, Pragmatic, Respectable

Self-Preservation Threes focus on building a life of security and success through independence and hard work. While they still manage their image, this is often hidden, even to themselves. These Threes are more likely to say things like "I don't care what others think," or "I only care about a job well done." A Self-Preservation Three event planner shared that she loved executing huge, complex events but would be mortified to be dragged onstage and honored for her work. However, she'd love nothing more than to overhear attendees describe the conference as extremely well done.

Being a good person is another key driver for Self-Preservation Threes. They are steadfast and committed to their people. They work hard to create stability for their families, providing for all their comforts. However, they sometimes move too quickly and overlook verbally communicating their love and care. They also believe good people are not flashy, so they feel shame around showing off their success. Yet they enjoy the experiences afforded by monetary resources, so they might choose the best quality product possible, while avoiding flashy brand markings.

In general, these Threes are more calculated and risk-averse than others, and they avoid making emotional decisions. For example, a Self-Preservation Three might maintain success at a job they are very good at, even though they hate it and dream of starting their own small business. While this approach may seem logical—and may be backed by numbers—it's still an emotional choice. It's driven by fear of losing their lifestyle and status at the cost of finding a way to align with their truest self. I often meet Self-Preservation Threes while attending inner work retreats after they've encountered a big life event. Maybe their body gave out, like in Charity's story, or they are grieving an unexpected loss, and this seismic shift has left them shaken and searching for purpose.

Growth Stretch for Self-Preservation Threes

BE A LITTLE IMPRACTICAL. There is more to life than a to-do list, but that can be difficult for Self-Preservation Threes to accept. Your perspective on practicality and efficiency is admirable, but these are not the only things of value in life. For these Threes, growth is not about forcing but relaxing. Find time for fun, for being a bit impractical, for feelings, and for play. You'll know you're growing as the anxious need to be productive quiets over time.

Social Three

Nickname: Prestige
At a Glance: Polished, Confident, Impressive

Social Threes are the quintessential Three depicted in most teachings of the Enneagram. They are enterprising, drawn toward situations where they can be at center stage and showcase their ideas, excellence, and abilities. Social Threes naturally influence and inspire those around them. Social Threes are comfortable talking about their accomplishments, and they often encourage others to brag a little, too. It can be difficult for these Threes to imagine that some people are not impressed by their success, poise, or hard work. They avoid exposing vulnerability, instead portraying a flawless, unflappable image.

While they are able to make genuine connections, they may not always be aware of the ways that they are putting on a performance. They recognize where their own interests and the group's interests intersect and step in to ensure success. Though they are concerned for the well-being of the group overall, they tend to be competitive, avoiding personal failure at all costs. As a result, others might experience their relationship-building as transactional. Their attention gravitates toward the "value add" in a given situation, including when they look in the mirror. Beneath the surface, this is fueled by the expectation that they are only as worthy as they are impressive, productive, or valuable. The key to more connected and authentic relationships is accepting themselves and others for the messy, complicated, unique human beings we are, rather than distilling worth to a few societally sanctioned functions.

Relationally, Social Threes are encouraging, confident, and positive. It can be difficult for them to let others see their truest selves, but they eventually allow a lucky few to truly see them.

Growth Stretch for Social Threes

SHOW YOUR FAILURE. Social Threes avoid revealing imperfection without an ulterior motive. Often, if they do show imperfection, failure, or setbacks, it takes the form of the past tense, and it can easily become just another stepping stone in their success story. Let people see you now, as you are, without your typical social filter. The acceptance you're ultimately seeking is self-acceptance, but it will help to recognize the ways that introducing a bit of vulnerability will invite others to move closer rather than push them away.

Sexual Three

Nickname: Charisma

At a Glance: Charming, Malleable, Supportive

Sexual Threes focus on being the epitome of perfection. They craft themselves to become the object of jealousy and desire. Sometimes this is described as becoming "Barbie" or "Ken," but it's also common for these Threes to perform the most enticing way to be in any sphere (work, home life, gym, academics, and more). The concept of attraction is not limited to external appearance and can encompass other elements of our personalities that are prized in specific groups. Intelligence, accolades, and other abilities can be part of the Sexual Three's enticing persona. Each individual's expression of this subtype is couched in their cultural concepts of success, attractiveness, perfection, and charisma. This subtype is not about *being* attractive but about how our energy naturally flows toward crafting a self that will attract specific people.

Sexual Threes merge strongly with their partner, and they often overidentify with this role as the perfect "catch." They lose themselves in this identity, leading to feelings of loss and confusion overall. While they are charming in getting what they want, they can lack self-esteem due to this conditional sense of self. Sexual Threes are more emotionally expressive, gentler, and more self-conscious than other Threes, seeking deep conversations and emotional intimacy with others. Though, as is the paradox of the sexual instinct, they can simultaneously be less poised because their attention is not on the collective experience (social), or their own scruples (self-preservation), but on the spark of connection they're kindling.

In relationships, Sexual Threes are supportive and encouraging, and they often find satisfaction in the success of those they support, in part because they merge with others to the extent that it's difficult to parse who is actually benefiting. They may fear abandonment if they let their partner down, assuming that others only appreciate them for their output, results, and help. These Threes need to get to know themselves better so that they can become more aligned with their true self and cultivate a life that is authentic and meaningful to them.

Growth Stretch for Sexual Threes
PRIORITIZE YOURSELF. Notice how often you focus your work and your efforts on being attractive or supportive to others. Do you have any hobbies or activities that are unrelated to building a persona? What can you do that's just for you? What's something you've always wanted to try that doesn't line up with how others see you? Make it a priority to engage in these activities, even if you're not good at them (and especially if you don't look good doing them).

Dynamic Movement Arrows

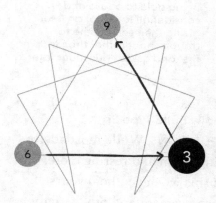

On the Enneagram, Type Three is connected to types Six and Nine. These are the Three's arrows, which means the other types the Three can move to and freely access. I often use the term *move to*, but this does not mean the Three becomes the other type—it simply means that the Three borrows characteristics and tendencies of the arrow types. If you've read other Enneagram books, you've likely heard this theory explained differently, so return to chapter 2 for further explanation if needed.

The most important thing to know here is that we can all borrow the higher (healthy) and lower (unhealthy) qualities of both arrow lines. When we're tired, stressed, overwhelmed, or otherwise not paying attention we tend to access these lower states. When moving intentionally, we can develop the higher side of our arrow lines.

RECOVERY POINT–TYPE SIX	
Unintentional Drift to the Lower Side Could Look Like . . .	**Intentional Movement to the Higher Side Could Look Like . . .**
• Frantic activity and feeling like everyone is out to get them • Becoming highly anxious, insecure, and uncertain, rendering them hesitant to take risks for fear of failure or letting their image slip • Getting stuck in analysis—decision-making is incredibly difficult because so many variables exist • Extensive overthinking and then doing something random or out of the blue to paper over the uncertainty they feel • Pervasive self-doubt	• Asking themselves the good questions they have been avoiding • Recognizing that some things are worth doing, regardless of the outcomes • Reevaluating what actually matters to them vs. what is supporting their image • Becoming aware of how they're feeling, whether or not things make sense or are aligned • Being able to pause and consider all facets of an issue, giving themselves time to troubleshoot rather than leaping first and asking questions later

Growth Stretch: Intentionally Build Type Six

• REEVALUATE YOUR EXPECTATIONS. While most advice for Threes includes slowing down and resting more, it's challenging to accomplish this when you hold yourself to expectations of continual achievement and productivity.

Take a moment to reflect on your expectations: Where have they come from? Are they truly helpful for you? Have you absorbed expectations from others? Use an analytical Six mind to tease apart the origins of these ideas and get a little suspicious about why they exist. Over time, release the expectations of others and prioritize what you want and need from your life.

- ASK YOURSELF GOOD QUESTIONS. For example, before making a plan, saying yes to a project, or starting something new, ask yourself: Does this make sense right now? Am I doing this for myself or for my image? Is this aligned with what I want to do moving forward? Is my emotional response telling me something? Even if this is a great opportunity, is now the right time?

TRANSFORMATION POINT–TYPE NINE	
Unintentional Drift to the Lower Side Could Look Like . . .	Intentional Movement to the Higher Side Could Look Like . . .
• Zoning out, numbing everything, perhaps collapsing on the couch and watching TV all weekend or being unable to get out of bed	• Slowing down to intentionally rest, which also allows them to connect with themselves and others
• Becoming overwhelmed and stuck in the belief that nothing they do matters	• Detaching worth from productivity, knowing they don't need to earn the right to exist
• Being unable to know or communicate what they need and want from others	• Being able to go with the flow instead of forcing the world to bend to their will
• Avoiding all the intricacies and challenging aspects of navigating day-to-day life	• Connecting to their gut instinct and inner knowing
• Internal hostility, annoyance, and stubbornness toward others' expectations	• Acting in accordance with the truth of who they are because they don't need to bend, shift, or cater to anyone else's metrics
	• Honoring their need for spaciousness, time to process, and daily downtime

Growth Stretch: Intentionally Build Type Nine

- MAKE YOUR CALENDAR MORE SPACIOUS. Threes often crash and burn to the low side of Nine when they've pushed themselves to the point of collapse. Rather than waiting until your body gives out, preemptively protect your time, energy, emotions, and mental health by planning downtime, rest, and space to process in your calendar. Schedule an introverted night in, say no to engagements, or go for a slow and easy walk.

- NOTICE WHAT YOU DON'T HAVE TO EARN. Threes tend to assume everything must be earned, but one of the beautiful things about Nines is that they don't believe they have to hustle to earn the right to exist. Simply being is enough. As you go about your day, notice the air you breathe or that your heart is beating; observe the natural beauty that surrounds you, look up at the sky, or smell a flower. Observe the little wonders of nature that do not require output from you to experience.

Communication and Relationships

In this section, we'll explore both sides of communication: the Three's side as well as those in communication with Threes.

How to Relate with a Three

- DO SOMETHING TOGETHER. Threes can have deeper conversations while they're doing something else, especially at the beginning of their growth journey or when they're first getting to know someone. Strengthen your relationship without the pressure: go for a walk, try a new activity, take a class, read a book to discuss, run errands, and the like. These activities can offer a gateway into deeper discussions. In some cases, a Three might jump straight into a deeper connection and may be more vulnerable, but they may need you to share first.

- BE UPFRONT. Threes typically appreciate direct communication, and they dislike when others bury the lede or communicate indirectly. Most Threes would rather not guess what the other person wants or needs, and they may convey anxiety if they sense they are expected to pick up some unspoken message. If you're at work, give them the bottom line first, then share other important details.

- HOLD VULNERABILITY WITH CARE. Threes don't want others to see behind the mask. Deep down, they're often unable to look at it themselves, believing that no one who sees what's there will stick around. Sometimes, Threes aren't even certain if there's anything there, and that's even more terrifying. Showing up imperfectly triggers a fear that others will use this vulnerability against them in the future. While Threes might seem sure and confident without outside input, they often feel like they're not doing enough, not working hard enough, or not moving quickly enough. If a Three lets you see their less polished side, resist the urge to poke fun or celebrate catching them on an "off" day and simply appreciate seeing them in their full humanity. Let them know you see and appreciate who they are and you love them, warts and all.

- DON'T PRESSURE THEM TO SLOW DOWN. Constantly being challenged, questioned, or hindered in what they're trying to accomplish can lead to conflict with Threes. Even when changing course is the best idea, Threes might be irritated initially. Similarly, urging them to slow down, rest, or relax can be challenging for Threes who have not yet learned to reevaluate their sense of worth. Affirming them when they are resting or relaxing is helpful, but if they feel shamed for not resting, that's just another thing they're failing at. (But Threes, you can work on this by developing your intentional movement to Six!) While slowing down is helpful for Threes, the shift must come from the inside to be genuine.

Communication Skills for Threes to Develop

• WORK ON INTEGRATING YOUR EMOTIONAL REALM. It often feels safest and most efficient for Threes to disconnect from their emotions as a way to move forward. However, this can cause various issues in communication, chief among them that Threes seem to lack empathy when they're so disconnected. Embracing a broader emotional experience can help you be a compassionate and genuine communicator.

• NOTICE YOUR SHAPESHIFTING AND HOW IT IS AND ISN'T WORKING FOR YOU. Sometimes shapeshifting is about being adaptable, but sometimes it's about image management. If you're able to observe this characteristic in yourself, you can notice when you begin to say or do things you don't believe because you're crafting an image.

Practice Self-Friendship

In any relationship, interpersonal and intrapersonal (that is, within the self) communication co-occur.[3] As a result, I find it helpful to develop our relationships with ourselves as we're working to improve relationships with others.

To me, the concept of self-friendship is simple: it's considering how we would respond to a friend who needed a little love and doing the same thing for ourselves. Here are a few ways you can practice self-friendship as a form of self-care.

- Save some time for yourself rather than giving it all away or packing your calendar to the gills.
- Validate your need for rest and remind yourself that your worth isn't based on others' opinion, approval, or admiration.
- Affirm your feelings. Extending extra kindness, grace, self-compassion, and empathy to yourself—and slowing down enough to let it sink in—is healing.
- Celebrate your accomplishments! It sounds cheesy, but a pat on the back or saying "I've done a great job" can go a long way.
- Banish guilt and say yes to new projects only when you really mean it.

Growth in Real Life

Growth practices for Threes include leaning in to the body's natural needs for rest, rejuvenation, and pacing. Many Threes believe that if they don't move quickly, they'll fall behind, so they demand an almost robotic level of efficiency and productivity from themselves. And to be honest, this often works for a while! At some point, however, many Threes begin to wonder if there's more to life. One great way to begin is by doing something no one else will see just because they want to, especially if that thing is "unproductive" and is fun or restful.

Thought Patterns That Might Be Keeping You Stuck

We all have thought patterns that keep us stuck. When they are subconscious, your initial response to the suggestion that these might not be helpful thoughts could be visceral discomfort. However, remember that we are focused on excavating and identifying these beliefs as a way to become free of them.

Notice how these thought patterns might come up for you:

- I am what I do.
- If I let people see the real me, I'll lose [fill in the blank] (status, success, my job, friends, family, admiration).
- Failing means I'm a failure.
- If I slow down or stop, everything will fall apart. I don't need rest. I'll sleep when I'm dead.
- I'm not an emotional person, and that doesn't really impact me.
- If others see me in a good light, I'm doing things right.
- If I show how hard I'm working behind the scenes, I'll be less impressive.

Examine your assumptions.

For each pattern above, journal about the following:

- Where does this belief come from?
- How long have I been attached to this belief?
- Is it true? Is it really true?
- What would be different if the opposite were true?

Everyday Practices: Looking Inward and Valuing Authenticity

Growth for Threes is getting in touch with the real self. Getting in touch with the true self will help them understand what they do and don't like, where they're performing and where they're genuine, and they'll be more able to slow down and enjoy life because worth isn't based on hustling.

Feel your feelings.

It might have surprised you when you first learned the Enneagram that type Three is in the heart center. Many Threes don't experience themselves as emotional (or if they do, they might say that OTHERS don't experience them as emotional). To begin to tap into your emotional realm, try these journaling exercises.

- USE EXPRESSIVE WRITING TO OPEN UP. Try the journaling practice listed in chapter 2.
- REFLECT ON THESE QUESTIONS. What does being separated from your emotions offer you? How does this help you be more productive or successful? How does this contribute to your image? Can you imagine how being separated from emotion might not be helping you?
- EXPERIMENT WITH NAMING YOUR FEELINGS. Naming feelings aids emotional intelligence, which can benefit your life overall. When you're unaware of what's going on beneath the surface, you might find yourself irritable or anxious but unaware why you feel off. When you're upset or unsettled, use an emotion wheel (find one in the resource guide at https://www.enneagramirl.com/resources) and name the emotion beneath the surface. To practice this while calm, choose an emotion from the wheel and journal about what it feels like in your body, when you experience it, and how you express it.

Reevaluate where worth comes from.

Threes tend to put a lot of stock in how others perceive them. Judging worth in this way can leave you on a roller coaster of self-esteem: sometimes you've got it, and sometimes you don't. Here are a few ways to reevaluate:

- REDEFINE WHAT SUCCESS MEANS. Respond to each of the following prompts in your journal.
  - In my family of origin, success was defined as . . .
  - Growing up, I remember hearing the following phrases about people who were successful . . . And these phrases about people who were not successful . . .
  - The society I live in defines success as . . .
  - Because of this, I assume success looks like . . .
  - My values differ in that I care more about . . .
  - When I think about my values and my future, success would look like . . .
- ENVISION HOW YOU'VE LET OTHERS DICTATE YOUR WORTH. Imagine a thin string of light attaching you to everyone who has ever weighed in on your worth. You might see your parents, teachers, employers, partners, ex-partners, friends, maybe even your barista. Now imagine you're taking all of that light back inside yourself. First, take a few deep breaths, and then, on your next in-breath, vacuum it all back in. What does it feel like to have all the light back inside you? What will you do with it? Where will you focus now that you're the one who gets to decide?
- SET INPUT-BASED GOALS. Threes get caught up in results. It's part of the reason you're so motivated and successful! But it can make you miserable because it's easy to fall into perfectionism, and you overwork yourself trying to hit goals that are outside of your control. Instead of "get 1,000 podcast downloads," make your goal "publish 2 podcasts a month for the next 6 months."[4]

Try a hobby that is just for you!
This hobby must be something you won't turn into a business, and you won't perform for anyone: something that is purely creative, fun, energizing, or enlightening. No metrics, numbers, or data al-

lowed. For me, this practice has unearthed plenty of fodder to process with my Enneagram coach, and it's made me wonder how much joy I've missed by only doing what I'm already good at.

Stop waiting for a better version of yourself.
Even though you'll likely continue to grow and become a truer version of yourself, that version is no more worthy than you are today. Go ahead and burn the good candle or drink your best wine or savor the chocolate you've been saving for a "special occasion." You don't have to wait until you get this part out of the way. You will always be a little bit imperfect, and there will always be ways you feel like you're not yet enough, but you are deserving of the best care, even now.

CHAPTER 10

Type Four

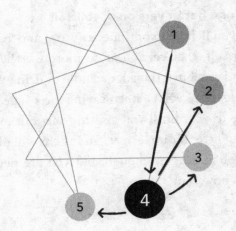

Lauren has always known the feeling of longing. Growing up, she thought if she had a less chaotic family, or lived closer to her school and friends, or didn't feel so *different* she'd be happier. She yearned to grow up and make her own decisions, and she often daydreamed about the life she would have someday. As an adult, though, the longing never dissipated, even as she built a community of friends, enjoyed various hobbies, and found a meaningful career.

One afternoon, Lauren was invited to a reunion for her high school volleyball team at a longtime friend's house. She'd just moved back to the area and was eager to reconnect.

Driving up to her friend's property, Lauren's heart sank. She assumed this friend had some property—enough for a sand volleyball court, a pool, and horses—but hadn't considered this particular gut-wrenching sensation. The house was beautiful, of course, and the view of the foothills. Before she even stepped out of the car, her mind was reeling with comparisons. *We went to the same school, technically had the same opportunities, and she has all this? What do I have?* Lauren thought.

As the afternoon wore on, Lauren felt like an outsider trespassing in this happy, golden world. She was certain her friends could sense the shame and envy emanating from her pores, but she tried to put it out of her mind as she volleyed the ball back over the net.

For days after, Lauren tortured herself, questioning every decision she'd ever made, and feeling utterly degenerate in comparison to this optimistic, kind, and clearly well-off friend. Lauren didn't want to live in the hills an hour from the city, she reasoned, but she wanted to be able to make that choice. She didn't envy the early mornings and mid-match diaper changes of a mom of three kids under three, but she couldn't help but feel *behind*. Like life passed her by, and nothing was going her way. Like she was doomed to feel this way forever because there was just something about her that precluded her from the charmed happiness she'd witnessed.

And then, another feeling arose. *You're so ungrateful! Look at the beautiful life you already have!* Lauren thought. Shame washed over her, spinning her into this cycle of longing and contempt.

A year later, nothing has changed in Lauren's life externally, but her internal landscape is shifting through her growth work. Sometimes the shame narrative pops up, but she has developed ways to compassionately reconnect with herself when it happens. She's found that getting in touch with her body is useful, but she also looks outside herself when this spiral begins. By being curious about others, like her "perfect" friend, she can see beyond her idealized notion of their lives and recognize their full humanity. In doing so, Lauren can step out of the comparison trap and appreciate that every person is complex, flawed, and beautiful, and so is she.

How Fours Show Up

Fours are **motivated** by a desire to know and express their truest, most authentic identity.

Fours are deeply introspective and are on a lifelong quest to understand the depths of their psyche. While some other types may resonate with the desire for self-understanding, for Fours, it's not a lack of self-knowledge but a depth of self-knowledge that propels them forward. The more they uncover, the more they find that they don't quite understand yet.

Fours are idealists who believe that more is possible: a perfect world, lacking nothing, could exist, but it's not here. Longing for this ideal leaves Fours feeling frustrated and disappointed over the lackluster reality around them. Sometimes, they feel they are the only ones who see the possibility of this more substantial, meaningful, or extraordinary existence. At the very least, they feel they are the only ones who care. Thus, they feel there's something essentially different about them. Being different can feel welcome, as Fours love feeling distinctive and significant, but sometimes Fours loathe being different, as they feel there is something missing in them that exists in everyone else.

This love/loathe dichotomy is common throughout the Four personality. They deeply desire connection and long to pull people in, but they also fear abandonment, and they ensure their psyche stays intact by pushing others away. Fours may feel socially awkward or unsteady because the desire for connection competes with the suspicion that anyone could ever truly mirror them in the way they need. Sometimes, Fours subconsciously make themselves inscrutable, as if being enigmatic will dull the sting of feeling misunderstood.

Fours are deeply connected to their emotional realm. Like all heart types, Fours rely on their emotional awareness to gather information in the world, so they are acutely aware of the emotional atmosphere around them. As an expert seamstress can instantly detect imperfections in a fabric, Fours can automatically sense gaps in understanding, resonance, and mirroring from others. It's disheartening for Fours to hear other people say they understand them, when they intuitively sense others don't.

Fours **avoid** being inauthentic, insignificant, or indistinguishable. Avoiding being inauthentic often means that Fours spend more time than most other types considering how they feel or what they think about things and why. They are attuned to minute misalignments and are more committed to acting in accordance with their inner truth than with external obligations. Sometimes Fours are described as inconsistent, but it's more accurate to say Fours are willing to adjust based on what feels most aligned and true.

Fours relish nuance. Their exceptional talent for identifying subtle differences in words, emotions, or understandings simultaneously helps and hinders them. Nuance aids creative expression, emotional articulation, clever wordsmithing, and more, but it also detracts from their ability to feel fully settled and content in the world because there's so little that feels just right. Expression and understanding can always be further clarified. When I write about Fours online, they'll often say, "It's almost that, but not quite. I'd actually say it this way . . ." Asking Fours how *they* would communicate an idea is more effective, as many Fours have a knack for choosing the perfect descriptors for their experiences.

From a young age, Fours may have felt alienated from their caregivers and loved ones. Fours often report feeling like they simply didn't fit in their family of origin, or that they felt abandoned or ridiculed because their interests and temperament varied from their parents and siblings. In adulthood, Fours subconsciously search for the mirroring they lacked in childhood. Because young Fours are acutely aware of the emotional timbre of their environment, feelings of otherness and fears of abandonment fractured their sense of belonging, leaving them to daydream that they might be rescued and welcomed into their ideal family.

The most common **misconception** about Fours is that they cannot be happy. Fours experience and express a wide range of emotions, including happiness, joy, and excitement. In general, the Four's emotionality is not static. They can experience a broad spectrum of emotions in a short time frame, or even simultaneously.

Furthermore, their emotionality is a strength, not a weakness. The Four's wide range of emotional experience and expression also lends to their resilience. Because they are accustomed to moving toward big emotions internally, they can often navigate these feelings in daily life without becoming so overwhelmed they crumble. This is their gift: being able to be present with emotional heaviness allows them to create that space for others who are suffering, too.

Thresholds

High Thresholds: Emotional Expression and Contentment

Fours have a **high threshold** for emotion and emotional expression. While some Fours feel overwhelmed by the strength of their emotions at times, they don't typically try to paper over or repress these feelings. Instead, they move toward emotions to understand them. Fours are more likely to be overwhelmed by internal pressure to dissect every single thought and feeling than they are to avoid them altogether.

Fours also have a **high threshold** for contentment because their attention naturally gravitates toward what they are lacking. Sometimes they notice what is lacking in their environment or situation, but even more frequently they notice what is lacking in themselves. They often perceive their lives as insufficient as they are falling short of their idealized life. Imagination guides Fours as they seek to understand the world, but defaulting to daydreaming can deepen their sense of despair. On their growth path, Fours can access more self-acceptance, which allows them to see that there's nothing deficient about them.

Low Thresholds: Being Misunderstood and Inauthenticity

Fours tend to have a **low threshold** for being misunderstood. Their eye toward nuance means they can detect ways their conversation partner does not understand, so they may seek to clarify how they're feeling. If that's not possible, they may find themselves frustrated by the lack of resonance.

They also have a **low threshold** for inauthenticity. Small talk, pleasantries, and surface-level conversations feel insignificant, and Fours would rather discuss soul-level topics. They can sense inauthenticity in themselves and others, and they'll do their best to get to the bottom of it. If they feel someone is incapable of delving beneath the surface with them, they may move on from the conversation or relationship in search of something more meaningful.

Type Four Personality

In this section, we'll dive straight into the type Four personality structure, but you'll find a detailed overview of the terms in this section (Passion, Defense Mechanism, Virtue) in chapter 2.

Passion: Envy

The passion of type Four is envy. Envy is driven by comparison and is the state of desiring what someone else has, especially in relation to how happy, competent, capable, or fulfilled others seem to be.

The predominant focus is not necessarily on taking something away from another person but on desiring what another has for themselves. For many Fours, envy is not centered on material possessions but their own perceived lack of some ineffable force that allows others to be functional or admirable or worthy while the Four feels mired in self-consciousness.

When living from envy, Fours believe that others have something that they lack. This missing piece is the key that is keeping them locked out of the land of contentment or goodness or fulfillment, but Fours may not be able to describe how this feels aside from the sense that it feels terrible. Comparison is woven throughout the Four psyche as well, and it constantly inflates and deflates their self-worth. Sometimes they feel superior, especially when they are suffering more than others or experiencing the world more acutely than most, and sometimes they feel inferior, unable to be happy as the deficient, lacking creatures they believe they are. Either way, there is now a new way to feel: being the one person who is uniquely superior OR inferior offers a sense of distinction and specialness that is a crucial adaptive strategy for type Fours.

The passion of envy could look like . . .

- Intense loneliness because no one else struggles as significantly as they do.
- Believing that they are lacking what others have, which allows others to be happier, better, more deserving, or more able to cope.
- Using comparison to determine whether they are inferior or superior, resulting in low self-worth when negatively comparing and a sense of being the chosen extraspecial one when positively comparing.
- A need to be special, significant, distinguishable in a unique way and becoming someone others will envy.

Reflecting on Your Passion Through Journal Prompts

How does the passion of envy show up in your life? If you can think of an example, write about it. What was happening when you saw envy show up clearly? How did it feel? What were you paying attention to? In what ways did envy serve you? In what ways did envy *detract* from what you needed or wanted in that moment?

Defense Mechanism: Introjection

The defense mechanism of introjection is a way for Fours to control their own suffering. Introjection allows Fours to cope with the pain of loss, envy, and lack by shifting the blame from external factors to their own inability to do anything well. Internalizing failures gives the Four evidence by which they can verify their own sense of deficiency, which propels them deeper into suffering. In a similar way, Fours swallow the words and criticism of others whole, as this allows them to defend themselves against external threats or rejection. This makes them feel better—if only marginally—because it enables them to avoid the devastation of abandonment because they abandon others first, pushing them away because they believe there's no other end. Believing in their own decrepitude in some ways confirms that they have introspected enough to see the dark, ugly center at their core. Suffering, whether they express it or not, can be a grounding force. Carrying around all that they've lost (and knowing for certain they're the reason why) is intensely painful. Few could thrive under these circumstances, let alone function. But Fours wear this sense of self-inflicted pain on their sleeves as they proclaim, "Look at my abject depravity. Look at how I've suffered. Look at how I'm still here." Depending on subtype, this defense is used in service of perseverance, victimhood, or competition.

Reflecting on Your Defense Mechanism Through Journal Prompts

How does the defense mechanism of introjection show up in your life? How does assimilating negative ideas about yourself as your own thoughts help you defend yourself from the world? In some ways, it's more comfortable to believe the world is good, and you're the only bad one. But what if that's not the case? Why do you think it's easier to absorb negative attributes as your own and difficult to recognize your positive qualities? What if you're actually not so bad?

Virtue: Equanimity

The virtue of type Four is equanimity. When living from the virtue, Fours see that nothing is lacking in them or in anyone else: all is equal and balanced. In this state, Fours no longer feel beholden to comparison as there's no use for it when no one is better or worse, and instead they rest in knowing they are among equals.

Equanimity is also marked by the ability to healthfully detach from emotions such that big emotional tides can rise and fall without taking up residence or causing internal upheaval. Instead, Fours simply ride the waves and let them go, knowing that they're tethered to their sense of self in a grounded, sober way. Fours are also able to rest in their inherent worth, unattached to the normal ways they create an internal identity that allows them to feel like a distinctive individual. Ironically, it is only in equanimity that Fours are able to access true integration and authenticity with the self. Rather than using expression as a way to stake a claim on their identity, Fours can be exactly as they are, loving what they love (even the unremarkable, common, or banal), and being a version of themselves their younger self never dared to be.

The virtue of equanimity could look like . . .

- Recognition that you have everything you need, and you aren't lacking anything. A pervasive serenity and feeling of fullness, gratitude, and satisfaction.
- A sense of balance or equality with regard to yourself and others: every human is unique and special in their own way, and we are all alike, too. No one needs to stand out.
- Mindfulness, which includes the ability to observe emotions without attaching to them.
- Being grounded in reality: nothing is overly idealized (the positive swing) or catastrophized (the negative swing). Healthy detachment from emotions as you no longer overidentify with experiencing them.

OPENing Up to Equanimity

As you recognize envy and apply the OPEN framework introduced in chapter 4, you'll begin to shake off the ways your personality structure is keeping you bound and slowly move toward the virtue of equanimity.

OBSERVE: Notice when your automatic activities are a function of envy. For example, notice how your mood changes when you're around others you perceive as better or worse than you. (Remember, it's natural to feel this way as this has been a strategy you've needed to survive. Try not to judge yourself for seeing others this way but use it as a curiosity on your growth path.)
PAUSE: Through reflection, then self-observation, you'll be able to slow your automatic reaction. As you get better at catching yourself in the act, you'll be able to find a pause. As you pause, simply take a breath and ground yourself.
ENGAGE CURIOSITY: Get curious about a different reaction: what else could you choose? As you consider new options, keep in mind

that this step is simply to think about how to step out of your normal reaction, which you'll try out in the next step. In our example, perhaps you begin to measure yourself against a co-worker or friend. What do you need in this moment? What makes you feel less than equal? How could you value yourself and your friend equally? NEXT RIGHT THING: Experiment with different responses or reactions. You don't have to get it right! This is a way to try out different things, and again, you want to start small. So perhaps in this moment, when you're feeling the desire to find fault in yourself or in your friend as a way to feel better in this instance, try extending gratitude, giving a compliment, or appreciating your differences.

Subtypes

The three subtypes of type Four represent different expressions of the passion of envy. If you're a Four, you'll likely see a bit of yourself in each description. To understand which subtype is dominant for you, look at the evidence in your life: How does your behavior align with each description? Which of the growth stretches feels most intolerable to you?

Self-Preservation Four

Nickname: Tenacity

At a Glance: Persevering, Refined, Discerning

Self-Preservation Fours are often mistyped because they don't express their emotions as described in most surface-level Enneagram explorations. Like all Fours, they feel deeply, but they convey just a fraction of their experience. They may choose to share vulnerably with just a few close people. They focus on being self-sufficient, and they work hard to obtain whatever they covet. These Fours set high standards for themselves and push themselves to reach for lofty goals.

In some ways, Self-Preservation Fours believe they deserve to suffer. They move toward painful experiences, grueling challenges, or intense expectations and subconsciously challenge themselves to tolerate suffering without flinching. They feel a deep need to be strong and to prove to themselves that they can endure. The self-inflicting aspect of this is twofold: they believe that if they were really "good" or worthy, things wouldn't be so hard for them, and they assume that others in the same scenario would have an easier time.

The preservation of self is the continual testing and challenging, ensuring they will survive any trial they could possibly face. Over-identifying with this suffering, and denying their own softness and emotionality as a result, offers security. Self-Preservation Fours are often unaware of these dynamics, though. A Self-Preservation Four friend and I endured the same difficult experience, and she continually brushed it off as "no big deal." Only once I shared my pain around it did she entertain acknowledging her own feelings. Overlooking struggle drives these Fours forward. Unfortunately, their inner dialogue can be harsh and cruel, and it can be difficult for them to imagine that self-compassion might help them heal.

These Fours need to be more in touch with how much they put themselves through mentally, physically, and emotionally, and they need to release their stranglehold on emotion that is keeping them from being fully in touch with what is happening beneath the surface. They must learn that what makes their lives worthy, significant, and meaningful is not that they chose the most difficult path but that they are worthy as they are.

 Growth Stretch for Self-Preservation Fours
LET OTHERS SUPPORT YOU. Self-Preservation Fours tend to reveal feelings only after they've been processed and no longer

need attention. It seems like the most "sensible" thing to do sometimes, but it often comes from your beliefs that you have to suffer, you don't deserve support, and you cannot need anything from anyone. Trying to get others to see how you're suffering while simultaneously trying to prevent them from truly seeing you can leave you lonely. You can't be truly known when entrenched in this cycle. Showing your needs and letting others show up for you will help you build connections with others. You don't have to push through all alone.

Social Four

Nickname: Shame
At a Glance: Melancholic, Enigmatic, Genuine

Social Fours are the subtype most often depicted in descriptions of Fours. Their introspective nature is accentuated by their eloquence and specificity as they describe their internal world. They are expressive, sensitive, and demonstrative. Though they are relational and emotionally attuned, their attention gravitates to what's missing in them that makes them less capable of happiness than others seem to be. Fours are often fairly self-critical, but Social Fours can have less of an abrasive or demeaning internal voice, and instead feel a low hum of worthlessness. They carry a deep sense of shame, believing that others can readily see their faults, so many Social Fours will lead with their faults overtly, getting it all out on the table. While all Fours struggle with comparison, Social Fours are acutely aware of how different or inferior they feel, resulting in big feelings of sadness, fury, and embarrassment.

Social Fours are convinced something is wrong or deficient about them. The social instinct incorporates themes of belonging, recognition of hierarchical structure, and power, and Social Fours identify themselves at the very bottom of the ladder. For this Four, life is full of high highs and low lows. While cataclysmic shifts can be welcome at times, these Fours are often unaware that their self-sabotaging and self-deprecating behavior fuel a cycle of feeling victimized by the world. This galvanizes their sense of abandonment, and they feel left alone without belonging, further neglecting their own agency, abilities, and brilliance.

Being so self-aware about their flaws can be helpful, but because they are incognizant of their negative bias, they assume their self-assessments are more accurate than they are. True self-awareness requires Social Fours to dedicate just as much energy to observing their many positive qualities.

Social Fours are gentle, kind, and empathetic. They are the best friends when life is hard because they can be present without needing to fix it.

Growth Stretch for Social Fours

EMBRACE YOUR OWN POWER. It's common for Social Fours to feel that they are powerless in the face of their suffering or in light of all that is happening in the world. You endure the pain, but taking action can be very, very difficult. Often, this is connected to an internal belief of powerlessness and deficiency. What would it look like to embrace your own power? How would it feel to remember that you have the power to change how you approach life?

Sexual Four

Nickname: Competition
At a Glance: Ardent, Dynamic, Indomitable

Sexual Fours are intense and passionate. Though they have the same emotional depth and sensitivity that other Fours do, it's buried beneath an external expression of anger and drive. Sexual Fours tend to be extreme: they are all in, or all out. Internally, they believe, "If I'm not superior, I'm inferior." These polarities can make it difficult to integrate the softer emotions beneath the surface that feel weak or vulnerable, but the ferocity behind them still needs to vent somehow. Anger and competitive energy guard against the sadness or disappointment of comparison, inferiority, and being misunderstood.

Competition can be focused on attracting an ideal mate, but it also offers these Fours exciting, dynamic feedback in their relationships. Sexual subtypes long for intimacy but use all sorts of tricks that unintentionally work against the truer connection they are seeking. Chasing chemistry, competition, and seduction can be indirect manifestations of this drive. For the Sexual Four, competing with their partner can feel like intimacy: they bring such intensity and dynamism to the table that they expect to feel more connected, but it doesn't last as they need it to. Sexual Fours also use their superiority—hard won through competition and being the only one who is the best—to buttress their self-esteem and attract specific others, but this tends to be counterproductive.

These Fours often minimize their own pain by inflicting pain on others through lashing out or making others feel less-than. They can be quite ambitious and motivated to excel, and they passionately pursue impact and success.

When working with Sexual Fours in a coaching context, I find these clients bring a lot of anger, contrarianism, and pushback into their sessions. They need space to vent their frustration, especially at the fact that the world does not understand them, even though they feel they've been so clear. At the end of the session, however, these Fours will often drop in to the underlying emotions in the last few minutes: they needed to dig through a thick layer of anger to recognize what was beneath it all along.

Growth for Sexual Fours is about getting more in touch with sadness and a fuller range of emotions. Going beyond that mask will help Sexual Fours feel more understood, and it will offer loved ones an opportunity to express more compassion for their experiences.

Growth Stretch for Sexual Fours

SIT WITH YOUR FEELINGS. Sexual Fours tend to immediately (and intensely) externalize their feelings. Increasing your ability to sit with your feelings and get curious about what's underneath them will help you expand your ability to process them. As you do this, you might find yourself less likely to lash out or take them out on others and more likely to moderate them, acknowledge them, and move through them within. Seeing them all as valuable will help you move through feelings in a more balanced way while also keeping the connections you long for.

Dynamic Movement Arrows

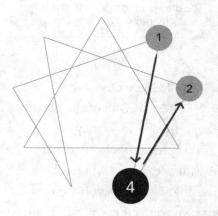

On the Enneagram, type Four is connected to types One and Two. These are the Four's arrows, which means the other types the Four can move to and freely access. I often use the term *move to*, but this does not mean the Four becomes the other type—it simply means that the Four borrows characteristics and tendencies of the arrow types. If you've read other Enneagram books, you've likely heard this theory explained differently, so return to chapter 2 for further explanation if needed.

The most important thing to know here is that we can all borrow the higher (healthy) and lower (unhealthy) qualities of both arrow lines. When we're tired, stressed, overwhelmed, or otherwise not paying attention we tend to access these lower states. When moving intentionally, we can develop the higher side of our arrow lines.

RECOVERY POINT–TYPE ONE	
Unintentional Drift to the Lower Side Could Look Like . . .	**Intentional Movement to the Higher Side Could Look Like . . .**
• Being intensely judgmental toward themselves and others, even to the point of self-loathing • Being picky and focused on what is not ideal • Forcing themselves to do things they don't want to do, believing they deserve the pain • Very erratic moods: anger, sadness, rage, melancholy • Extreme black-and-white thinking: if they feel slightly misunderstood, it's all for naught	• Becoming more practical, structured, and focused as they lean on discipline and systems to accomplish their dreams • Doing the things they need to do, even when they don't feel like it, because they recognize that the aim is still aligned, even if they'd rather do something else in this moment • Staying committed to their purpose • Feeling more confident in their choices and their abilities • Being able to connect with their bodies and move with greater decisiveness

Growth Stretch: Intentionally Build Type One

• **USE ACTION TO BUILD SELF-EFFICACY.** One of the biggest hurdles for Fours is recognizing their own agency in changing their circumstances. Taking action helps Fours see their own abilities and skills as valuable, powerful tools to move in a direction of their choosing. Use skills you are most confident and clear in, and then give yourself encouragement for doing it well. To get started, it might help to embrace this connection to the body center by getting moving: yoga, walking, stretching, or more intense exercise can all be ways to bolster your sense of self-efficacy.

• **NOTICE YOUR ACCOMPLISHMENTS.** Regardless of how an individual One feels about lists, list-making and crossing off is a pervasive type One stereotype. Let's lean in to it: when you do anything today, notice it! Instead of creating a to-do list, try creating a "done" list. This technique can help you observe how far you've come rather than noticing what you're lacking. Everything counts, even brushing your teeth! We all have seasons that feel like making it through a day is a feat, so this is a way to embrace yourself with kindness even in those seasons.

TRANSFORMATION POINT–TYPE TWO	
Unintentional Drift to the Lower Side Could Look Like . . .	Intentional Movement to the Higher Side Could Look Like . . .
• Shapeshifting to appease others, and avoiding conflict by sugarcoating or hiding what they feel or think	• Seeing the good in others: everyone is worthy, loved, and valued exactly as they are (even themselves)
• Demanding that others see them and meet their needs	• Seeking connection with others by being more likable and friendly without fearing the other person will abandon them
• Becoming needy or pouting to hint at needing attention or connection (we all need connection, but there are more helpful ways to communicate that)	
	• Focusing their curiosity on how someone else is doing, how they're feeling, and what they need
• Expecting others to be able to read their minds and becoming incensed when others misunderstand; then remaining unwilling to clarify because they "should" know	• Seeking to be of service and support others
	• Recognizing that who they truly are has many shades, thus being more open to being flexible and willing to compromise
• Attempting to buy love or affection at their own expense by giving lavish gifts or doing something extravagant they would like others to do for them	

Growth Stretch: Intentionally Build Type Two

• LOOK UP, LOOK AROUND. Fours focus on suffering to a fault. Whether this suffering is internal or external, it's easy to notice these aspects of the world. But Twos are often quite optimistic, and they take action to help and serve others. Access your inner Two by creating good in the world where it feels like it's lacking: instead of mourning that lack exists, identify ways you can serve and lace up your boots. Go plant vegetables in a community garden, join a local after-school tutoring program, or volunteer at a nonprofit you love. The most important aspects of this activity are engaging with other humans to accomplish a common goal and taking positive, optimistic action.

• FIND LOVING COMPROMISE. If there's one thing Fours don't like, it's knowingly choosing that things will fall short of their expectations. Compromise can feel like something that is out of your hands: a way that you're at the mercy of others' preferences without agency. That's not what we're doing here. Instead of feeling like things are out of your hands (and holding on to the sadness or frustration that things didn't go as you planned), intentionally choose to compromise with someone. Whether it's deciding what color to paint the living room or picking out a movie, note the differences of opinions aloud and then decide to work together on a solution.

Communication and Relationships

In this section, we'll explore both sides of communication: the Four's side as well as those in communication with Fours.

How to Relate with a Four

• TAKE THE TIME TO DEEPLY UNDERSTAND. Fours are sensitive to being misunderstood, and when they can tell others aren't taking the time to truly understand them, they can feel frustrated and rejected. Check in throughout the conversation by saying something like, "What I'm hearing is . . ." or paraphrasing what they've shared and then asking, "Is that right?" Don't assume you get it—rely on them to share if you've understood or if they need to explain further.

- SHOW THEM YOU CARE ABOUT HOW THEY'RE DOING. A Four's emotional sensitivity can be beautiful as they express their ideas and resonate deeply with others, yet it can also mean sometimes small things make them feel a little off. If they seem "off," and you genuinely want to know, ask questions like "How are things going for you?" "How are you feeling?" "What's on your mind?" This can show a Four you care. It's possible they're not sharing because they have so much happening beneath the surface, and they don't want to share if you don't have time to help them feel heard. Fours have excellent radar for genuine interest and may resist answering questions if you seem to be going through the motions.

- DON'T TRY TO CHEER THEM UP! Sometimes others have a hard time with a Four's moods and attempt to make it all go away. But for a Four, the inability to be with challenging or uncomfortable emotions is a "you" problem. They're doing just fine, and they recognize their ability to process all sorts of feelings as an asset. This is not to say you have to become pensive or melancholy, too: Fours love a well-timed joke, and they can have a wicked, occasionally morbid, sense of humor. If you can really "go there" with them and be with some of the darkness, rather than shortcutting because it's uncomfortable, that helps the process feel more complete and less alienating. Fours love to be with people who are willing to be truly honest and resist glossing over the hard stuff.

- BE GENTLE. While Fours want the authentic truth, they can also be very sensitive. Criticism can be tough, especially if it pertains to areas in which they already feel deficient or self-conscious, because Fours often feel something missing inside them anyway. Offer genuine encouragement when you can, and be compassionate with feedback, especially when your feedback incites a big reaction.

Communication Skills for Fours to Develop

- NOTICE WHEN YOU'RE EXPERIENCING REACTIVITY IN YOUR CONVERSATIONS. Spend some time alone understanding your reactions: What is going on beneath the surface? Are there specific words or circumstances that are triggering these emotions? How can you take time to process these feelings and take gentle care of your sensitivity? Being so emotionally aware all the time can feel like being a live wire, and anything can set you off. Creating space for emotional hygiene is a way to honor your sensitivity without letting it rule your life. Sensitivity is a precious resource worthy of protection; energetic boundaries can help you navigate emotionally charged conversations without feeling so swept away.

- NOTICE WHEN YOU ARE SHARING A STORY BECAUSE YOU'RE TRYING TO RELATE. Sometimes this self-disclosure can be helpful, but often it can make others feel like you're just turning the conversation back to yourself (when you're actually trying to make them feel heard!). Take some time to notice this tendency and when it's helpful versus when it's not helpful in conversations. Experiment with other ways to make your conversation partner feel heard, like saying something like, "Wow, that sounds so —— (nuanced emotional word)" or "I can sense how challenging that was for you."

Practice Self-Friendship

In any relationship, interpersonal and intrapersonal (that is, within the self) communication co-occur.[1] As a result, I find it helpful to develop our relationships with ourselves as we're working to improve relationships with others.

To me, the concept of self-friendship is simple: it's considering how we would respond to a friend who needed a little love and doing the same thing for ourselves. Here are a few ways you can practice self-friendship as a form of self-care.

- Practice self-compassion to step out of constant comparison or pervasive critiques of yourself and others.
- Honor your feelings through journaling, meditation, or prayer. Sometimes, the only way to feel validated is to believe your feelings are valid.
- Affirm what you know to be true of you out loud, and note what you love about yourself and your surroundings.
- Remind yourself that you don't have to have it all together (no one does).
- Bring to mind something you've been wishing could be different, and take action on making a change or genuinely accepting it.

Growth in Real Life

Growth for Fours is about moving away from the tendency to believe they are lacking what others have and toward a sense of inner confidence and self-belief. Fours tend to expand, intensify, and extrapolate emotions as a way to attach to them and truly feel something (even though sometimes this can be used as a distraction). Growth, then, means moving toward calm, composure, and evenness: they don't lose their sensitivity and emotional depth, but they are able to observe and experience emotions without holding on to them so tightly.

Thought Patterns That Might Be Keeping You Stuck

We all have thought patterns that keep us stuck. When they are subconscious, your initial response to the suggestion that these might not be helpful thoughts could be visceral discomfort. However, remember that we are focused on excavating and identifying these beliefs as a way to become free of them.

Notice how these thought patterns might come up for you:

- Others have something that I don't; there's something different about them that makes them able to be happy.
- I need to be rescued.
- No one will ever truly understand me. Being different is my burden to bear.
- I am ruled by my emotions.
- The ideal I'm searching for is out there, I just have to keep searching.
- I'm not enough. I'm too much. There's something wrong with me.
- Suffering and self-loathing make life feel real. Who will I be if I'm not broken?

Examine your assumptions.
For each pattern above, journal about the following:

- Where does this belief come from?
- How long have I been attached to this belief?
- Is it true? Is it really true?
- What would be different if the opposite were true?

Everyday Practices: Appreciating That You Are Enough

Fours spend a lot of time considering what's happening for them internally, so it will be helpful to consider your own bias as you work through these practices. Notice areas that still feel challenging to address or identify.

Notice the needs behind big expressions.

Sometimes Fours believe that if they don't fill out every corner of an emotion with bigger and bigger expression of that emotion, they won't have truly, authentically felt it. This can leave Fours dwelling in emotions and unable to separate from them; for many Fours, this is the coziest, most natural place to be. However, this often keeps you from moving forward into the real work you need to be doing. Journal about the following:

• Bring to mind a recent time when you accentuated your emotional experiences. What was happening for you in that moment? What need did it meet? How did you feel after you've felt an emotion all the way through in this way? Are there times when other issues or emotions might be hiding beneath these outsized expressions?

Challenge your assumptions about yourself and about the world.

One of the pitfalls of envy is that it leads you to believe there's something wrong or deficient about you. Try the following journaling exercises.

• WHAT IS BENEATH THIS FEELING? What might be different if you believed you were fully capable, competent, and strong? What issues come up for you when you think about yourself that way?
• REEVALUATE YOUR SELF-CONCEPT. While Fours tend to be fantastic at seeing nuance and living in the gray area, sometimes Fours can be black and white about their worth. Using this thought process, if you're measuring up, you're great. If you're anything less than perfectly enough, you suck. Measuring yourself this way traps you in comparison. Question your assumption that no one is equal: everyone is either better or

worse. How can you affirm your value as you are, regardless of how you measure up?

- WHAT ARE YOU ALREADY GOOD AT? Spend some time brainstorming what you're great at. If you can't think of anything, draw a Venn diagram on your page, and look at the intersection between what you do often and may get good feedback for AND what feels fulfilling, energizing, and inspiring for you.
  - What strengths do you already possess that make you great at these things?
  - How might these strengths support you as you shift your mindset about your own capabilities?
  - What would you like to do more of (especially from the "energizing" list)?
  - What would you like to do less of?

Recognize your inner critic's message.
Fours can have harsh inner critics. If this is you, wonder what the critic might be telling you. Is your critic trying to warn you? Protect you? Keep you safe? What purpose is the critic serving in your life? One step toward growing self-compassion is embracing and acknowledging that sometimes we've felt we've needed this little voice, but now we're trying a different way to move forward. To begin growing in self-compassion, you might also try observing your critical inner voice: "Wow, that's a harsh way to speak to myself," "Ouch, that hurts to hear those words," or "Ah, I see you're trying to keep me safe, and I appreciate that, but I've got this." All of these phrases can help you notice, observe, and then slowly begin to shift when you're ready.

Make the problem the problem (not you).
Fours tend to overidentify with and internalize their problems. You start telling yourself the story that your problems are all your fault,

that other people don't have these problems because they are better or more functional, and that you're destined to live this problem-filled life. In *Already Enough,* therapist Lisa Olivera suggests that externalizing our stories can help us cope and craft new narratives for our lives.[2] Here's a journaling practice to try this out:

1. Give the problem a name.
2. Depersonalize it by writing it from a third-person perspective.
3. Use time-oriented language to establish that this problem is transitory. For example, "He's having this problem right now," or "She hasn't found a solution yet."
4. Use the phrase, "The story I'm telling myself is . . ."[3]

Part IV

The Mind Types: Overview

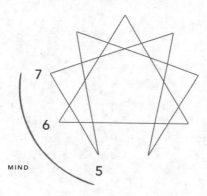

MIND TYPES	
Central Themes	Security, strategy, rationale, logic, mental modeling, planning, idea generation, problem solving, analyzing
Underlying Emotions	Fear, anxiety
Common Experiences	• Anticipating what might happen next: can inspire troubleshooting, feeling on edge, or escapism • Suspicion, not taking what others say at face value, needing to look into rationale on their own • Spinning thoughts
Aversions	• Overtly emotional reasoning without backup • Being swept up in others' plans • Things that don't make sense to them

Type Five

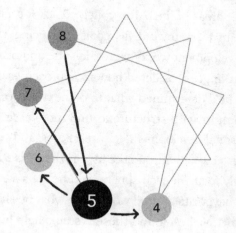

When Zack was in college, he noticed himself rotating through the same limited items in his wardrobe, even though he had more options to choose from. Being a practical—bordering on ascetic—Enneagram Five, he figured he ought to either wear all of his clothes or pack the extraneous items off to Goodwill. Upon further investigation, Zack recognized that repeating outfits was a method for minimizing his daily decisions, which afforded precious energy for more important tasks.

Zack designed a creative approach to expand his outfits without going full Steve Jobs (in a black turtleneck and jeans every day) or taxing his busy mind with sartorial choices. He developed a date-based system that would dictate which shirt, undershirt, pants, and shoes to wear each day. For example, on the third of the month, he would wear the shirt three to the left of the hanger for yesterday's shirt. The system worked. He found new outfits he likely never would have tried, and over the years he's added another caveat to avoid looking like a roll of a die picked his outfit: he gives himself three tries "in case the system picks something absolutely hideous." This fail-safe is rarely necessary though as he's collected a wardrobe that seamlessly works together with his system in mind.

Zack's systematic life started with his wardrobe but has since expanded into other areas of life. After college, Zack found a similar approach helped him work toward his goals. Balancing a full-time job with personal development work, chores, leisure, and other daily tasks meant he painstakingly considered how to approach each hour of the day. By the time he'd determined what to do next, he was drained. He leaned on his comfort with structure to find more ease here, too. For each sphere (personal development, leisure, chores, and such), Zack has a list, and he adds new activities to the lists as they arise. A randomizer app selects a daily focus in each sphere, and he feels steady balancing it all because he never sits around wondering what he should do next.

Now in his thirties, he's found these systems help him stick to his intentions while providing mental spaciousness. Of course, some daily tasks fall outside the structure because they call for attention. Even if the app didn't land on "shovel the driveway" this morning, he still has to do so after heavy snowfall so that he can leave for work. For the most part though, this system keeps each day fresh and interesting while keeping Zack on track toward his goals and ensuring he gets plenty of leisure time as well.

Enneagram Fives have all sorts of ways to lessen the load of daily tasks without sacrificing what matters to them. While Zack's specific method might be unique to him, most Fives have systems to avoid overwhelm and maintain margin in their lives.

How Fives Show Up

Fives are **motivated** by a need to be competent and self-sufficient. Fives experience resources as limited, so they protect their reserves, including space, time, physical, mental and emotional energy, finances, and other personal resources. To ensure they can take care of themselves, Fives may confine their desires to match their capabilities. By being independent and capable, Fives ensure they won't need much from others, and others will not ask for too much from them.

Fives spend time processing information, parsing through it in their minds, and ensuring they can make a thoughtful next step. Mental modeling helps Fives predict how much of a given resource an action will cost them.

Knowledge is one resource that is not finite to a Five. Their insatiable curiosity combined with their capacity to hold vast swaths of information provides fertile ground for endless learning. Though cerebral, some Fives do not identify with being "intellectual," even if they love to learn. Fives often prefer learning from key expert sources and drawing sound conclusions to relying on someone else's summary. Paradoxically, Fives look for hard data from others, but they tend to deal in abstractions when communicating their ideas. Clarifying the real-world meaning of their ideas is of less concern, unless they are specifically tasked with doing so. In moments of unhealth, stress, or exhaustion, Fives may disconnect from reality, seeing everything as a construct of their minds without any real bearing on existence.

Fives **avoid** experiencing depletion or intrusion. Many Fives sense that their "battery" for each day is limited. They carefully consider how to make daily life less demanding, knowing their energy will need to last all day until they can be alone to recharge. Often, Fives have a deep fear that if they need resources from others, they'll risk inviting encroachment. Withdrawing from others and securing their own lifelines is much more stable. This reaction often feels innately important for survival, even when the Five cognitively knows that the people around them are not trying to overwhelm or inundate them.

Fives find solace in their alone time as it affords them time and space to recharge and process their day. Fives sometimes report that they will stay up late or get up very early to ensure they have enough alone time. If unable to carve out enough time, Fives sometimes withdraw into their minds even while they are physically present with others. Withdrawal is not necessarily about others, and at times it can be painful for a Five to realize their loved ones have taken their need for alone time personally. However, when withdrawal feels essential for survival, they will often meet that need even if it disappoints others.

Sometimes even when Fives are open to spending time with others, concerns about their boundaries keep them away. Navigating boundaries can take a lot of emotional energy from Fives, especially since most have found themselves in situations where their preferences were disregarded.

Fives highly value privacy. Many Fives share that they mentally sort their relationships, and their closest relationships are committed, loyal, and comfortable. Those in the innermost circle are privy to more intimate details, but even then, Fives keep some things to themselves. This privacy can feel like a small bit of freedom.

From a young age, Fives noticed that they fared best in life by meeting their own needs. As children, they may have perceived their caregivers as unable or unwilling to adequately care for them, and they concluded that they must care for themselves. Therefore, the core motivation underpinning the Five personality is organized around ensuring their needs are met, depending solely on their own abilities.

A common **misconception** about Fives is that they are devoid of emotions. Many Fives report connecting to their emotions, but they prefer to process them alone, storing them away to be unpacked in solitude. Once alone, Fives internally dissect their emotional experiences into disparate parts, breaking them down further and further until the experience is manageable, understandable, and intellectually sound. It's typical for Fives to think their feelings until they develop the skills to access them experientially. Creating this mental distance can help a Five maintain the steadiness that feels secure. Having their wits about them is a top priority. Emotional expression can feel destabilizing for a Five, and they don't share readily, even though they can be deeply affected by life.

Thresholds

High Thresholds: Expertise and Importance

Fives have a **high threshold** for what qualifies as competence or expertise. Fives are voracious learners. They're often the type of people who decide to read a bit more about legal contracts before starting a business and end up becoming a lawyer along the way. Or they want to write a novel and go back to school for an MFA in creative writing. "Fake it until you make it" is not an approach Fives appreciate. Therefore, they have a high bar for expertise for themselves and others, and they cringe inwardly when others purport to have unwarranted expertise.

Fives also have a **high threshold** for what feels worth their time and energy. Fives are acutely aware of their limitations. No one can do everything they want, and Fives focus only on the things that are highly important, interesting, or valuable to them.

Low Thresholds: Violation of Privacy and Socialization

Fives have a **low threshold** for what feels like an infringement on their privacy. Once I wrote on Instagram that Fives tend to dislike personal questions. A Five responded in a comment, "I actually don't mind personal questions as long as they're not too personal. For example, if they're asking me what books I'm reading, that's gone too far." While asking about books might not be too intimate for all Fives, this quick comment revealed a clear difference in how Fives might engage in conversation differently from other types.

Fives also have a **low threshold** for social needs being met. It doesn't take long to fill their social tank, and they are drained by pointless small talk. However, they have a higher threshold in certain contexts. For instance, if social engagements are organized around a defined purpose and the Five understands the rules of engagement and their expected role, they'll be more likely to actively participate. Similarly, Fives appreciate delving into conversations that are intriguing, mentally stimulating, or informative.

Type Five Personality

In this section, we'll dive straight into the type Five personality structure, but you'll find a detailed overview of the terms in this section (Passion, Defense Mechanism, Virtue) in chapter 2.

Passion: Avarice

The passion of type Five is avarice. In this context, avarice is not money-hungry greed but the hoarding of resources to ward against feeling emptied or without. By taking in information, they can possess more and more knowledge about topics, places, theories, or even people, and they begin to feel whole. However, this is a bottomless well, and they always thirst to collect more.

Avarice serves Fives as it ensures they have enough resources to get by, and it's fueled by an early life experience of finding that they can't rely on others to get what they need. Avarice fuels scarcity, and it fosters stinginess (the mental fixation of Fives), which motivates Fives to avoid giving too much away. Thus, Fives hold back love, attention, and emotion. In an ideal world, they would freely give, recognizing that what they give will be returned, but that's not the world Fives have known.

The passion of avarice could look like . . .

- Being closed off to emotion, love, and outside nurturance, and even minimizing wants and needs to avoid needing anything from anyone else.
- An excessive desire to acquire or possess more than you need, especially with regard to knowledge.
- Overfocusing on maintaining steadiness to manage anxiety that something may come up that you don't know how to handle.
- Not allowing yourself to give or receive love because it could require emotion and deplete energy.

Reflecting on Your Passion Through Journal Prompts
How does the passion of avarice show up in your life? If you can think of an example, write about it. What was happening when you saw avarice show up clearly? How did it feel? What were you paying attention to? In what ways did avarice serve you? In what ways did avarice *detract* from what you needed or wanted in that moment?

Defense Mechanisms: Isolation and Intellectualization

Isolation helps Fives avoid feeling completely empty and depleted. It also helps them avoid being overwhelmed by life. Isolation is, in part, about isolating themselves from others, but it's also about isolating parts of themselves from other parts. In this sense, it's more like compartmentalization: their mental focus is detached from their feelings, their work life is detached from their home life, and even specific relationships can be compartmentalized.

Another common defense mechanism used by Fives is intellectualization. This serves to keep ideas in theoretical existence, split off from real life. Psychologist Joseph Burgo describes this defense mechanism as keeping "the entire emotional spectrum at bay,"[1] allowing the Five to believe that rational thought is the only force beneath the surface. Recognizing a broader emotional range is useful, and Fives may be able to access this first through sensing where they feel pressure or tightness in their bodies. However, noticing bodily sensations can also be challenging when Fives are less aware, as all of their attention is focused on thinking. Fives tend to overemphasize the wisdom in remaining objective while disregarding the wisdom their body or heart could offer.

Reflecting on Your Defense Mechanism Through Journal Prompts

How do the defense mechanisms of isolation and intellectualization show up in your life? How do these forces uphold your desire for more information and your tendency to withhold yourself? What makes you want to withdraw? When do your energy resources feel threatened? How does this pattern of compartmentalization mode serve you well? How might compartmentalization create a different outcome than what you truly want?

Virtue: Nonattachment

The virtue of type Five is nonattachment. Nonattachment is marked by a Five allowing themselves to open up and be affected by the world. Emotion, energy, and resources are part of life, and they rise and fall, but the Five living from nonattachment is connected to the dynamic of this flow, rather than being so connected to squirreling resources away.

It may seem nonsensical to imagine breathing only by inhaling and never exhaling, but this is the life of avarice. Nonattachment integrates an abiding faith that each exhale makes space for the next inhale. Moving with this constant ebb and flow allows Fives to open up more to find that engaging, not withholding, brings life. Their withdrawal keeps them safe from being ruffled by external factors, but a real, full experience of life requires engagement with others in the world.

A Five I interviewed said that when she moved away from avarice and toward nonattachment, she found that the limit on her energy that once felt so concrete was actually a figment of her imagination. When she stopped focusing on how she must withhold, she started finding herself more energized by being fully engaged with the world.

The virtue of nonattachment could look like . . .

- An open-handed approach to life: seeing life as an ebb and flow— neither fullness nor emptiness will last forever.
- Allowing yourself to give and receive, to nurture and be nurtured.
- Believing everything is plentiful, including enough energy, connection, love, or attachment. Fives often believe enough knowledge exists, but these other components are challenging to connect with.
- Recognizing that abundance is an option, not just theoretically but practically. Thus, you are able to be sublimely generous.

OPENing Up to Nonattachment

As you recognize avarice and apply the OPEN framework introduced in chapter 4, you'll begin to shake off the ways your personality structure is keeping you bound and slowly move toward the virtue of nonattachment.

OBSERVE: Notice when your automatic activities are a function of avarice. For example, notice how often you collect information from the world around you but refuse to give anything back. Perhaps this takes shape in conversations with a friend or loved one. You offer something small, which makes it seem like you're being personal, but in reality you're not sharing as much as they are.

PAUSE: Through reflection, then self-observation, you'll be able to slow your automatic reaction. As you get better at catching yourself in the act, you'll be able to find a pause. As you pause, simply take a breath, and ground yourself.

ENGAGE CURIOSITY: Get curious about a different reaction: What else could you choose? As you consider new options, keep in mind that this step is simply to think about how to step out of your normal reaction, which you'll try out in the next step. In our example, what could you gain by engaging rather than withholding? How might the relationship flourish if you were able to give a bit more of yourself?

NEXT RIGHT THING: Experiment with different responses or reactions. You don't have to get it right! This is a way to try out different things, and again, you want to start small. So perhaps in this moment, when you're feeling the desire to limit how much emotional energy you expend, try something different.

Subtypes

The three subtypes of type Five represent different expressions of the passion of avarice. If you're a Five, you'll likely see a bit of yourself in each description. To understand which subtype is dominant for you, look at the evidence in your life: How does your behavior align with each description? Which subtype do you see in action? Which of the growth stretches feels most intolerable to you?

Self-Preservation Five

Nickname: Castle

At a Glance: Respectful, Steadfast, Independent

Self-Preservation Fives focus on creating a comfortable life well within their limitations. By erecting boundaries around themselves, they create margin and avoid intrusion. These boundaries can be physical—like creating their own sanctuary space in their home or office—or emotional and mental. These Fives are sensitive to intrusions, and they need ample alone time to process and to feel settled.

Self-Preservation Fives like predictability, which allows them to remain steady amid life's daily demands. They might spend their morning mentally preparing for the day by envisioning what they expect will happen. This practice helps Fives appropriately allot their energy, which ultimately allows them to be more present and makes life more manageable. Unfortunately, things don't always go as planned. Self-Preservation Fives can experience a lot of anxiety, though they might describe this as an inability to slow down their thoughts or difficulty finding mental space. It helps if they understand why changes need to occur, but sometimes they just need time to recalibrate.

A Self-Preservation Five who grew up riding horses said that riding was a powerful experience because it helped her connect to her body. Her horse would notice where she was holding tension and would react accordingly, even if she, as a Five, was unaware. Over time, she became more attuned to her body, and it improved her riding and her sense of solidity in the rest of her life. Sometimes claiming to "feel" something is almost giving themselves too much credit, since they are technically *thinking* about feelings. Integrating their emotional experience often also includes recognizing physical sensations and connecting them to feelings.

Though they limit their social sphere, Self-Preservation Fives are warm and kind with their close people. They don't always express how they feel, but they deeply value these relationships, and they are endlessly loyal.

Growth Stretch for Self-Preservation Fives

TRUST YOUR ABILITY TO NAVIGATE BOUNDARIES. Self-Preservation Fives place highly rigid self-protective boundaries that don't allow them to fully experience life. For example, you might say, "No, you can't come over" because saying something like "I'd love to see you but only for an hour" would allow uncertain perimeters. The hard-and-fast boundary is comfortable, but it doesn't leave space to experience life and relationships. When you set a hard boundary, what are you protecting? What might you be missing? What if you trusted that you have all the tools you need to navigate boundaries as they come up? What might happen in your life and relationships?

Social Five

Nickname: Idol

At a Glance: Astute, Purposeful, Professorial

Social Fives are principled and idealistic. They tackle life's biggest questions as they seek to understand the meaning of life, and they foster conversations around what they see as the most important issues in society. These Fives seem more dynamic than the other subtypes, vigorously debating concepts and sharing their ideals. They are more comfortable at the helm of a given social engagement, such as in the role of teacher or facilitator, than they are mingling without a defined purpose. Social Fives look for esteemed experts in their field or area of interest, and they align themselves to learn from that individual, often idolizing them and their expertise.

While Social Fives can be direct and selectively energetic, they maintain boundaries around their innermost workings, often preferring to discuss spiritual or emotional topics in an intellectual way, rather than an experiential way. This pattern can easily morph into spiritual bypassing, which is marked by learning and teaching others how to apply practices without doing it themselves. They may subconsciously meet social needs through learning from experts or even developing parasocial relationships (which are inherently one-sided) instead of building healthy, interconnected relationships among peers or partners. Though it feels safer to withhold themselves, avoiding personal entanglements, they miss out on meaningful life experiences.

For Social Fives, growth looks like getting more in touch with a sense of humility around what they're learning and seeing the tendency for bypass. An unaware Social Five may feel that they don't need to be able to apply concepts if they can teach them, but when it comes to spiritual growth, personal mastery, or other development work, that's not the case.

In relationships, Social Fives can seem detached or even impersonal, even though they care deeply for the people they are closest with. They might assume that if they've shared their feelings once, their position is clear and remains unchanged. But sometimes their loved ones need more reassurance than these Fives naturally offer.

Growth Stretch for Social Fives

ENGAGE THE EMOTIONAL ASPECT OF YOUR SEARCH FOR KNOWLEDGE. Social Fives are often reluctant to access their emotional side, which is a natural part of doing Enneagram work. Notice your tendency to skip past the hard emotional inner work and jump straight to teaching or expert mode. What might you be able to access if you stayed in the transformation stage? What emotions are the most uncomfortable for you? What can those feelings teach you that you can't get by intellectualizing the information you're collecting?

Sexual Five

Nickname: Confidant
At a Glance: Sensitive, Curious, Idealistic

Sexual Fives are warmer and more relational than other Fives, as they are concerned with idealism in the sphere of love and finding a partner. They may collect data and information about others, and they often enjoy delving deeper with people once they've sensed a spark of chemistry or intrigue.

They are more emotionally expressive and artistic than the other Five subtypes. Even if they are not interested in creating art, music, poetry, or similar creative outputs, they may view their approach to whatever they do (science, relationships, philosophy, business) as an art form. Part of this expression is a more open display of their passion and sharing their ideas with others.

Though they seem less distant than other Fives, Sexual Fives still look for fulfillment in inanimate objects, like books or sources of information, finding solace in consuming by themselves to be safer than seeking support in other humans.

Sexual Fives face internal tension between their desire to merge with another person, which coexists with a desire to push others away. They seek an ideal love connection in which they can give of themselves fully, but being so unprotected triggers a deep fear of abandonment. In this sense, emptiness is not just being without resources but experiencing the loss of a relationship that has given them fulfillment. Holding back, even just a little, prevents them from experiencing total loss. Avarice manifests in grabbing for the relationship and bringing that person closer with no intention of giving more of themselves.

Growth for Sexual Fives requires integrating themselves into reality more. Rather than seeking an ideal that doesn't exist, these Fives can move toward embodied presence and find a deeper sense of connection. Being a "seeker" can be a way of avoiding vulnerability, which exists in the present moment. Moving away from the pursuit of ideal connection can allow the Sexual Five to look internally for the sense of self they may have lost, and it can help the Sexual Five to be more emotionally available for the relationships they've already cultivated.

Growth Stretch for Sexual Fives

EMBRACE REALITY RATHER THAN IDEALIZING. When you are searching for a relational spark, it's easy to fall into a pattern of finding aspects of an ideal partner in various people. In your mind, you might even create a spliced-together version of the ideal you're searching for. Underneath this tendency is often a deep-seated fear of being unsafe, coupled with a belief that only the ideal will be safe. Notice your closest relationships: How do you already feel safe in these relationships? How does their "human-ness" contribute to you feeling safer than you are with your idealized picture? Embrace what is already good and even enough in these relationships.

Dynamic Movement Arrows

On the Enneagram, type Five is connected to types Eight and Seven. These are the Five's arrows, which means the other types the Five can move to and freely access. I often use the term *move to*, but this does not mean the Five *becomes* the other type—it simply means that the Five borrows characteristics and tendencies of the arrow types. If you've read other Enneagram books, you've likely heard this theory explained differently, so return to

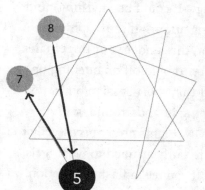

chapter 2 for further explanation if needed.

The most important thing to know here is that we can all borrow the higher (healthy) and lower (unhealthy) qualities of both arrow lines. When we're tired, stressed, overwhelmed, or otherwise not paying attention we tend to access these lower states. When moving intentionally, we can develop the higher side of our arrow lines.

RECOVERY POINT–TYPE EIGHT	
Unintentional Drift to the Lower Side Could Look Like . . .	Intentional Movement to the Higher Side Could Look Like . . .
• Becoming more confrontational and black and white about arguments • Asserting dominance over others as a way to feel intellectually superior • Strong, impenetrable barriers • A lack of trust in others, believing, "I'm the only one I can trust" • Being completely shut off from emotions, especially from vulnerability	• Feeling grounded and embodied • Being able to move into action, even before they feel fully ready • More awareness of their physical body • Taking direct action not driven by fear but by conviction (rather than against what they're avoiding, they move toward what they want) • Seeing the power in their knowledge, experience, and expertise, rather than always looking for more

Growth Stretch: Intentionally Build Type Eight

• **SENSE YOUR CONNECTION TO YOUR PHYSICAL BODY.** It's not uncommon for Fives to disconnect from what's happening for them physically, even in the midst of exercise or other forms of movement. Get moving (walking, running, yoga, tennis, gardening, cleaning—it could be anything) and spend at least five minutes paying attention to the physical sensations: feet on the pavement, dirt under your fingernails, scents or other surroundings. Try to hold off on queuing up your audiobook or podcast until this short session ends. Just notice all the sensations happening in and around you.

• SHOW MORE AUTHENTIC EMOTION. Eights aren't necessarily the most emotional type, but they are fairly attuned to what feels authentic to them at a gut level. If you feel a flash of emotion, try expressing it rather than immediately detaching from it. This might be a bit much at first, but if you can start by naming it and then leaning into it a bit internally, you can start to grow that ability to express it outwardly. Embody confidence in yourself, your abilities, and your skills.

TRANSFORMATION POINT–TYPE SEVEN	
Unintentional Drift to the Lower Side Could Look Like . . .	Intentional Movement to the Higher Side Could Look Like . . .
• Sporadic and gluttonous action, especially around knowledge pursuits • Escaping into mental fascinations • Finding focusing challenging, which can interrupt effective action or clarity • Never feeling they have enough: feeling unsatisfied with life as it is • Frantically searching for experiences of steadiness, satisfaction, and stability	• Embracing lightness, quick wit, and exuberance • Opening up a bit more about who they truly are and what's beneath the surface, trusting that others want to know them • Engaging in the world and being able to be flexible because they've sensed abundance • Flexing their creativity to think outside the box beyond what "makes the most sense" or is "rational" or "logical"—do what they want for pleasure even when it doesn't make sense • Seeing the ebb and flow of resources as part of life and being open-handed about it because it'll all work out

Growth Stretch: Intentionally Build Type Seven
• JUST DO IT! Sevens trust themselves to figure things out, so they say yes when they feel inspired, even if they're not sure how it'll all come together. Practice saying yes and moving into action before you're ready. To begin, try giving yourself a deadline rather than leaving things open-ended, and start with low-stakes endeavors.

- LEAN INTO YOUR FUN, ADVENTUROUS SIDE. That line to Seven means that part of you exists, even if you haven't discovered it yet. What sounds fun to you? Is there anything you've considered but thought it seemed too impractical or overwhelming? If we're assuming energy is abundant and discovery is guaranteed, what would you try? Maybe it's attending a local beer-making event, or studying the history of a specific cuisine and trying the dish all over the world, or training to hike the Appalachian Trail—apply your curiosity, and lean into your interest with the gusto of a Seven.

Communication and Relationships

In this section, we'll explore both sides of communication: the Five's side as well as those in communication with Fives.

How to Relate with a Five

- DON'T FORCE IT. Fives are comfortable with silence. They don't need to fill in every lull with more talking, and they abhor inane chatter or gossip. Talking to a Five about what they're interested in is often welcome, especially if the interest is mutual. For Fives, sharing their thoughts feels like offering up a part of themselves. If it's instantly disregarded, they might choose not to share anything else.
- PRIVACY IS A PRIORITY. Fives prefer to process feelings when they are alone. Even when they are very comfortable, Fives tend not to share all their personal details and reserve a bit for just themselves. This is not secrecy, which connotes an ulterior motive, but privacy, which feels like a necessary boundary for survival. When they withdraw, their relationship partner may pursue, which feels like an encroachment. Fives on a growth

path will work on this, but it can be helpful for others to take a position of inviting rather than pursuing. Mutual trust and respect are foundational to any relationship with a Five.

- LET THEM PROCESS. When approaching decision-making, don't expect an immediate response or decision from your Five. Their thorough processing takes time. If there's a deadline, explore that with openness with a Five and work to set a deadline together. If you want to persuade a Five, emotional pleas will not work. Giving facts, data, sources, and time for them to look into it on their own is more helpful. Because Fives value objectivity, communicating in a way that is rational, logical, and calm will get the best results, and you'll get the same in return.

- REMEMBER THEIR SENSITIVITY. Because Fives don't often show their emotions, others sometimes assume they don't exist. This is not the case. Fives are quite sensitive, and they spend much of their time observing everything and everyone around them. Their sensitivity could be emotional, or it could be in relation to their environment (lighting, scents, space, sound), feeling inadequate to meet expectations, timelines shifting unexpectedly, or any other factor that is important to them. This doesn't need to be a topic of conversation, but it can be helpful to keep in mind, especially when a Five doesn't want to go to a certain restaurant or participate in an activity. By assuming it's only withdrawal, you'll miss an opportunity to connect with a Five on a different level.

Communication Skills for Fives to Develop

- COMMUNICATE YOUR NEED FOR ALONE TIME. You know you need more time to be alone and think than many others do. It can be helpful to let others know when you need space.

In a close relationship, you might even develop a routine or a word to signal you are going to go be alone. This will help them understand you and your needs a bit more. You can't ensure that no one ever feels hurt, but you can do your best to let them know you need to be alone for you, not to avoid them.

- GIVE YOURSELF A TIME FRAME FOR COMING TO CONCLUSIONS. It can be difficult to feel like you've gathered enough understanding because the more you know, the more you learn that you don't know. But stretching yourself by deciding you'll come to a decision in a certain time frame can help you determine when to stop analyzing and move on.

Practice Self-Friendship

In any relationship, interpersonal and intrapersonal (that is, within the self) communication co-occur.[2] As a result, I find it helpful to develop our relationships with ourselves as we're working to improve relationships with others.

To me, the concept of self-friendship is simple: it's considering how we would respond to a friend who needed a little love and doing the same thing for ourselves. Here are a few ways you can practice self-friendship as a form of self-care.

- Give yourself space not to have all the answers.
- Do something alone that you enjoy, and take an exploratory approach, rather than going in with certain expectations for your time.
- Process what you're learning out loud and think of questions you'd like to consider. As different ideas arise, give yourself time to process your thoughts rather than jumping into research mode.

- Listen to music that makes you feel something, and allow yourself to explore those emotions as you listen.
- Explore new activities you might enjoy.

Growth in Real Life

Growth for Fives is about getting out of their heads. For most Fives, being in their minds is the most comfortable, safe, and satisfying place to dwell; however, being so cut off from everything else leaves Fives isolated and less connected. Growth means connecting with their bodies and truly interacting with the world in a literal, rather than theoretical, way. It also means seeing how logic and reasoning are not the only things that are important in the world.

Thought Patterns That Might Be Keeping You Stuck

We all have thought patterns that keep us stuck. When they are subconscious, your initial response to the suggestion that these might not be helpful thoughts could be visceral discomfort. However, remember that we are focused on excavating and identifying these beliefs as a way to become free of them.

Notice how these thought patterns might come up for you:

- If I run out of energy, I can never refuel.
- Anything I share is like a part of me I've given away and can never have again.
- I don't have enough information—I need to keep thinking and researching before I move forward.
- When I really think about it, I know I'm truly alone in this world.
- I must be competent at all times. Incompetence is unacceptable.

- My knowledge will protect me from feeling fear. I must avoid fear because emotions make me less rational, logical, and calm.
- If I let others see my needs, that will give them the opportunity to intrude.

Examine your assumptions.

For each pattern listed, journal about the following:

- Where does this belief come from?
- How long have I been attached to this belief?
- Is it true? Is it really true?
- What would be different if the opposite were true?

Everyday Practices: Embodiment and Expansion

Growth practices for Fives can be tricky because Fives carefully think through their approach to life, and many Fives love that they've found the most logical, comfortable, and controlled way of living. Enneagram inner work offers the possibility that more fulfillment, awareness, and consciousness are available to you. The growth practices here focus on opening up to what is possible. Rather than shifting from a scarcity-only mindset to an abundance-only mindset overnight, it's about seeing abundance as an option, too.

Get back in your body.

Not everyone enjoys exercise (and many Fives are sick of being told to work out for personal growth!), but getting back into your body is about more than hitting the gym. Instead, getting back into your body could be:

- Taking a walk in nature and paying attention to where your feet are hitting the ground, what that feedback feels like, how you're breathing, how you're feeling physically, and other sensations.

- Doing an activity you enjoy for the pleasure of it that also involves movement, like cooking, baking, gardening, working on a hobby, building something, or other similar activities. As you move, notice how you're feeling, how you're holding your posture, what you're paying attention to, what you're able to do when you're connected to your body, and so on. Notice when you're escaping into your mind, and draw your attention back to your body.

- Breathing exercises and meditation: noticing how you're breathing, where your attention goes, what it's like to breathe deeply, and so on.

- Various types of exercise: yoga, HIIT workouts, strength training, and such. If you're a Five who loves distance activities, such as long-distance running or biking, try being fully mindful of your body for a few minutes every hour.

Notice when you're compartmentalizing your world,
especially your emotional world from your mental, thinking world. Sometimes this tendency can make it difficult to have deep relationships because the other party feels like they never truly know their Five. Additionally, conflict can be quite challenging because some Fives find themselves focused on puzzling through how to solve the problem (or prevent problems in the first place) rather than being present in the more difficult emotional aspects of the conflict. When this happens, it can drive a wedge in the relationship. Is there someone in your life you'd like a deeper relationship with? Is there someone you'd like to get to know better? What would it be like to share just a little bit more with them? Or, if they're sharing, what would it be like to be fully present with them without intellectualizing it?

Invite close loved ones to experience life with you.

Fives often have particular interests, but at times, they can feel uncertain about sharing them. Sometimes, this is because sharing an interest feels too personal: it's the only safe or private space the Five has (and if that's you, that's okay—you're not expected to share everything). But at other times, Fives can feel like it's just easier to go alone rather than going through the vulnerability of opening up and sharing something they're interested in. If you love beer, try asking a loved one to go to a beer festival with you the next time there's something like that in your city. If you love seeing movies, try asking a friend to watch and discuss a film with you. These simple experiences might show you that being with people isn't always so exhausting. You might notice that you feel wiped out after being with others because you only do activities you enjoy when you're alone; when you're with other people, you do what they like. It makes sense that it sometimes feels too intimate to share what you love, but close, trusted relationships are the perfect playground for trying this out.

Notice when you're thinking your feelings versus feeling your feelings.

At first, it might be helpful to think your feelings when you first begin to notice them, but your development includes learning to feel them, too. The difference between thinking and feeling them often has to do with physical and physiological reactions to them. Instead of thinking through why you feel sad, feeling sadness might mean noticing heaviness in your chest or weight in your gut, or allowing tears to come to your eyes, or even visualizing making space in your chest for sadness to grow. This will likely look different for each person. Start by noticing first, and then move into experimenting with creating more space for emotional expression.

CHAPTER 12

Type Six

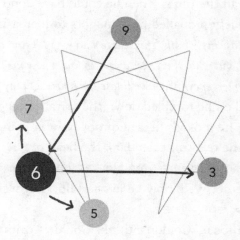

Joey is a model employee. He is proactive, punctual, and responsible. So when he got an urgent email from his company's chief technology officer, his stomach dropped. The email was a final reminder to complete their company's cybersecurity training. Because Joey is so proactive, his email filters had archived the previous reminders. He responded to confirm he'd complete it right away. Unfortunately, as a remote employee, there were issues with logging in to the company's VPN, which further delayed completion.

The following morning, when he still couldn't log on, he started to wonder if something else was amiss. He had a performance review scheduled with his manager the following day, and he requested to move the meeting up. Her schedule was typically open, but she sent a terse reply back: "Can't, busy today."

Hmmm . . . he thought. In their years working together, she'd always been more verbose. The head of Human Resources wasn't responding to emails, either, and Joey was starting to panic. Despite his stellar track record, a voice in his head whispered doubt and insecurity.

Throughout the day, Joey meticulously reviewed recent assignments, noting all the times when he could have done more. Second by second, anxiety propelled his thoughts to increasingly worrying scenarios. *If I lose my job like this, there's no way I'll find a new one soon. We have savings, but what if it takes a year to find a new job? And what if we have a medical emergency? Then we'll lose the house. Oh my god, where will we live?* On and on he tumbled down the spiral of concern.

Everywhere he looked, he saw proof he was going to get fired. He pulled up the relevant calendars: the head of HR, CTO, and his manager all had the same time blocked on their calendars. Head of accounting, too. Well, now he felt certain: they were going to let him go.

He couldn't focus. Couldn't think. Couldn't calm his pounding heart, and he couldn't see this situation from any other angle. That night, he stared at the ceiling above his bed. The next morning, he braced himself for the news. Before his meeting with his manager, he felt like a shell of himself.

"Hey, Joey!" His boss smiled. It was unnerving. She was happy about firing him? Or was she just as uncomfortable with the confrontation as he was? His entire performance review, he waited for the words, "We're letting you go." But at the last second, she instead said, "So you're getting a promotion." This was the one eventuality he had not anticipated. His boss pointed to his proactive nature, his continued high performance, and repeated her frequent assertion that the department could not function without him.

Though he had received almost exclusively positive feedback over the five years he'd been with the company, all of that went out the window when he felt uncertain. His brain could no longer think logically, and he started finding linkages between coincidental but unrelated events. Sixes like Joey prefer to be one step ahead. They hate to be caught off guard by a possibility that could negatively affect them. Fear, like Joey's, does not feel unwarranted but reasonable. He is trying to predict what might happen so that he can be safe.

Unfortunately, this fear is common for Sixes. They feel certain of nothing except the fact that they are about to lose their job, despite a mountain of evidence to the contrary.

How Sixes Show Up

Sixes are **motivated** by a need to experience safety, stability, and certainty. For some Sixes, that means managing their physical surroundings, but many Sixes ensure safety through monitoring their relational connections, understanding and adhering to rules, planning for various scenarios, and questioning the world around them. Sixes are difficult to describe because the subtypes, which we'll explore later in the chapter, are vastly different. However, the common experience of Sixes relates to their constant awareness of what might happen next, which manifests in a keen intuition, allowing them to skillfully sniff out inauthenticity. In overdrive, this awareness morphs into hypervigilant dread. Even though Sixes appreciate pragmatism and analytical thinking, they can be unaware of the way their subconscious mind imagines threats to manage that their logical mind would otherwise discount.

Sixes crave predictability and consistency from their environment and relationships. Establishing trust is challenging for Sixes, especially because they can easily envision that others have ulterior motives. Sixes want community, and deep down, they sometimes wish everyone else would be more consistent and trustworthy. Unfortunately, humans are fickle, and Sixes are hypersensitive to moments when they observe people are not who they've said they are. Finding people who are consistent and predictable is one way for them to feel a little more steady. But Sixes aren't always so steady and predictable themselves: sometimes they are quite reactive, especially when faced with conflict. Sixes are fiercely honest and resistant to putting on airs. They are transparent about who they are, and they are frequently the first to joke about their predisposition to hypervigilance.

Sixes **avoid** their concept of the worst-case scenario coming to fruition. If this happens, they can instantly recognize how their failure to manage the threat allowed this moment to materialize. In their minds, Sixes rarely think "sometimes bad things happen," instead defaulting to "I should have seen this coming." This reinforces the assumption that they will be able to mitigate any threat, which amplifies their vigilant preparedness. Forethought and troubleshooting are powerful strengths, but they become limiting when overdeveloped.

Sixes also avoid sticking their necks out, believing instead that safety is in numbers. Many Sixes have shared that while they care passionately about a cause, they don't want to be the one to go out on a limb all alone.

Sixes tend toward contrarian thinking. At times, taking the opposite perspective can be innocuous. If you ask a Six if they had a good day, they might tell you all the bad things about their day before saying, "Overall, it was a good day!" Sixes hate to mislead, so this brief mental investigation allows nuance and clarity that feels more honest to the Six. When you share good news with a Six, they'll likely be thrilled for you, but they may also use those first moments to say, "Just make sure you . . ." This is not pessimism or ill will but a way of sharing they want the best for you and can sense a way it will all fall apart.

At other times, playing the devil's advocate can be a way of exploring other ideas, and it can be a defense against being swept away by a convincing argument. Testing, questioning, and doubting offer a Six some solace in knowing they've thoroughly investigated various perspectives. When dealing with authority figures, Sixes are slow to trust. They like to understand the rules and the reasoning behind the procedures in place prior to submitting to them.

From an early age, Sixes may have experienced the world as unpredictable. Since they felt very little safety in their environment, anticipating what might come next helped them to feel a modicum of control over their lives. In general, Sixes believe they are responsible for more than is reasonable, so all of these mechanisms serve to avoid blame as well.

A common **misconception** about Sixes is that they are constantly overcome with fear. While many Sixes feel fear, Social and Sexual subtypes in particular leverage various coping mechanisms designed to avoid the experience of fear. Other types sometimes assume that Sixes can't handle difficult news because of their general apprehension, and they withhold information to protect them. However, for a Six, the worst of all worst-case scenarios is being lied to. It's useful to remember that Sixes are also skilled problem-solvers who are happy to help figure things out.

Thresholds

High Thresholds: Certainty and Readiness

Sixes have a **high threshold** for what feels like certainty. They assume curiosity and culling information will lead to a deeper sense of certainty overall, but unfortunately it rarely works that way. Instead, they find themselves with more information to sort through and less clarity on which way to go. Looking for reassurance from others can be futile as well, unless their outside committee verifies the same direction the Six already thought they wanted to go. It's a tricky game that unaware Sixes don't realize they're playing.

Sixes also have a **high threshold** for readiness. Even if they are the most prepared, the most qualified, or the most skilled, they rarely feel ready for the next step. They project long timelines for themselves and delay getting started until they've sorted it all in their minds. Sixes want confidence they will know how to navigate obstacles before they begin. Doubting is second nature, whether aimed at themselves, the process, the project, or others. Because of this, they can get stuck thinking that everything will always be as it is now or worse.

Low Thresholds: Betrayal and Dishonesty

Sixes have a **low threshold** for what counts as suspicious behavior. While they are loyal, committed friends and partners once trust is built, establishing that foundation is slow. In the interim, they engage in testing, a subconscious relational pattern in which the Six is attempting to identify the trustworthiness of a new relationship. While Sixes desire good relationships, they want to know as soon as possible if a new friend is going to let them down.

Sixes also have a **low threshold** for what feels like dishonesty. When people first learn the Enneagram, they often assume Sixes are way too anxious and fragile to handle the truth. But being hyper-aware does not build weakness but strength. Sixes have already imagined all of the worst things that might happen, and they're prepared to navigate them, even if others are afraid. A Six camp director shared his experience with navigating camp emergencies. Though he might be frequently uncertain and vigilant about what might happen, he knew exactly what to do in emergency situations. He was able to stay calm and do what needed to be done, even if that meant finding situations he'd rather never happen upon. For a Six, dishonesty is always more alarming than the truth, even when the truth is frightening.

Type Six Personality

In this section, we'll dive straight into the type Six personality structure, but you'll find a detailed overview of the terms in this section (Passion, Defense Mechanism, Virtue) in chapter 2.

Passion: Fear

The passion of type Six is fear. When living from the passion of fear, Sixes can find themselves spinning their wheels: they are constantly thinking of something new to add to their considerations, and they struggle to make decisions with finality. One of my Enneagram colleagues, Teresa, calls it a "quivering heart."[1] The sense that one can never be certain about anything is so unnerving and destabilizing for a Six that they spend their days trying to manage everything. Sixes are often known for being over-responsible because the more they are in touch with fear, the more they check and recheck, making sure they haven't missed anything. At times, this may seem like One-ish perfectionism, but it's driven by a sense that if they lapse in judgment just for a moment, things might fall apart.

The passion of fear also drives Sixes to be highly self-protective to shield themselves from harm. Scanning for threats leads Sixes to find them everywhere. The world Sixes inhabit is not more dangerous, but Sixes are more aware of all the reasons to be afraid. Depending on subtype, fear can make Sexual Sixes intense, reactive, and frenzied, Social Sixes detailed, responsible, and contained, and Self-Preservation Sixes cautious, worried, and stuck in inaction.

The passion of fear could look like . . .

- The feeling that the world is "out to get you," leading to suspicion and concern.
- Overthinking and overanalyzing, focusing on surfacing options to the point of feeling frozen, and even taking the contrary stance when thinking through things in your mind.
- Reluctance to make a definitive decision, or pausing a project at the last second to double check or reevaluate.
- A subconscious need to protect yourself through being suspicious of others and having a hair-trigger "distrust" mechanism.

Reflecting on Your Passion Through Journal Prompts

How does the passion of fear show up in your life? If you can think of an example, write about it. What was happening when you saw fear show up clearly? How did it feel? What were you paying attention to? In what ways did fear serve you? In what ways did fear *detract* from what you needed or wanted in that moment?

Defense Mechanism: Projection

Projection is a psychological defense mechanism in which individuals unconsciously attribute their own unacceptable, unwanted, or disowned thoughts, emotions, motivations, attributes, and/or behaviors to others.[2] While the projection may be positive, negative, or neutral, it occurs because the individuals who are projecting perceive the projected attributes as difficult to acknowledge or threatening to believe about themselves. Although Sixes use projection as a way to create some certainty and thus reduce their anxiety in ambiguous, uncertain, or potentially dangerous situations, ironically, these projections—particularly if they are negative in nature—raise the Six's anxiety level. In addition, when Sixes project something either negative or positive that is untrue, they create a false reality without knowing they are doing so.

Consider our opening story. Joey was fearful that his job no longer wanted him, yet further reflection revealed his own dissatisfaction at work. In reality, *Joey* wanted to end his employment, but his subconscious projection assigned this desire externally. In the type Six personality pattern, projection is a way to manage fear without actually feeling it. If Sixes project that the world is full of scary people and bad things are always happening, they don't have to feel the fearful trembling inside them. And, they can plan ahead to make it all better.

Reflecting on Your Defense Mechanism Through Journal Prompts

How does the defense mechanism of projection show up in your life? How might projecting your fears or suspicions onto others make life feel more manageable? How would things be different if you could consciously own these feelings rather than projecting them? In some ways, feeling under threat can be more comfortable. When things feel nice and sorted, it's easy to wonder if unseen dangers are lurking. How does splitting (sharply categorizing good versus bad) work in concert with projection to help you feel more safe, even if that safety is keeping you stuck?

Virtue: Courage

The virtue of type Six is courage. In this context, courage refers to feeling fear and moving forward anyway. Sixes connected with courage trust themselves and their ability to choose well for themselves, so they take the reins to lead their own life. Anxious self-protection is replaced with openness, vulnerability, and confidence in their own ability to handle whatever comes their way. Rather than focusing on reasons to mistrust, courage shows Sixes the path toward trust and goodness. Sixes desperately want to believe the world is full of good, kind people who do the right thing and serve the common good, but fear obscures this vision, rendering Sixes skeptical and worried. Courage restores their vision of humanity and allows them to move forward with ease and wonder intact.

The virtue of courage could look like . . .

- Standing in self-assurance based on your own merit, rather than using ideologies, principles, or others to feel secure.
- Reckoning with the existential unknowability and uncertainty in life, and moving forward anyway.
- Awakening to your inner knowing and intuitive guidance, even if it seems inexplicable or illogical.
- Remembering your power, knowledge, and preparation, and taking definitive action.

OPENing Up to Courage

As you recognize fear and apply the OPEN framework introduced in chapter 4, you'll begin to shake off the ways your personality structure is keeping you bound and slowly move toward the virtue of courage.

OBSERVE: Notice when your automatic activities are a function of fear. For example, notice how often you take the opposite perspective of whoever you're conversing with. Sometimes this can be helpful for problem-solving, but sometimes it's a tool used to investigate from a place of fear.

PAUSE: Through reflection, then self-observation, you'll be able to slow your automatic reaction. As you get better at catching yourself in the act, you'll be able to find a pause. As you pause, simply take a breath and ground yourself.

ENGAGE CURIOSITY: Get curious about a different reaction: What else could you choose? As you consider new options, keep in mind that this step is simply to think about how to step out of your normal reaction, which you'll try out in the next step. In our example, perhaps you can identify that the suspicion and fear you're experiencing are fueling this contrarian reaction. What need are you trying to meet? What fear are you trying to calm? What else could meet that need? These questions can help you identify when fear is misplaced.

NEXT RIGHT THING: Experiment with different responses or reactions. You don't have to get it right! This is a way to try out different things, and again, you want to start small. So perhaps in this moment, when you're wanting to mentally examine something by taking a different approach, you could share how you're feeling about it, empathize with your conversation partner, or say out loud, "I'm wanting to push back on this because I'm afraid of—."

Subtypes

The three subtypes of type Six represent different expressions of the passion of fear. If you're a Six, you'll likely see a bit of yourself in each description. To understand which subtype is dominant for you, look at the evidence in your life: How does your behavior align with each description? Which subtype do you see in action? Which of the growth stretches feels most intolerable to you?

Self-Preservation Six

Nickname: Warmth

At a Glance: Hesitant, Kind, Perceptive

The Self-Preservation Six is the most "phobic" Six. They are in touch with fear, worry, and concern, and they are most likely to present as anxious. Their fear manifests as insecurity, and they often find themselves feeling guilty or ashamed, even if they've done nothing wrong. Pervasive self-doubt leads to second-guessing, and they often outsource their power by projecting it onto others. Anger can be particularly unnerving for Self-Preservation Sixes. When they are angry, they present a warm, charming demeanor to keep themselves safe. When others are angry, they move away as a form of self-protection. Despite this internal tension, these Sixes are warm, kind, and relational. They are loving friends who tend to be loyal, consistent, and supportive. While it may be easy to overlook their expertise, especially when Self-Preservation Sixes overlook it themselves, they are curious people who develop a deep level of competence. Part of their work is owning their power and agency in their lives and reclaiming their confidence in their own decision-making.

Like other Sixes, Self-Preservation Sixes are sharp analyzers, looking for deeper answers through questioning and investigation. They tend to build alliances with others as a way of connecting with the group and creating a well-protected team environment, and they tend to appreciate strong, competent authority. However, if they find the authority or their alliance untrustworthy or unethical, they become suspicious and paranoid, certain that others are out to get them. In personal relationships, they are drawn to protective people who will take them under their wing.

Self-Preservation Sixes habitually unearth information and possibilities, but they remain ambivalent about what is the right way to move forward. It's hard to choose what is next when so many options swirl around, and exponentially more possible outcomes pop up on their mental map.

Notice how you may be working extra hard to make sure you've thought of everything, and pay attention to the ways that you might be able to find more ease if you could move forward with the first plan rather than the twentieth.

Growth Stretch for Self-Preservation Sixes

REMEMBER YOUR POWER. Self-doubt can be a constant for Self-Preservation Sixes. In some ways, this is just their critical thinking brain in overdrive—they can't stop deconstructing the issue, seeing different sides of it, and taking the opposite side to make sure their choice is correct. Unfortunately, cycles of self-doubt and second-guessing can leave you feeling powerless because you end up outsourcing decisions, which might feel safer in the short term. Part of the growth path is learning to lean on your own competence, preparation, and power as a guide. Instead of "I'm not sure I can do this," call attention to the part of you that believes you can. You might not believe it at first, but over time you may begin to find your inner knowing.

Social Six

Nickname: Duty

At a Glance: Dependable, Structured, Skeptical

The Social Six is known for being a more structured character, relying on rules and systems to avoid feeling afraid. They are often more intellectual and analytical than spontaneous, though they enjoy a good time. These Sixes habitually manage uncertainty by seeing life in more rigid and black-and-white terms, believing that if they follow the rules, everything will be okay. Social Sixes take on extra responsibility to add layers of stability in their lives. While Social Sixes aren't necessarily extremely sociable, they focus on the collective good, making sacrifices to serve the good of the group. It's not uncommon to find Social Sixes in leadership roles, as they tend to be direct, transparent, and competent. Considering contingencies is second nature, and they create solid procedures to make dropping the ball highly unlikely. One Social Six leader I worked with created detailed procedures for the frequent emergency situations in the role.

When something happened, she didn't panic: she reached for the binder. If followed properly, the first point person could disappear, another could step in, and everything would still run smoothly. Preparing for these situations made alarming situations manageable. Even though Social Sixes might not enjoy being the one to make big decisions, sometimes they know that they are the best person for the job, because at least they can trust they'll do it right.

Social Sixes are keen observers of social hierarchies and power relationships. Typically, a Social Six would love nothing more than a competent, assertive, ethical authority who can guide the ship, easing the Social Six's over-responsibility and hypervigilance, and allowing them to relax for a change. Unfortunately, this is a rarity. Often, trustworthy authorities are hard to come by, and Social Sixes look to their ideologies and principles more than an individual. In lieu of a worthy leader, Social Sixes can overfocus on doing everything just so, becoming controlling of others in the process.

Social Sixes tend to exhaust themselves with their high level of responsibility. They can be deeply self-sacrificial, focusing so much on making everything okay for others that they don't consider themselves.

Social Sixes don't always recognize their compulsion to seek control. By taking a step back, Social Sixes may find they need new ways to cope with the stress of feeling unsupported or unstructured. Becoming more tolerant of their fear and uncertainty through connecting with their emotional center is an important part of the work.

Growth Stretch for Social Sixes

TRUST YOUR INNER KNOWING. Social Sixes can find themselves completely dependent on their intellect and unaware of their body or heart intuition. Social Sixes can be very intuitive but prefer to tamp down that skill and related emotions in favor of feeling certain through logic. When you're making a decision, tune in to your sense of inner knowing—carve out a quiet space and listen to yourself. What can your emotions tell you that your head can't? What feelings surface for you as you make decisions? Incorporate your emotional state as a way to trust yourself as you move through your life.

Sexual Six

Nickname: Intimidation
At a Glance: Assertive, Lively, Inquisitive

The Sexual Six is known for their strength and assertiveness. This subtype is the most "counterphobic" Six, and they often are unaware of the way that fear is running their lives. Sexual Sixes encounter threats in life like they've just seen a bear in the forest: they make themselves look as big and intimidating as possible. They subconsciously silence fear and opt for confidence and invincibility. These Sixes tend to be quite contrarian and have a deep sense of rebellion. While this can be directed at corrupt authority figures, their own fears are a primary focus. A Sexual Six who is afraid of heights will go skydiving as a way of confronting the thing that scares them the most, as if to challenge death or even fear itself.

The pattern of taking the opposite side is even more pronounced in this subtype. They can be quite reactive and are often called intimidating or intense because they move toward life with such force. For a Sexual Six, the best defense is a good offense. In a meeting, they may spit out their first reaction, even if it's emotionally charged and fiery, which often earns this subtype a reputation for being more like type Eight. However, unlike Eights, Sexual Sixes are driven by fear.

In relationships, Sexual Sixes love connecting with their specific people—they can't get enough. It can be challenging for these Sixes to find relationships that meet these needs, especially because their trust can be more fickle than the other two subtypes. Finding a partner who is consistent, trustworthy, and morally good will help this Six feel at ease. Once they establish the relationship, some of their natural testing and questioning behaviors may subside as they feel more secure.

Unlike many other Sixes, Sexual Sixes trust themselves implicitly and may be unaware of their fear. Jumping right in and giving a big reaction can seem like the best plan, but it tends to be chaotic and destabilizing. A knee-jerk reaction can destroy relationships they've carefully built.

Growth for Sexual Sixes is about being more open to their emotional side, allowing themselves to feel fear, pain, deficiency, and other challenging emotions they often numb. The most challenging part of the work can be the very first step of observing how they are driven by fear.

Growth Stretch for Sexual Sixes

SLOW YOUR REACTIONS. Reactivity can be an issue for all Sixes, but this is especially true for the Sexual Six. This might look like big anger, big emotions, or even being a little "scary" and intimidating to someone else. Often, this reaction is instantaneous, so it might surprise you and leave lingering regret. When you're not in a confrontation, work to slow things down a bit by moving at a slower, gentler pace and paying attention to your soft feelings, especially fear. When a stressor occurs, use the skills you've developed to pause and take a beat before reacting.

Dynamic Movement Arrows

On the Enneagram, type Six is connected to types Nine and Three. These are the Six's arrows, which are the other types the Six can move

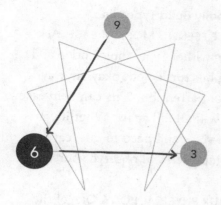

to and freely access. I often use the term *move to,* but this does not mean the Six becomes the other type—it simply means that the Six borrows characteristics and tendencies of the arrow types. If you've read other Enneagram books, you've likely heard this theory explained differently, so return to chapter 2 for further explanation if needed.

The most important thing to know here is that we can all borrow the higher (healthy) and lower (unhealthy) qualities of both arrow lines. When we're tired, stressed, overwhelmed, or otherwise not paying attention we tend to access these lower states. When moving intentionally, we can develop the higher side of our arrow lines.

RECOVERY POINT–TYPE NINE	
Unintentional Drift to the Lower Side Could Look Like . . .	Intentional Movement to the Higher Side Could Look Like . . .
• Seeing even more sides of every issue • Becoming even more stuck in indecision because they have more information but less motivation to move forward • Becoming resigned, frustrated, and dismissive, thinking, "Nothing will work out, so why try?" • Even less belief in themselves and their ability to impact reality • Feeling anxious about upsetting the status quo	• Being able to relax and let things unfold • Believing everything will work out • Becoming more trusting rather than being suspicious and self-protective • Becoming accepting and open-handed because they can see all that is good • Relaxing their need to be the responsible or practical one

Growth Stretch: Intentionally Build Type Nine

• CONSCIOUSLY PRACTICE FEELING MORE AT EASE. Ask yourself: What is unfolding without your intervention and going well? What went wrong but turned out okay anyway? Bring whatever is good into your attention. This can help ease a little of the fear that things will all fall apart. What if you were not responsible? What if you don't need to take care of everything? Mentally take a step back and observe yourself from afar.

• GET MORE IN TOUCH WITH YOUR PHYSICAL BODY. One of the challenges for Sixes is that they live in their heads, and often their minds are spinning with what might happen, what if, what's next, what do I need to do, and such. But getting into your body can help connect to what you're experiencing in the moment. Turn your attention to what feels calming—it could be your breath, your feet on the ground, or a slow movement. Breathwork and yoga could help here.

TRANSFORMATION POINT–TYPE THREE	
Unintentional Drift to the Lower Side Could Look Like . . .	**Intentional Movement to the Higher Side Could Look Like . . .**
• Frenetic activity, more anxious than purposeful	• Being able to step into direct, decisive, well-prioritized action
• Letting others dictate what they "should do" as a way to buttress their worth and security	• Feeling more optimism and seeing success as a probable outcome
• Becoming impatient and snippy	• Embodying courage through seeing all the risks and moving forward anyway, supported by confidence in their own abilities
• Feeling more vulnerable to feelings of insecurity due to fears of failure	
• Competing with others' success and strategically using others to get ahead, believing others have ulterior motives, too	• Recognizing their capabilities and trusting their resourcefulness and preparation
	• Taking action and joining teams without as much questioning or investigating

Growth Stretch: Intentionally Build Type Three

- WHAT'S DONE IS DONE. While Sixes habitually second-guess their decisions and often find themselves stuck in regret, Threes tend to think, "what's done is done." It's not that they never regret, but they find regret to be counterproductive. Instead, they learn what they can from their experiences, and move on. Instead of ruminating, consider a takeaway or actionable learning for next time. If the regret is circular or not actionable, consider that you can't change it, and you did the best you could with what you had at the time.

- CONFIDENCE COMES WITH ACTION. One of the keys to personal growth is self-efficacy, which is a belief in your own ability to make the change you want in your life. Borrow from this type Three habit: do what you think is best, and see how it goes. When it goes well, consider you are building confidence in your abilities. When it doesn't go well, consider you are building confidence in your resourcefulness.

Communication and Relationships

In this section, we'll explore both sides of communication: the Six's side as well as those in communication with Sixes.

How to Relate with a Six

- STAY OPEN AND CONNECTED. Sixes often desire frequent contact with close friends and loved ones. When they're not doing well, this consistency acts as a security blanket. If too much time elapses between moments of connection or checking in, a seed of fear could undermine trust. When Sixes are more aware of the impact of fear in their relationships, they can offer themselves the reassurance they look for in those frequent check-ins. Staying connected is helpful, but it can be more beneficial to discuss expectations around communication and find a cadence that works best for both of you.

- SHOW UP. Sixes show up for their people, and they look to establish relationships where others show up, too. Follow-through, even on little things, can go a long way. This doesn't mean you have to abandon your own life to live side by side with a Six, but consider how a Six might show up for you and do the same. The type Six can be the archetype for a good friend, and other types can learn from their example.

- TREASURE THE RELATIONSHIP. Sixes invest in strong friendships and want to have good relationships with people who return their loyalty, care, and commitment. Sixes sometimes say that past friends have taken advantage of their loyalty, fostering hesitation around new relationships. This experience, as well as other contrarian tendencies, can cause a push-pull dynamic in which moments of building trust alternate with moments of panic and thoughts like, "I've trusted too much, I'm too far in, and now if they back out the rug will be pulled out from under me." This can be destabilizing, but it doesn't always mean the relationship is doomed. Sometimes it just needs more time to mature.

- DON'T TALK THEM OFF THE LEDGE. When Sixes communicate concerns, it's tempting to make it better by attempting to talk them out of their fears. This is both ineffective and invalidating, as Sixes often need to talk through their thoughts and stop circling around them in their minds. If they feel someone will not tolerate their state of mind, they may distance themselves, but that won't reduce their level of anxiety. Sixes are known for being great troubleshooters, and this ability to think through so many options is a boon to their troubleshooting process.

Communication Skills for Sixes to Develop

• NOTICE WHEN YOU'RE PUSHING BACK and questioning because you are actually wanting to improve the issue at hand versus when you're pushing back because something else is going on (like feeling anxious in general or lacking trust in an authority). Addressing underlying causes will help you be more influential when problems arise.

• RECOGNIZE HOW HYPERVIGILANCE SHOWS UP IN YOUR COMMUNICATION. Sixes are often hyperaware of minute shifts in relationships with others. This is often a useful survival strategy, but sometimes it gets overused. When others act in a way that is contrary to how you expect, or when others take a different stance on an issue, work on having more understanding. Different perspectives and motivations are not necessarily indications that they're not on your side anymore.

Practice Self-Friendship

In any relationship, interpersonal and intrapersonal (that is, within the self) communication co-occur.[3] As a result, I find it helpful to develop our relationships with ourselves as we're working to improve relationships with others.

To me, the concept of self-friendship is simple: it's considering how we would respond to a friend who needed a little love and doing the same thing for ourselves. Here are a few ways you can practice self-friendship as a form of self-care.

• Give yourself time to rest and not feel responsible for others; be sure to care for your mental and physical health.

• Allow yourself to change the plan or the schedule, especially when it is self-imposed.

- Do something creative that you can enjoy as a way to step out of the constant mental chatter in your head.
- Create habits of self-soothing when you are processing worries and concerns.
- Practice leaning in to your internal guidance and doing what is best for yourself.

Growth in Real Life

Growth for Sixes is about connecting with their inner, courageous self. Sixes can be hindered in life by their constant thoughts that there's something they haven't thought about yet, their indecision, and even their resistance to taking decisive action. Sixes might want to think through everything to move away from feeling worry or concern, but thinking often leads to more worry. Instead, it's helpful for Sixes to zoom out a bit, either by imagining themselves as a thoughtful observer or by taking a physical break from whatever they're trying to puzzle through.

Thought Patterns That Might Be Keeping You Stuck

We all have thought patterns that keep us stuck. When they are subconscious, your initial response to the suggestion that these might not be helpful thoughts could be visceral discomfort. However, remember that we are focused on excavating and identifying these beliefs as a way to become free of them.

Notice how these thought patterns might come up for you:

- I must be totally, 100 percent certain before I move forward.
- If I put myself out there, I risk being stranded and vulnerable to attack.

- I'm not sure if I can rely on my thoughts or ideas as the final answer, so I have to check that it's accurate.
- I have to think of everything. There's probably something I've not thought about yet.
- At the end of the day, everyone is out for their own interests. Being suspicious of others keeps me safe.
- Others are either for me or against me—there's no in between.
- Trust is extremely fragile and can't be rebuilt.

Examine your assumptions.

For each pattern above, journal about the following:

- Where does this belief come from?
- How long have I been attached to this belief?
- Is it true? Is it really true?
- What would be different if the opposite were true?

Everyday Practices: Facing Fear and Finding Intuition

Growth practices for Sixes include tapping into the side of you that is ready to trust, ready to take action, and ready to make decisions. This side of you might have some clarity, insight, or awareness to share, but it often gets drowned out by all the other parts that are questioning what you're not seeing, what you haven't looked at yet, and what else might be overlooked.

Look for reasons to trust (not just reasons not to).

It's easy to tally up reasons not to trust people: when they were late, when they weren't completely authentic, when they didn't follow through, and so on. Of course, sometimes, these can be good warning signs for us! But at other times, this can cause Sixes to lose trust in people who are trustworthy since they often keep track of why NOT to trust someone. Rather than only looking for reasons not to trust, also look for reasons to trust! You don't need to indiscriminately trust people—you can keep your awareness—but also look for reasons why people can be trusted and weigh those, too. Being gracious with others is an important component of learning to trust. It can feel risky at times, but it's necessary to build trust as you build relationships.

Get it out of your head.

When your thoughts are swirling, it can be helpful to put it all down on paper. Use whatever method that works for you (many Sixes like decision trees), and map out your concerns, what might happen, the information you have, and what you can do next. Notice when questioning, doubt, and rechecking are the most obvious response but maybe not the response you need. At times, it might feel comfortable to use one of these familiar strategies when trying to meet a different need. What action can you take based on the information at hand? What is your fear telling you? Thank your fear for trying to keep you safe, and choose a step you can take right now.

Allow for ambiguity.

This is most relevant for Sexual and Social subtypes. Sixes often seek to squelch ambiguity and uncertainty through gathering information. Unfortunately, life just doesn't work that way. Notice where you're seeking to stomp out any gray area, and invite it back in. Notice when you're even oversimplifying an issue because that's the most tolerable way to look at it. How can you see things differently? How can you make more space for feelings like fear or uncertainty that might show up when things aren't cut and dry? How can you feel that fear and move forward anyway?

Climb the fear ladder.

This exercise is adapted from a similar practice by Dr. Julie Smith.[4] First, identify a situation that you need to move toward that scares you. Write down the scariest version of this, and below it, write other variations that are still difficult but more manageable. The most manageable iteration will be at the bottom. For example:

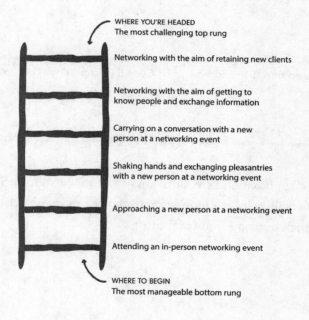

WHERE YOU'RE HEADED
The most challenging top rung

Networking with the aim of retaining new clients

Networking with the aim of getting to know people and exchange information

Carrying on a conversation with a new person at a networking event

Shaking hands and exchanging pleasantries with a new person at a networking event

Approaching a new person at a networking event

Attending an in-person networking event

WHERE TO BEGIN
The most manageable bottom rung

In this example, the bottom rung might be attending a virtual networking event. Slowly work your way up as you develop skills. The important part here is to allow yourself to get comfortable, but get started now, rather than waiting until you feel ready to start.

When something is uncomfortable, you'll gain more momentum by beginning than by thinking about it.

Weigh the pros and cons.
This is a technique used in motivational interviewing.[5] The purpose of this exercise is to untangle your fears, motivations, expectations, and desires regarding a specific decision. On a sheet of paper, draw a large box. Then draw a line down the middle of the box vertically and another across the center horizontally. Label the boxes:

Pros if I make X change	Cons if I make X change
Pros if I keep things the same	Cons if I keep things the same

Fill in each box honestly. This might not make your decision for you, but it will help you look at your choices more objectively and decide which outcome you want most.

CHAPTER 13

Type Seven

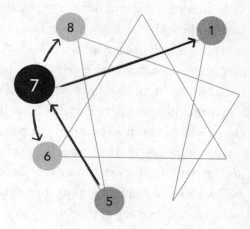

"Hi Suzi, it's nice to see you today."

"Good moooorning!" Suzi singsonged back. It was her first therapy appointment in a long while. The prolonged isolation of the pandemic, work stress, and loneliness were weighing on her. Every fiber in her being hates being tethered, and suddenly, her office was closed, and stay-at-home orders limited her options. An unfamiliar existential angst settled in. Suzi was beginning to see cracks in her cheerful demeanor.

"Let's start with a grounding exercise," her therapist suggested through the screen. *Ugh*, Suzi thought. *We've barely started and already this?!* Suzi had tried meditation before and found it enjoyable, if a little dull. So she didn't expect this short exercise to be groundbreaking.

But as the therapist directed her to breathe, to notice her feet on the floor, to feel her back in the chair, to be fully present in her body, something strange happened. Suzi began to cry. It was like she was feeling her body for the first time, and at last relief, sadness, fear, and peace poured out in big, heavy sobs.

This moment marked a change for Suzi. She'd never recognized how deftly she intellectualized her emotions. She could feel excitement and joy coursing through her body easily, but anything else turned into a cognitive puzzle in need of a quick, ingenious solution.

She'd always been the person her family and colleagues relied on to fix things. Her resilient spirit, upbeat perspective, endless positivity, and sheer will to make things work meant that most things could be worked out or reframed. Trade show booth in shambles? Suzi will befriend the guy with the power tools two booths over. Co-worker who constantly doubts her sitting in the front row during her presentation? Suzi will mischievously highlight his questions and show how to problem-solve on the go. Project timeline in jeopardy? Leave it to Suzi to rescope and make it work with limited resources. Her determination was contagious, and she naturally found herself surrounded by others who were working together toward mutual success. By showing up with resilient energy, creative spark, a can-do attitude, and quick humor, Suzi could solve any sticky situation. In general, Suzi was accustomed to getting good feedback, and she always took constructive comments in stride. She's always believed in her ability to craft the world she wants to live in.

Becoming grounded felt unsettling. Suzi began to wonder what would happen if she began tapping into her emotionality. *Will my strengths disappear? How will I be effective without these shiny, sparkly coping mechanisms?* Committing to growth work was fascinating to Suzi. Who doesn't want to learn new things? But gaining access to "negative" emotions contradicted her internal narrative. After this fortuitous therapy session, she realized she'd been skirting these scary, disconcerting emotions, and it was no longer serving her. This new therapist could instantly perceive how disconnected she was from her body, and this time, she couldn't outrun it.

How Sevens Show Up

Sevens are **motivated** by a need to be free to explore every possibility at their fingertips. Though they are often identified as fun-chasing and whimsical, at their core Sevens are seeking mental stimulation. Intellectual pursuits, novel experiences, adventures, and the like offer Sevens the constant cognitive immersion they seek. Sevens are cerebral, innovative thinkers who are quick to solve problems using creativity and imagination.

In all their forward-thinking and activity, Sevens **avoid** being trapped in pain or boredom, though many Sevens don't connect with the idea of avoiding pain when they're beginning their inner work. Pain isn't even on their radar. Thus, it may be helpful to note that boredom can be panic-inducing and even painful for a Seven. Optimistic Sevens exhibit pessimism[1] in the underlying suspicion that if they do experience pain, boredom, fear, or profoundly painful emotions, they will become mired in them and unable to experience anything else ever again. This sense of feeling trapped is so aversive that their psyches hide this concept away. The result is an internal state that some Sevens describe as a treadmill: if they don't find that next thing soon, they'll be thrown off the treadmill into a listless limbo of anxiety. So even though it seems pleasurable to be so keen on new opportunities and silver linings, the dark side of this motivation is that looking for the next thing sometimes feels like a huge pressure; they must find the next thing before this moment ends.

Sevens eschew limitations. Externally imposed limitations may inspire Sevens to push back, but many Sevens look for intrinsic motivation to abide by the rules in a way that fits their objectives, especially in a job or academic setting they appreciate. For example, a type Seven lawyer shared that he "played the game" as he was supposed to throughout law school because he was excited about the financial freedom in his future as a lawyer. Opting in was a calculated choice, indicating internal motivation rather than external imposition. This dissolved the sense of limitation because he was able to mentally reframe the constraints. Sevens tend to prefer a flat hierarchy and are not overly deferential to authority. They see everyone as essentially equal, regardless of societal roles or power structures.

In other scenarios, however, Sevens avoid restrictions by quietly rebelling. "You didn't say I couldn't" is a common refrain for Sevens who deftly find loopholes in written rules and can abide by the letter of the law without following the spirit of it. While this habit can be maladaptive at times, most Sevens avoid causing societal or communal harm and instead use these skills to showcase absurdity, inequity, or the need for change.

From an early age, Sevens recognized they would have to meet their own needs in life. Even if they weren't literally left to their own devices, young Sevens often felt that no one else would provide for them in the way they needed. By becoming independent and taking care of themselves, Sevens created an approach to life that works for them.

Sevens exude positivity, so their humorous, light approach to life can give the impression that they are not serious. This is a **misconception**. Sevens are cerebral, sharp, innovative thinkers who are fully capable of taking their work seriously while also enjoying the process. When given the choice, Sevens will opt for the most intriguing option, so they can seem noncommittal, but many Sevens are deeply loyal and sustain cherished lifelong friendships.

When it comes to other emotional experiences, such as sadness, grief, disappointment, or doubt, a Seven's mind may habitually shield them from seeing their internal impact. However, the more they wake up to how their personality patterns are keeping them stuck, the more Sevens can develop a sense of this broader emotional range. When they have close, safe people who will hold space as they process deeper things, they will share. Experiences of profound grief, chronic pain, and other adversities can shift the way Sevens approach the world. In the face of tragedy, moving through pain can still feel like a conscious choice, but it has a grounding effect on Sevens who choose to deeply experience and examine their suffering.

Because of their positivity and optimism, others often overlook how sensitive Sevens can be, especially because they rarely share with others when their feelings are hurt. Sevens can also be more self-critical than they let on. Sometimes their constant flurry of activity helps them avoid experiencing the pain of sensitivity and inner criticism.

Thresholds

High Thresholds: Possibilities and Activity

Sevens have a **high threshold** for what feels possible. It's not uncommon for Sevens to think of the most outlandish ideas and chase after them full force. Often simply believing they can bring an idea to fruition influences the outcome: instead of spending time asking if it will work, they pay attention to how they can make it happen. Every little inroad is a small victory that propels them forward. When Sevens want something, they'll apply their innovative, creative, dynamic problem-solving skills toward that end.

Sevens also have a **high threshold** for activity. They are sometimes unaware of how many different hobbies, commitments, and tasks they've piled on their plate until they suddenly find themselves getting exhausted and burning themselves out. They don't say yes just to be agreeable: part of the problem is that they genuinely want to try so many things. Sevens can be disconnected from their bodies, using it as a tool to carry them along to satisfy their mental pursuits, and they may not notice when their battery is getting low. Even though Sevens don't want to miss out on activities out there in the external world, they can be unaware of what they might be missing if they never slow down and look inward.

Low Thresholds: Celebration and Emotionality

Sevens have a low threshold for what is worth celebrating. Even small thrills can be something to celebrate. They make a habit of celebrating their friends, too, and can be effusive with their praise. Being less focused on the downsides means that Sevens highlight all the amazing qualities in their friends and sometimes overlook the less positive qualities, as long as they're still able to feel great after hanging out with that friend.

Sevens can have emotional conversations, but they tend to have a low threshold for how much they want to handle in a moment. In a group setting, they can solve this discomfort by cracking a joke to lighten the mood. To the Seven mind, this behavior feels helpful—why would anyone want to feel bad when they can feel good? But as Sevens grow, they can recognize the merit in enduring heavy emotional experiences longer than they'd like. In therapy or coaching, Sevens can be masters of distraction without even realizing it—they use topics of fascination as intellectual exercises to avoid talking about the real stuff of life. Looking at the negatives can be painful, especially when it triggers self-criticism.

Type Seven Personality

In this section, we'll dive straight into the type Seven personality structure, but you'll find a detailed overview of the terms in this section (Passion, Defense Mechanism, Virtue) in chapter 2.

Passion: Gluttony

The passion of type Seven is gluttony. In this case, gluttony is not about consumption of food or beverages but the habitual chasing of mental stimulation through novel experiences. Gluttony manifests as a life without limitation, soaking up all that life has to offer until they've tried a little bit of everything. This is why Sevens have a reputation for being world travelers. However, even Sevens who are less adventurous find ways to explore through learning, reading, and experiencing. The world is full of millions of options to sample. Sometimes gluttony can drive Sevens to exhaustion because they feel they will get stuck if they slow down or stop—they feel stressed trying to plan for the future and are rarely able to be present. Sevens in this mode can struggle with choosing one path because of the opportunity cost of forgoing other options.

Gluttony holds the Seven captive because it is self-reinforcing. It feels incredible to be delighted by a constant stream of novelty. Gluttony says, "the world is your oyster," and Sevens wholeheartedly agree. This vice is difficult to shake because it works so well in allowing Sevens to procure the life they've always imagined with relative ease. When they can't, they can reframe on a dime to prove that the way things turned out is better.

The passion of gluttony could look like . . .

- Seeking indulgence and becoming irritated at others who suggest real or imposed limitations.
- Sampling a little of everything in life, as evidenced by your inability to rest or settle in a particular job, home, vacation, project, or other limitation.
- A resistance to being stuck, trapped, or settled, instead enjoying feeling a bit untethered.
- Intense but unidentifiable fear lurking beneath the surface, triggered by being pushed or forced to slow down. Some Sevens describe this as panic, an "icky" feeling, or anxiety.

Reflecting on Your Passion Through Journal Prompts

How does the passion of gluttony show up in your life? If you can think of an example, write about it. What was happening when you saw gluttony show up clearly? How did it feel? What were you paying attention to? In what ways did gluttony serve you? In what ways did gluttony *detract* from what you needed or wanted in that moment?

Defense Mechanism: Rationalization

Rationalization is a psychological defense that allows Sevens to create positive feelings after things have gone awry. This defense mechanism is ubiquitous in our society, as the encouragement to make the most of what we can't change can be a useful tool to move forward in life as we learn. But this usefulness is precisely why it's so pernicious. Many self-help books encourage such behavior as a path toward happier and more productive living. Sevens read the advice and think, "Done! What's next?" They seem to sail through life with the wind at their backs because they can solve almost anything and then reframe the rest.

But rationalization can also distract them from dealing with hard truths. This isn't necessarily a bad thing, though it can be frustrating to deal with someone who is unwilling to see things as they are. The potential trouble with rationalization is even more stark when Sevens rely on it to justify their bad behavior, deftly shifting the narrative around their choices to make their decisions the only logical response. Thus, they didn't do anything wrong! Whether the shift is conscious or not, it enables the Seven to avoid the sting of harming someone else. The growth path for Sevens requires seeing more of life as it is, without the constant idealization or reframing.

 ### Reflecting on Your Defense Mechanism Through Journal Prompts

How does the defense mechanism of rationalization show up in your life? In many ways, rationalization meets your needs; after all, there are many things in life that we can't change, but we can change the way we think about them as a way to move forward. However, this can create an illusion of life that is always good while short-circuiting other processes like grief, anger, disappointment, or fear. When do you notice rationalization most frequently? How might this habit stand in the way of your growth?

Virtue: Sobriety

The virtue of type Seven is sobriety. Sobriety is a state of being that is entirely present, grounded, and serene. When in touch with this virtue, Sevens can face reality as it is, without the sparkly sheen of excitement cast on it by their habitual patterns of finding the bright side and making everything more interesting. Sobriety allows Sevens to stay present, even in the face of fear, grief, anxiety, or sadness. In a sense, suffering can be a gateway to sobriety for Sevens. They don't have to experience a specific tragedy to know suffering, they just have to allow themselves to feel the deep impact of the pain they've kept at bay. Sometimes this simply means looking at their lives without the rose-colored glasses to see instances of loneliness or childhood adversity or loss.

Sobriety opens a world of possibilities: when they are no longer driven to plan the future or optimize their time to sample as many things as possible, Sevens can stay in the moment. Instead of building experiences a mile wide and an inch deep, they do the opposite: they go deeper into their sense of self, deeper into their experience of life, and deeper into the true fulfillment that comes when they are fully awake and accepting of all their emotions. They stop chasing joy outside of themselves and return to the essence of who they are.

The virtue of sobriety could look like . . .

- Recognizing painful experiences as part of life and staying present with them, without the need to alleviate or solve anything.

- Finding support in limitations and restrictions.
- Returning to a sense of calm and inner wisdom, and away from the need to move faster than time itself. Feeling undistracted and truly present with life as it is.
- Experiencing wholeness, joy, and fulfillment as a precious gift, sweeter because you hold suffering in tension, too.

OPENing Up to Sobriety

As you recognize gluttony and apply the OPEN framework introduced in chapter 4, you'll begin to shake off the ways your personality structure is keeping you bound and slowly move toward the virtue of sobriety.

OBSERVE: Notice when your automatic activities are a function of gluttony. For example, recognize when you start to get antsy about finding the next pleasurable experience before the current one fades.

PAUSE: Through reflection, then self-observation, you'll be able to slow your automatic reaction. As you get better at catching yourself in the act, you'll be able to find a pause. As you pause, simply take a breath and ground yourself.

ENGAGE CURIOSITY: Get curious about a different reaction: What else could you choose? As you consider new options, keep in mind that this step is simply to think about how to step out of your normal reaction, which you'll try out in the next step. In our example, perhaps you can identify that the desire for more has more to do with wanting to fully settle into an experience than to sample many different experiences. What if the answer is not in the future but in the current moment? How could this moment meet your desire?

NEXT RIGHT THING: Experiment with different responses or reactions. You don't have to get it right! This is a way to try out different things, and again, you want to start small. So perhaps in this moment, when you want to hop into the next experience, you sink more into this one. What are you tasting, touching, smelling, seeing, or hearing right now that makes you feel alive? How do the more challenging aspects of this moment make life feel more vibrant?

Subtypes

The three subtypes of type Seven represent different expressions of the passion of gluttony. If you're a Seven, you'll likely see a bit of yourself in each description. To understand which subtype is dominant for you, look at the evidence in your life: How does your behavior align with each description? Which subtype do you see in action? Which of the growth stretches feels most intolerable to you?

Self-Preservation Seven
Nickname: Advancement
At a Glance: Resourceful, Enterprising, Adaptable

Self-Preservation Sevens are focused on fulfilling their core survival need for unlimited freedom. While they exude the classic Seven cheerfulness and magnetism, they are also more grounded and pragmatic than the other Seven subtypes. Many Self-Preservation Sevens easily envision the long game: by saving money and working hard now, they can establish a future of limitless freedom. In this subtype, the cerebral nature of the Seven is most apparent, and they are strategic forward thinkers who focus on building a life of pleasure through career success. Hard work greases the wheels of life so that Self-Preservation Sevens encounter less resistance. Everything is an exchange. By working deals and being fun and charming, these Sevens make it easy on others to get what they want. They easily find mutually beneficial ways to move forward.

Self-Preservation Sevens often have a tight-knit group of people around them, and they tend toward enduring relationships filled with love and loyalty. Self-Preservation Sevens may not fall in love as easily as other Sevens, and they may be wary of people and practices that engage too much magical thinking. If they are members of a faith practice, they tend not to be too spiritual, preferring to remain in the practical realm of reality. While fully engaged with their close people, these Sevens avoid getting too touchy-feely with anyone outside their circle.

In comparison to other Sevens, Self-Preservation Sevens more easily see the shadow side of a given situation, and they tolerate longer delays in gratification. They tend to finish projects and so don't resonate with the stereotype of the flighty Seven leaving a plethora of half-painted cabinets in their dust. They also tend to be more likely to move toward action rather than focusing on idealizing and dreaming.

Growth Stretch for Self-Preservation Sevens

LET YOUR LOVED ONES SEE THE REAL YOU. Sevens let others think they're superficial, and an open book. But Sevens, especially Self-Preservation Sevens, hold a lot back. Perhaps there are deeper emotions that are difficult to express, experiences you'd rather forget, or fears you don't want to think about. But your loved ones want to support you, to know you, and to carry your burdens with you. Practice opening up to a trusted person: let them know it's difficult but that it's important for you to share. If needed, you could agree on a defined end time for the conversation so you know you'll be able to move on to more pleasant things soon enough.

Social Seven

Nickname: Sacrifice
At a Glance: Altruistic, Convivial, Virtuous

Social Sevens move against the innately self-serving nature of the passion of gluttony by becoming self-sacrificial. They focus on being a good, pure, generous person in society who maintains a standard of morality for themselves and the group. They consider the needs of others first, and they may be unaware that sacrificing themselves for others can actually be a different form of self-serving. Subconsciously, they don't give others what others need; they give others what will serve the broader social context or their own desires. For example, they might host a party and float about the room refilling champagne glasses when the party starts to wind down. It's a kind gesture, but it also supports extending the gathering and fostering happy feelings, all of which make the Seven feel good. Social Sevens are idealists who fear seeing the world—and themselves—as they truly are. They engender a world that is filled with good by working hard to alleviate pain and brokenness wherever they see it.

Social Sevens are warm and compassionate, and they are often mistyped as Twos. They are frequently found in helping professions and aid work. Relationally, they offer warmth and connection, and they can be unaware of the ways they put themselves last. Being so quick to reframe while also resisting any scent of selfishness can make these Sevens unaware of how little they do that actually adds to their own fulfillment.

Social Sevens differ from the other subtypes of Seven in that they are often more self-critical and more sensitive to others' feelings. Even though they are self-referencing, they pay close attention to what is happening with others. While it doesn't define their worth, they will move toward suffering to make it better.

Social Sevens seem to be more in touch with pain, but the truth is that they are still not in touch with their own pain. Growth requires Social Sevens to allow themselves to fully acknowledge the parts of life that hide in the shadows. Some Social Sevens can seem a bit sad, as if they are carrying more weight than they're meant to. As they heal, they have to learn to let that go. As they begin to recognize their patterns, it can be painful for these Sevens to also realize they're not as altruistic as they thought. While their patterns can work well for them, they avoid seeing how eternal optimism, taking away pain, and being unwilling to see internal darkness all inflict harm, however unintentional.

Growth Stretch for Social Sevens

INTEGRATE WITH SELF-COMPASSION. Social Sevens abhor the idea that they could be selfish. To combat this, you might find yourself sacrificing for everyone around you. Notice the ways you put yourself last to compensate for your fear that deep down, you are quite selfish. Introduce some self-compassion here. What if you *do* act selfishly sometimes? Take a moment to let that sink in. Should every person be reduced to their most despised traits? What if both can be true: you *sometimes* act from self-interest, AND you are a beautiful, good human who does not have to constantly sacrifice to make up for it. Go for a walk and meditate on how opposites offer balance.

Sexual Seven

Nickname: Suggestibility

At a Glance: Whimsical, Intuitive, Radiant

The Sexual Seven infuses lightness and enthusiasm into the world. Life is never boring because they believe magic could be behind the next corner. This is the rose-colored-glasses-wearing Seven who sees the best in everyone and everything. Everything is more amazing when that's your default setting. The world is filled with beautiful possibilities, even if they sometimes project their imagined world onto reality, driving a sense of detachment from reality. Sexual Sevens can seem naive because they seem to live with their head in the clouds, but they are still clever and strategic head types. Sevens seem to float on the surface, but whimsy is countered by rationality, though the definition of the most rational approach to life depends on the Seven. Deep down, their busyness can be driven by anxiety. Inner work challenges their assumptions about the world as it can be difficult for Sexual Sevens to recognize the utility of bringing downsides into their perspective.

They may be more likely to move toward an ideal of a romantic relationship than an actual person. They desire love and admiration, but the ideal of a spiritual connection with a partner both scares and thrills them. Becoming intertwined sounds intoxicating, but in practice it can be destabilizing. Sexual Sevens imagine they'll forgo their independent streak when they find the perfect person. Even very good relationships fail to meet that standard, sending the Seven off to look for a connection that will meet that ideal. After a few tries, these Sevens may realize that the ideal doesn't exist, and that the love they're seeking is in front of them, waiting to be explored in all its imperfection. In communication, these Sevens want to get to the interesting part. Conversations that are tedious and mundane are exhausting, but Sexual Sevens love to learn, so if they're able to find something new within a conversation, they're highly attentive. If an interaction lacks spark or intrigue, they tend to opt out or stir the pot.

Sexual Sevens differ from the other subtypes in that they are often the most spiritual or mystical type. They are content to connect with intuition as a guide, and their curious nature leads them down many paths of learning. Many Sexual Sevens have dabbled in varied careers. A dear friend of mine has been, among other things, a technical recruiter and herbalist and stunt car driver in the past few years. She excels at each, and then she finds the next strike of fancy to pursue. Sevens possess an admirable indifference toward the opinions of others: if they like the life they're living, who cares what anyone else thinks! This perspective allows them to be wildly experimental in their path to proficiency, which aids their overall success in any endeavor.

Growth Stretch for Sexual Sevens

RECONNECT TO REALITY. Notice how you automatically highlight positivity while ignoring everything else. What might happen if you slowed down and allowed yourself to see reality as it is? How does fear keep you in this perpetual state? Perhaps you fear getting stuck, or perhaps you fear that taking off the rose-colored glasses will mean you will no longer be able to see anything good. Move toward sobriety by seeing the world as it is and embracing all of reality in the present. How are you idealizing those around you? How are you idealizing your life?

Dynamic Movement Arrows

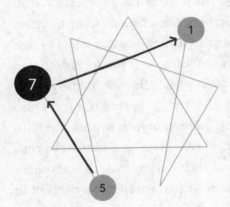

On the Enneagram, type Seven is connected to types Five and One. These are the Seven's arrows, which means the other types the Seven can move to and freely access. I often use the term *move to*, but this does not mean the Seven becomes the other type—it simply means that the Seven borrows characteristics and tendencies of the arrow types. If you've read other Enneagram books, you've likely heard this theory explained differently, so return to chapter 2 for further explanation if needed.

The most important thing to know here is that we can all borrow the higher (healthy) and lower (unhealthy) qualities of both arrow lines. When we're tired, stressed, overwhelmed, or otherwise not paying attention we tend to access these lower states. When moving intentionally, we can develop the higher side of our arrow lines.

RECOVERY POINT–TYPE FIVE	
Unintentional Drift to the Lower Side Could Look Like . . .	Intentional Movement to the Higher Side Could Look Like . . .
• Feeling reticent and withdrawn, unable to break out of the box of limitations	• Choosing to add depth of knowledge rather than breadth of knowledge
• Self-isolation, especially when experiencing pain	• Seeking to be an expert in their field
• Focusing to the point of exhaustively researching and struggling to move into action	• Speaking on their expertise after thoroughly considering their ideas
• Increased anxiety about their freedom, especially with regard to not getting what they need	• Exhibiting humility and wisdom by thoroughly considering the impact of their decisions
• Feeling uncomfortable in the world	• Openness to change one's mind when met with new information

Growth Stretch: Intentionally Build Type Five

• BUILD DEPTH RATHER THAN BREADTH. One of the incredible things about your brain is your ability to know something about every topic. Your curiosity and intellect allow you to hold so much information! But sometimes Sevens go a mile wide and one inch deep. Instead, pick a topic and dive in. Find a method to formulate your findings into concepts. For example, you could write about it, make bullet points, or extract themes from everything you've learned.

• PAY ATTENTION TO YOUR INNER WORLD. Get curious about yourself and study yourself like a Five would study a favorite topic. Analyze what's driving you, what you like and don't like, where you want to go, what you're feeling, your purpose in life, and so on. No right or wrong answers here: this is simply an exercise in looking inward.

| TRANSFORMATION POINT–TYPE ONE ||
Unintentional Drift to the Lower Side Could Look Like . . .	Intentional Movement to the Higher Side Could Look Like . . .
• Frustration, irritation, and resentment when things don't work out as planned	• Making a difference in the world through bringing their ideals and principles to fruition
• Rigidity around ideas, especially with regard to how things will work out	• An awareness of all that is good and ability to let go of the rest
• Perfectionism and a harsh inner critic	• Living in a way that is authentic and aligned with their purpose
• Strict ideas of how things should be, how people should be, how you should be	• Becoming more focused and seeing things through to the end
• An all-or-nothing mentality	• Prioritizing effectively with recognition that solid parameters can be a help rather than a hindrance

Growth Stretch: Intentionally Build Type One

• CHANNEL YOUR MOST PRACTICAL SELF. Staying in the realm of ideation is intriguing and comfortable to you, but like all head types, you need to download the mental model from your mind into the real world. Use the practicality and body-oriented nature of type One to connect with realistic next steps on the way to your goal.

- SUPPORTIVE SELF-LEADERSHIP. Use stress, fatigue, or frenetic energy as feedback to let you know it's time to reel things in. Exercise self-leadership by creating practical structures that support your well-being. Sometimes your self-care habits fall by the wayside because routines can be a bit boring, but your One arrow might call repetition reliable or effective. Be resourceful and stay curious as you take good care of yourself.

Communication and Relationships

In this section, we'll explore both sides of communication: the Seven's side as well as those in communication with Sevens.

How to Relate with a Seven

- BUILD A POSITIVE RELATIONAL CONNECTION. Sevens don't want to be in places or relationships that make them feel emotionally drained. Of course, at times, Sevens might choose to connect with people who see things differently as a way to bring balance and perspective, but they tend to avoid surrounding themselves with people they experience as negative. Sevens don't like to look at the downsides.
- DON'T ASSUME THEY FEAR COMMITMENT. Contrary to popular stereotypes, Sevens can be quite committed and loyal in close relationships. Even if romantic relationships are challenging, many Sevens report having lifelong friendships. The challenge with long-term relationships is not commitment but an aversion to being stifled or smothered, along with a sensitive internal warning system around that experience.

- CONFLICT CAN BE TRICKY. Sevens look for the quickest solution to conflict, which could include anything from looking on the bright side until it passes to engaging in a lively mental debate. When issues must be acknowledged, Sevens can struggle to deal with the underlying emotional truth of the conflict. While some Sevens are more direct in conflict, many find it intolerable, avoiding it until avoidance is more upsetting than helpful. If a relationship is consistently conflictual, Sevens might disengage from it entirely. To engage productively with a Seven, highlight your shared goal, including why it's important to work this out, and affirm your commitment to relationship.

- STAY OPEN. Sevens gravitate toward high-energy exchanges of ideas. These conversations invite spontaneity, inspiration, and curiosity. Rather than attempting to bring them back to earth, get curious with them! Throwing out concepts can be fun, and it doesn't mean they actually intend to paint the kitchen neon orange—it's just a bit of mind candy. Sevens love to be around people who say, "Yes, and," and they are master improvisers. While this might not seem like a relational activity to some, it can be a simple way to connect with a Seven.

- LIKE ALL MENTAL TYPES, SEVENS EXPERIENCE THEIR THOUGHTS AS MOVING A MILLION MILES A MINUTE. While this can be fodder for their imaginative and creative ventures, it doesn't necessarily work all that well in communication. Sometimes a Seven will say something that seems entirely unrelated, even though they could probably backtrack through the web of ideas that brought them there. Knowing this can help you exercise more understanding when Sevens seem to be all over the place.

Communication Skills for Sevens to Develop

- PRACTICE STAYING WITH WHATEVER IS HAPPENING IN THE MOMENT by getting more comfortable with a broad range of emotions. When facing discomfort, Sevens can slip into distracting themselves and others to lighten the mood. Even though you want to be taken seriously, this tendency to gravitate toward distraction can undermine that desire.

- SLOW DOWN WHEN YOU GET ANTSY. This is counterintuitive, but it's a crucial skill to develop for success in life and at work. When you feel yourself getting antsy in conversations, meetings, or prolonged tedious tasks, practice grounding yourself instead of moving on. While you may not intend to be rude when finishing someone's sentence or interrupting to add a thought, pay attention to the context. In some contexts and cultures, that's perfectly acceptable. In others, it's not. While you want to show you're excited, your conversation partner might misunderstand. Instead, ask relevant questions and respond to what they're saying instead of blurting out the tangentially related (but interesting!) concept you developed while they were talking.

Practice Self-Friendship

In any relationship, interpersonal and intrapersonal (that is, within the self) communication co-occur.[2] As a result, I find it helpful to develop our relationships with ourselves as we're working to improve relationships with others.

To me, the concept of self-friendship is simple: it's considering how we would respond to a friend who needed a little love and doing the same thing for ourselves. Here are a few ways you can practice self-friendship as a form of self-care.

- Become your own coach as you navigate difficult emotions, giving encouragement when you stick with a feeling longer than is typically comfortable.
- Spend time alone to unwind.

- Keep promises to yourself, even if something more interesting comes along.
- Let yourself experience frustration when things don't go as planned rather than reframing immediately.
- Offer compassion to yourself, especially when looking at the ways your typical habits might be driven by self-centered motives.

Growth in Real Life

Growth for Sevens is about slowing down and being able to be with the present moment. Sevens are seeking fulfillment, but by constantly skimming the surface, they sometimes miss the deeper level of fulfillment they could find by actually sinking into what's happening right now.

Thought Patterns That Might Be Keeping You Stuck

We all have thought patterns that keep us stuck. When they are subconscious, your initial response to the suggestion that these might not be helpful thoughts could be visceral discomfort. However, remember that we are focused on excavating and identifying these beliefs as a way to become free of them.

Notice how these thought patterns might come up for you:

- Everything is fine! Everything will work out.
- If I keep moving, I won't have problems.
- I can meet my own needs on my own.
- Being upbeat and optimistic is what makes me a good friend.
- If I start to go inward, I'm not sure what I'll find. I'm secretly afraid of what might be there.
- Once I notice pain, I'll never be free of it again.
- Life is pretty good. I don't really have a lot to work through.

Examine your assumptions.

For each pattern above, journal about the following:

- Where does this belief come from?
- How long have I been attached to this belief?
- Is it true? Is it really true?
- What would be different if the opposite were true?

Everyday Practices: Slowing Down and Feeling Your Feelings

Growth for Sevens includes noticing reframing and intentionally choosing a different pattern. It can be incredibly challenging for Sevens to step out of this pattern because their natural personality patterns are intrinsically rewarding: who wouldn't want to feel happy, excited, enthusiastic, or unlimited? Reframing, rationalization, pleasure-seeking, and escapism give satisfying, reliable feedback to Sevens. Moving out of this pattern takes conscious, willful effort, or it might be instigated by a painful experience the Seven can't shake. As you read these, Sevens, keep in mind that you can start small: you don't have to immerse yourself in everything you've been avoiding and stay there forever. Instead, start with feeling 1 percent more for 1 percent longer.[3]

Give yourself permission to say no.

While Sevens enjoy being on the go, they can also feel pressure to be that way at times, and when they're overextended, they can find themselves in extreme periods of withdrawal. Instead, practice noting when you're getting tired, and give yourself permission to turn down the volume on life just for a bit. Retreat, say no, and remember that everything you need from the world will still be available when you reemerge, but right now, you need your own attention most.

Make room for stillness.

Notice how often you're using movement to distract yourself. Even if you're not doing something "active," maybe you're searching for new information, stimulation, or entertainment? Every day, intentionally make time for silence. To begin, you might try walking in nature, doing the dishes, or simply sitting still. In any case, focus on your activity for five minutes in silence—no music, no TV, no podcasts, and so on. If you're actively moving while being in silence, it's likely that ten minutes will be doable at the beginning. If you feel the need to entertain yourself, jump out of this quietness, or change things up, just notice that, acknowledge it, and mentally set it aside. If you begin by combining your silence with movement (walking, chores, and such), eventually try to do this exercise while simply sitting. Notice your breath, notice your attention, and notice what's coming up for you.

Think about other perspectives.

Sevens often resonate with the common flight safety instruction to put their own oxygen mask on first. This isn't necessarily a bad thing—in a lot of ways, it's what you've needed to do to survive! The issue is when this is out of balance. When you're making decisions, consider others a little more often. It doesn't always have to be your first instinct, but learning to balance your own self-interest with the good of others will help you make decisions that improve your world and your relationships.

Stay a little longer.

When you begin to feel pain or emotion coming up, it's tempting to think (or say), "NOPE! Not today!" and figuratively or literally run in the opposite direction. This has served you well in life, and it's often kept you safe psychologically. However, the rich life you're looking for requires deeper integration with yourself. So when you start to feel that pain or emotion come up, observe your desire to jump out of it. To begin, simply notice this desire. After you can reliably see it, start to stay just a little longer: get curious about what's really going on here. What is the root of this emotion? Why is this feeling so intolerable? What might that emotion be communicating to you? Leaning in to this a bit might help you settle your mind. Showing yourself that you can feel a feeling without getting stuck can also help build tolerance here.

Investigate the present.

In his book *Four Thousand Weeks: Time Management for Mortals*, author Oliver Burkeman reflects on the concept of being truly present. We often think of presence as a state of mind rather than a fact of life, but Burkeman suggests that in the here and now is all you can ever be. "Living in the past" or "living in the future" are figments of our imagination, but we're never truly anywhere but here.[4] Sevens can be especially prone to conceiving of themselves in an imagined future, or "living in the future." Rather than relying on this thrill, what if you genuinely questioned what you're looking for? What is that imagined future offering to you? What is the idealization of future events giving you that the present moment is not? If it's an emotional need, a mental state, or a physical change, get curious about how that imagination is serving you. Now, consider how the present might be able to offer you the same if you focused on it. Are you looking for joy and rejuvenation? How can you get that right here where you are? Are you seeking stimulation? How can the present moment give you that same spark?

Author's Note

As an Enneagram writer, I am indebted to the authors and teachers who have shown me the way. My ideas have been shaped by Beatrice Chestnut, Uranio Paes, David Daniels, Don Riso, Russ Hudson, Sandra Maitri, A. H. Almaas, Helen Palmer, Ginger Lapid-Bogda, Claudio Naranjo, Stacey Ruff, Shelley Prevost, Elle Pugh, Marta Gillilan, Scott Allender, Jessica Denise Dickson, my *Enneagram in Real Life* podcast guests, interviewees, typing, coaching, and course clients, the @NineTypesCo Instagram community, and many more.

No matter your Enneagram type, I hope you found courage, enlightenment, and perspective in these pages. As you continue to walk this path, remember that growth and healing might not be immediate, but you can trust your capacity for change. Also remember this: you don't always have to be growing. Just like a garden, sometimes dormant seasons are part of the process.

If you love the Enneagram, I hope you'll share your passion with others. The most transformational learning I've experienced has taken place in groups, both in casual discussion and formal retreats. No matter where this learning takes you, take good care.

Still in your corner,

Steph

Acknowledgments

My favorite thing about the Enneagram is this beautiful community of curious and thoughtful humans. When I started @ninetypesco in 2017, I never could have imagined I'd be here, writing, podcasting, and teaching about the Enneagram. I am eternally grateful to every person who has liked, commented, messaged, or shared my posts. You inspire me with your dedication to your own personal development journeys, and our shared passion for the Enneagram. I have learned from all of you.

Authors always write, "It takes a village," and this has always seemed to be a massive overstatement to me. It's not. It really does take a whole pack of people to deliver this into your hands. Thank you to my agent, Alex Field, for being in my corner every step of the way. Thank you to the editorial team at HarperOne, especially Katy Hamilton for saying yes to this project, Ghjulia Romiti for carrying it through the messy middle, and to Angela Guzman and Maya Alpert for the final push. You are each brilliant, and I am grateful for your partnership in crafting this book. Special thanks to Stacy Erdman and Heidi Critz for your help editing the Enneagram content of this book, and to my writing buddy, Pidge Meade, for perfecting the introduction.

And thanks to Heidi Critz again for being my right hand and for keeping Nine Types afloat while I was in a writing/editing hole. Your professionalism, kindness, and expertise are unmatched, and I deeply appreciate every moment you've dedicated to working with Nine Types and the Enneagram. Thank you.

Thank you to the interviewees who offered their time, stories, and wisdom to this project. This book is better because of you, and I'm so grateful you shared a glimpse of your types with me and our readers. Thank you, Jacqui, Ericka, Justin, Stacey, Lauren, Dana, Najiba, Michael, Liz, Brian, Katie, Mel, Bryan, Robbie, Ashlyn, Charity, Tom, Augustus, Lauren, Heidi, Zack, Vanessa, Audrey, Teresa, Brandon, Chris, Joey, Kevin, Cheynna, and Suzi.

This book was also made possible by a village of loving and encouraging friends. My endless gratitude to the EnneaB*tches, my Bubble Friends (especially my Bay Area Bubblers), and the Heart Courage Pod. It has been a privilege to learn, grow, and teach alongside you. Thank you to my teachers, Beatrice Chestnut and Uranio Paes, and my mentor coach, Janaina Weiss.

Thank you to Amanda Steed for your never-ending support, compassion, and friendship. I swear, every Three needs an Eight like you in their lives.

Thank you to my family. To my parents (Alan and Christin, Rick and Miranda) for asking how the book is going, and also, thank you for not asking half as much as you might have liked. It's going! And it's here, so hope you like it. Thank you to my siblings, especially Haley for putting up with my constant changes and frantic deadline brain melt. And to Elliot, Maggie, and Joanna for being a little spot of joy delivered via FaceTime.

And the very most thanks to Brandon. I could not have done this without you. Truly, there are no words to describe how thoroughly unfinished this project would be without your emotional and practical support, and how grateful I am that you walked with me through it all. So thank you for holding down the fort during all these months. And for keeping the fort clean. And for making sure the fort never ran out of toilet paper. Ilysm.

Notes

Introduction

1. B. Brown, *The Gifts of Imperfection: Let Go of Who You Think You're Supposed to Be and Embrace Who You Are* (Center City, MN: Hazelden Publishing, 2010), 101.

Chapter 1: Laying the Groundwork

1. J. Wagner, *Nine Lenses on the World: The Enneagram Perspective* (Evanston, IL: NineLens Press, 2010), 15–16.
2. Wagner, *Nine Lenses*, 24.
3. R. Hanson, *Hardwiring Happiness: The New Brain Science of Contentment, Calm, and Confidence* (New York: Harmony, Crown Publishing Group, Penguin Random House), 17.
4. B. Van der Kolk, *The Body Keeps the Score: Brain, Mind, and Body in the Healing of Trauma* (New York: Penguin Random House, 2014), 76.
5. B. J. Allen, *Difference Matters: Communicating Social Identity*, 2nd ed. (Long Grove, IL: Waveland Press, 2011), 11–12.
6. Dr. Little calls these "personal projects." B. R. Little, *Who Are You Really? The Surprising Puzzle of Personality* (New York: Simon and Schuster/TED Books, 2017).
7. Allen, *Difference Matters*, 12.
8. C. Agorom, *The Enneagram for Black Liberation: Return to Who You Are Beneath the Armor You Carry* (Minneapolis: Broadleaf Books, 2022), 21.
9. Learning and unlearning are important parts of our inner work. I highly recommend picking up *The Enneagram for Black Liberation* by Chichi Agorom for more information, especially if you have questions about these concepts.
10. C. Agorom, *The Enneagram for Black Liberation*, 17.
11. C. Agorom, *The Enneagram for Black Liberation*, 13.
12. C. Dweck, *Mindset, the New Psychology of Success: How We Can Learn to Fulfill Our Potential* (New York: Ballantine Books, Penguin Random House, 2006).
13. R. Boyatzis, "An Overview of Intentional Change from a Complexity Perspective," *Journal of Management Development* 25, no. 7 (2006): 607–23.
14. K. Neff, *Self-Compassion: The Proven Power of Being Kind to Yourself* (New York: William Morrow, HarperCollins, 2011).

Chapter 2: How the System Works

1. D. R. Riso and R. Hudson, *The Wisdom of the Enneagram: The Complete Guide to Psychological and Spiritual Growth for the Nine Personality Types* (New York: Bantam Books, 1999), 9.
2. S. David, *Emotional Agility: Get Unstuck, Embrace Change, and Thrive in Work and Life* (New York: Avery, Penguin Random House, 2016), 43–62.
3. Riso and Hudson, *Wisdom of the Enneagram*, 53–54.
4. Riso and Hudson, *Wisdom of the Enneagram*, 56–57.
5. Riso and Hudson, *Wisdom of the Enneagram*, 58–59.
6. D. C. Funder, *The Personality Puzzle*, 8th ed. (New York: W. W. Norton and Company, 2019), 316.
7. Riso and Hudson, *Wisdom of the Enneagram*, 37.

8. Wagner, *Nine Lenses*, 88.

9. D. J. Siegel, *The Developing Mind: How Relationships and the Brain Interact to Shape Who We Are*, 3rd ed. (New York: Guilford Press, 2020), 341–351.

10. N. McWilliams, *Psychoanalytic Diagnosis: Understanding Personality Structure in the Clinical Process*, 2nd ed. (New York: Guilford Press, 2011), 27–31.

11. R. C. Schwartz, *No Bad Parts: Healing Trauma and Restoring Wholeness with the Internal Family Systems Model* (Boulder, CO: Sounds True, 2021), 32.

12. This concept is well illustrated in *The Science of Stuck*. B. Frank, *The Science of Stuck: Breaking Through Inertia to Find Your Path Forward* (United States: Tarcher-Perigree, Penguin Random House, 2022), 31–39.

13. S. Maitri, *The Enneagram of Passions and Virtues: Finding the Way Home* (New York: Tarcher/Penguin, 2015), 15.

14. McWilliams, *Psychoanalytic Diagnosis*, 100–103.

15. S. Maitri, *The Spiritual Dimension of the Enneagram: Nine Faces of the Soul* (New York: Tarcher/Penguin, 2000), 30–32.

16. Find more information in the accompanying PDF: https://www.enneagramirl .com/resources.

17. B. Chestnut and U. Paes, "Developing Powerful Enneagram Skills" (class), Chestnut Paes Enneagram Academy Professional Certification, March 2021.

18. Add note here about B Chestnut. B. Chestnut, *The Complete Enneagram: 27 Paths to Greater Self-Knowledge* (Berkeley, CA: She Writes Press), 25–33.

19. B. Chestnut and U. Paes, *Enneagram 2.0*, S2 Ep03, "What Does the Self-Preservation Repressed Instinct Look Like?," podcast, https://podcasts.apple.com/us/podcast /enneagram-2-0-with-beatrice-chestnut-and-uranio-paes/id1499745500.

20. B. Chestnut and U. Paes, *Enneagram 2.0*, S2 Ep14, "What Does the Social Repressed Instinct Look Like?," podcast, February 2, 2023, https://podcasts.apple .com/us/podcast/enneagram-2-0-with-beatrice-chestnut-and-uranio-paes/id 1499745500.

21. J. Luckovich, *The Instinctual Drives and the Enneagram* (Enneagrammer Imprints, 2021), 18–21.

22. Chestnut and Paes, "Developing Powerful Enneagram Skills," (class).

23. B. Chestnut and U. Paes, *Enneagram 2.0*, S2 Ep21, "What Does the Sexual Repressed Instinct Look Like?," podcast, May 11, 2023, https://podcasts.apple.com/us /podcast/enneagram-2-0-with-beatrice-chestnut-and-uranio-paes/id1499745500.

24. Chestnut, *Complete Enneagram*, 41–43.

25. Maitri, *Spiritual Dimension of the Enneagram*, 245–262; B. Chestnut and U. Paes, *The Enneagram Guide to Waking Up: Find Your Path, Face Your Shadow, Discover Your True Self* (Charlottesville, VA: Hampton Roads Publishing, 2021), 11–12, 37–38, 65–66, 93–94, 121–122, 149–150, 177–178, 205–206, 233–234.

26. Chestnut, *Complete Enneagram*, 86.

27. B. Chestnut and U. Paes, *Enneagram 2.0*, S2 Ep33, "Wings versus Arrows as Paths for Growth," podcast, November 16, 2023, https://podcasts.apple.com/us/podcast /enneagram-2-0-with-beatrice-chestnut-and-uranio-paes/id1499745500.

28. Chestnut and Paes, "Wings versus Arrows as Paths for Growth."

29. F. Anderson, *Transcending Trauma: Healing Complex PTSD with Internal Family Systems Therapy* (Eau Claire, WI: PESI Publishing, 2021), 4–5, 63–64.

30. J. W. Pennebaker, *Opening Up: The Healing Power of Expressing Emotions* (New York: Guilford Press, 1997), 39.

31. J. W. Pennebaker and C. K. Chung, "Expressive Writing: Connections to Physical and Mental Health," in *The Oxford Handbook of Health Psychology*, ed. H. S. Friedman (New York: Oxford University Press, 2011).

32. Pennebaker, *Opening Up*, 40–41.

33. F. Sirois, *Procrastination: What It Is, Why It's a Problem, and What You Can Do About It* (Washington, D.C.: American Psychological Association, 2022), 127.
34. F. M. Sirois, C. B. Stride, and T. A. Pychyl, "Procrastination and Health: A Longitudinal Test of the Roles of Stress and Health Behaviours," *British Journal of Health Psychology* 28, no. 3 (2023), 860–875, https://doi.org/10.1111/bjhp.12658.
35. J. Smith, *Why Has Nobody Told Me this Before? Everyday Tools for Life's Ups and Downs* (New York: HarperOne, HarperCollins, 2022), 38.
36. D. Siegel, *Aware: The Science and Practice of Presence: The Groundbreaking Meditation Practice* (New York: TarcherPerigree, Penguin Random House, 2018), 19.

Chapter 4: OPEN: A Framework for Sustainable Change

1. J. Smith, *Why Has Nobody Told Me This Before?* 46–47.

Chapter 5: Type Eight

1. Jacqui Acree shares this story on the Enneagram IRL podcast (https://www.ninetypes.co/blog/enneagram-irl-podcast-interview-episode-6) as well as in her email newsletter, which can be found on her website, https://jacquiacree.com/experience/.
2. Chestnut, *Complete Enneagram*, 113.
3. J. N. Ervin, J. A. Bonito, and J. Keyton. 2016. "Convergence of Intrapersonal and Interpersonal Processes across Group Meetings." *Communication Monographs 84* (2): 200–220. doi:10.1080/03637751.2016.1185136

Chapter 6: Type Nine

1. KC Green, *Gunshow by YR Friend KC Green*, 2013, https://gunshowcomic.com/648.
2. J. N. Ervin, J. A. Bonito, and J. Keyton, "Convergence of Intrapersonal and Interpersonal Processes across Group Meetings," *Communication Monographs* 84, no. 2 (2016): 200–220, doi:10.1080/03637751.2016.1185136.
3. Adapted from various examples in M. Urban, *The Book of Boundaries: Set the Limits That Will Set You Free* (New York: Dial Press, Penguin Random House, 2022).

Chapter 7: Type One

1. J. N. Ervin, J. A. Bonito, and J. Keyton, "Convergence of Intrapersonal and Interpersonal Processes.
2. E. Kross, *Chatter: The Voice in Our Head; Why It Matters, and How to Harness It* (New York: Crown Publishing, Penguin Random House), 72–73.
3. Schwartz, *No Bad Parts*, 89–95; A. Gazipura, *On My Own Side: Transform Self-Criticism and Doubt into Permanent Self-Worth and Confidence* (Brooklyn, NY: B. C. Allen Publishing and Tonic Books, 2019), chapter four.
4. E. Nagoski and A. Nagoski, *Burnout: The Secret to Unlocking the Stress Cycle* (New York: Ballantine Books, Penguin Random House, 2020), 13.
5. C. Williams, *Move: How the New Science of Body Movement Can Set Your Mind Free* (Toronto: Hanover Square Press, 2021), 131.
6. Williams, *Move*, 122–123.

Chapter 8: Type Two

1. For more on this concept, see chapter three of *Emotional Agility*.
2. Chestnut, Paes, *The Enneagram Guide to Waking Up*, 54.
3. You'll recognize this term if you like CliftonStrengths, formerly Strengths Finder by Don Clifton.

4. J. N. Ervin, J. A. Bonito, and J. Keyton, "Convergence of Intrapersonal and Interpersonal Processes across Group Meetings," *Communication Monographs* 84, no. 2 (2016): 200–220, doi:10.1080/03637751.2016.1185136.
5. A. Nerurkar, *The 5 Resets: Rewire Your Brain and Body for Less Stress and More Resilience* (New York: HarperOne, HarperCollins, 2024).
6. This is called box breathing.

Chapter 9: Type Three

1. M. Cartwright, "Midas," *World History Encyclopedia*, last modified June 23, 2021, https://www.worldhistory.org/midas/.
2. McWilliams, *Psychoanalytic Diagnosis*, 114–115.
3. J. N. Ervin, J. A. Bonito, and J. Keyton, "Convergence of Intrapersonal and Interpersonal Processes.
4. A. Abdaal, *Feel-Good Productivity: How to Do More of What Matters to You* (New York: Celadon Books, Macmillan Publishers, 2023), 123.

Chapter 10: Type Four

1. J. N. Ervin, J. A. Bonito, and J. Keyton, "Convergence of Intrapersonal and Interpersonal Processes."
2. L. Olivera, *Already Enough: A Path to Self-Acceptance* (New York: Simon and Schuster, 2022), 63–83.
3. Paraphrased from *Rising Strong*. B. Brown, *Rising Strong: How the Ability to Reset Transforms the Way We Live, Love, Parent, and Lead* (New York: Random House, 2015), 19.

Chapter 11: Type Five

1. J. Burgo, *Why Do I Do That? Psychological Defense Mechanisms and the Hidden Ways They Shape Our Lives* (Chapel Hill, NC: New Rise Press, 2012), 148.
2. J. N. Ervin, J. A. Bonito, and J. Keyton, "Convergence of Intrapersonal and Interpersonal Processes."

Chapter 12: Type Six

1. Teresa McBean, Enneagram Coach, Practitioner, and Pastor, teresamcbean.com.
2. McWilliams, *Psychoanalytic Diagnosis*, 111.
3. J. N. Ervin, J. A. Bonito, and J. Keyton, "Convergence of Intrapersonal and Interpersonal Processes."
4. Smith, *Why Has Nobody Told Me*, 170.
5. W. R. Miller and S. Rollnick, *Motivational Interviewing: Helping People Change*, 3rd ed. (New York: The Guilford Press, 2013), 238.

Chapter 13: Type Seven

1. B. Chestnut and U. Paes, "Providing Effective Enneagram Solutions" (class), Chestnut Paes Enneagram Academy Professional Certification, October 2021.
2. J. N. Ervin, J. A. Bonito, and J. Keyton, "Convergence of Intrapersonal and Interpersonal Processes."
3. This concept adapted from chapter 1. J. Clear, *Atomic Habits: An Easy and Proven Way to Build Good Habits and Break Bad Ones* (New York: Avery Books, Penguin Random House, 2018).
4. O. Burkeman, *Four Thousand Weeks: Time Management for Mortals* (New York: Farrar, Straus and Giroux, 2021), 135.